PSYCHOLOGICAL ISSUES

VOL. XII, Nos. 1/2   MONOGRAPH 45/46

HYSTERIA: THE ELUSIVE NEUROSIS

by

ALAN KROHN

INTERNATIONAL   UNIVERSITIES   PRESS,   INC.
315 Fifth Avenue   •   New York, N.Y. 10016

Library of Congress Cataloging in Publication Data

Krohn, Alan
    Hysteria, the elusive neurosis.

    (Psychological issues ; v. 12, nos. 1-2: monograph 45-46)
    Bibliography: p.
    Includes index.
    1. Hysteria. I. Title. II. Series.
RC532.K74   616.8'52   76-45546
ISBN 0-8236-2426-9
ISBN 0-8236-2425-0 pbk.

Manufactured in the United States of America

PSYCHOLOGICAL ISSUES

HERBERT J. SCHLESINGER, *Editor*

Editorial Board

. . . an hysteric makes sexuality out of the therapist's science, while the therapist makes science out of sexuality. In this affair, the hysteric has the advantage, there being more sex to science than vice-versa.

—FARBER, *The Ways of the Will*

CONTENTS

Acknowledgments   ix

Introduction   1

1 FREUD'S THEORY OF HYSTERIA   9

2 DEFINITIONS OF HYSTERIA   46

3 ETIOLOGY OF HYSTERIA   129

4 HISTORICAL AND CROSS-CULTURAL PERSPECTIVES
       ON HYSTERIA   156

5 COMPREHENSIVE DEFINITION AND
       CASE ILLUSTRATION   212

6 CONCLUDING REMARKS   328

References   330
Index   339
About the Author   345

ACKNOWLEDGMENTS

I would like to express my appreciation to all whose teaching, guidance, and encouragement made it possible for me to complete this project. I am indebted first and foremost to my clinical teachers and supervisors, Drs. Joseph Adelson, Alexander Guiora, Ira Miller, David Pryor, George Richardson, Frederick Wyatt, and Mrs. Katia Schorger. I also want to extend my appreciation to Drs. David Gutmann and Martin Mayman, who had a profound influence on my professional growth.

I would like to thank Mr. Paul Wiener for his editorial suggestions on earlier drafts. The greatest effort was surely put in by the many secretaries who typed what must have seemed to be endless drafts of the manuscript, Miss Helen Hershberger, Mrs. Lynn Housewright, Mrs. Pam Kosinski, and Mr. Paul Wiener. I am grateful to all of them.

I would like to express my appreciation to the Editorial Board of *Psychological Issues* and its Editor, Dr. Herbert Schlesinger, for the thorough, wholeheartedly constructive, and excellent suggestions for revisions of the monograph. I want to thank especially Ms. Suzette H. Annin for her thoughtful and candid observations on the manuscript and for her superb editorial work on it.

Most of all I am indebted to my wife Janis who helped me as editor, typist, and soul mate throughout this project.

INTRODUCTION

A systematic reappraisal of hysteria and hysterical personality demands first a consideration of the place of diagnosis in theory and clinical practice. Misuses of diagnosis are legion. At its worst, it reflects a cursory, idiosyncratic, gross labeling process involving a simplistic use of signs or symptoms, and often obscuring as much as it attempts to clarify. Unfortunately, such misuse has led to prejudice against diagnosis itself (Shevrin and Shectman, 1973). As Menninger, Mayman, and Pruyser (1963), Shevrin and Shectman (1973), and Pasamanick, Dimitz, and Lefton (1959) have strongly urged, however, rather than throwing up our hands in despair at diagnostic confusion and misuse, we need to redouble our efforts to delineate and delimit the nature of psychiatric illness. To quote Menninger et al. (1963):

> we vigorously oppose the view that treatment, other than first aid, should proceed before or without diagnosis. On the contrary, we feel that diagnosis is today more important than ever. The very fact that psychiatric designations have become so meaningless by conflicting usage makes it more rather than less necessary that we approach the specific problem in illness with a cautious, careful scrutiny and appraisal that has characterized the best medical science since the early days. It is still necessary to know in advance, to plan as logically as we can, what kind of interference with a human life we propose to make [p. 6].

Diagnosis need not be a static, superficial, merely descriptive label. If diagnosis is regarded as pinpointing a general psychological pattern, an ideal type that is neither a narrow

1

description of rigidly defined symptoms nor a gross and overabstract concept, it continues to be vital for clinical practice. Diagnosis need not exclude a conception of "dynamics," nor need it demand that any patient meet *all* the criteria of a diagnostic category. Indeed, a clearly delineated diagnosis that is rooted in the phenomena of the patient's clinical presentation serves as a starting point for viewing that particular patient. A valid diagnostic category should capture certain enduring psychological and/or behavioral constellations that will orient the clinician and provide him with a reference point for his continued diagnostic investigations. To criticize diagnosis because any patient fails to fit perfectly into a diagnostic category, or to misuse diagnosis by considering only those characteristics of the patient that fit into the ideal diagnostic type, are both common and serious pitfalls in diagnostic practice. Although neither is inherent to the process of diagnosis, both have served as ready excuses for its abandonment.

The conceptualizations of hysteria exhibit the difficulties found throughout the field of psychodiagnosis. Indeed, hysteria presents the diagnostic pitfalls dramatically, for during its long history it has been prey to them all. This monograph, then, while directed specifically to the problem of hysteria, also has implications for a more fruitful approach to diagnosis.

My central task in this monograph is to study a set of psychopathological and personality types called hysteria, conversion hysteria, anxiety hysteria, hysterical character, hysterical personality, hysteroid personality, etc. These terms are used every day by clinicians. At best, they are defined imprecisely, and at worst, completely arbitrarily. Hysteria has been defined by such diverse symptoms as the presence of phobias or psychologically based somatic symptoms, by character traits such as coquettishness or labile affects, and by intrapsychic dynamics such as the presence of Oedipal conflicts.

My synthetic effort in the monograph is focused on the psychoanalytic study of character as distinguished from the study of symptoms. Psychoanalysis began as a study of the psychology of symptom formation. While later psychoanalytic work has to some extent dealt with the psychology of character, and most clinical psychoanalysis and intensive psychoanalytic psychotherapy are in large part oriented toward the analysis of character problems, there have been very few attempts to examine systematically a particular personality type from a modern psychoanalytic viewpoint.[1] A central aim of this monograph is, therefore, to bring a psychoanalytic approach to bear on the hysterical personality and the hysterical neurotic.

It seems to this author that effective psychoanalytic diagnosis and assessment rest on two simultaneous approaches to the patient, one oriented toward the analysis of individual factors in his personality, and the other toward assessment of the personality as a total constellation. First, different sectors of the patient's personality must be carefully assessed. The nature of specific ego functions, the choice of defensive modalities (and which modalities in which intrapsychic circumstances), the quality of object representations and actual object ties, the resiliency of the ego, cognitive functioning, superego pathology, the capacity to delay under the pressure of impulses, are examples of the areas that demand the psychoanalytic diagnostician's careful attention. The Adult and Developmental Profiles (A. Freud, Nagera, and Freud, 1965) and the Metapsychological Assessment Profile (for assessment of analyzability) (Greenspan and Cullander, 1973) are two scales that facilitate this sort of approach. Second, the personality must be viewed as a constellation of these traits, as a working unit in which the elements studied in the first phase of the assessment are seen in a total context. These two points of view permit the analytic diagnostician to triangulate on the patient's personality and problem, to view the clinical phenomena both in terms of the parts and in terms of the whole. The psychoanalytic study of personality types would provide these latter points of reference. If regularly occurring constella-

---

[1] It is interesting to note that in the last ten years there has been more systematic psychoanalytic study of borderline and narcissistic characters than there has been of neurotic personalities.

tions of intrapsychic patterns can be identified and substituted for the superficial descriptive traits of psychiatric syndromes, then the analytically oriented clinician will have useful points of reference for his diagnostic work.

The two viewpoints have a mutually corroborating, self-correcting, and exploratory function. A specific ego defense, say projection, tends to occur along with a particular pattern of superego and ego-ideal development, a characteristic pattern of thinking, etc. (This may be because of a common point of fixation of ego and superego development, or because of the mutual influences of these various structures during development.) A tendency to find X defense along with Y pattern of thought and Z pattern of superego development is the foundation of the psychoanalytic psychology of character. The discovery that certain personality traits, each carefully and systematically defined and assessed, tend to occur together will further the psychoanalytic study of character. Such a finding has, first of all, basic psychoanalytic research interest. In addition, the psychoanalytic clinician can approach his patient with the hypothesis that certain constellations of defenses, unconscious fantasies, structural defects and assets, etc., will exist in a fashion that makes sense as a total working unit and will probably tend to conform to regularly observed clinical phenomena. This will help him to focus better on the patient's psychodynamics and psychic structure. If the patient presents X defense without the Y cognitive mode usually found with X, then the clinician is faced with an important psychodynamic question to answer. Such a question may lead to a revision of his assessment of the patient's defenses or to a new and better assessment of his cognitive functioning, to an understanding of some other significant intervening factors (such as an important identification), or to a rethinking and refinement of the concept of the character type itself. In this way a model of specific psychoanalytic dimensions, such as is found in the Adult Profile, along with a model provided by a modern psychoanalytic study of character that addresses the inter-relationships of these functions, would seem to have an optimal potential both for mutual corroboration and for useful, hypothesis-generating contradictions in day-to-day clinical work.

The best application of this sort of approach awaits a modern psychoanalytic investigation of character and personality structure. It is in this spirit that the essential and repeatedly observed psychoanalytic dimensions of one character type, the hysterical personality, are here presented.

THE ORGANIZATION OF THE MONOGRAPH

The monograph begins with a review of Freud's theory of hysteria. Chapter 2 analyzes various definitions of hysteria: (1) descriptive, behavioral, symptom definition, (2) definition based on assessment of character traits and character structure, (3) empirical research on the disorder, (4) definition based on psychodiagnostic testing, and (5) ego-psychological approaches to the syndrome. This chapter concludes with a discussion of the areas of dispute and consensus in the various definitions, and a provisional definition of the disorder based on themes that seem to appear, under different labels, in several approaches.

Chapter 3 discusses the problem of the etiology of the disorder. Parental influence and family constellations that promote the syndrome are explored. The role of loss or death of important people is examined. The role of constitutional factors and sex-specific personality traits in the development of hysteria are also noted. The oft-noted prevalence of hysteria in women is explored, along with hysteria occurring in men.

Chapter 4 explores hysteria from cross-cultural and historical points of view. The enduring, universal features of the disorder are distilled from the study of hysteria as it existed during the seventeenth century, the Victorian era, and the early twentieth century, and as it exists currently in other cultures, such as that of the Apache Indians of the western United States. The specific nature of the ego in this particular disorder demands a special consideration of socio-cultural forces, as illustrated in this chapter. An enduring definition of hysteria has been elusive because the forms of the disorder, more than those of any other psychopathology, have shifted with changing social and cultural currents. The changing definitions of hysteria reflect its most basic feature: its complex use of contemporaneous cultural and social forms. When, through a historical and cross-cultural survey of the disorder, this process is understood, the enduring ego processes and instinctual conflicts that lie at the root of this syndrome become clear, and the diagnosis becomes viable.

Chapter 5 presents a comprehensive model of the hysterical personality and hysteria. It builds on the provisional definition presented in Chapter 2 and integrates the universal aspects of the disorder that emerge from the cross-cultural and historical analysis. The definition of hysteria and the hysterical personality is then illustrated with the initial psychiatric evaluation and early portion of a psychotherapy of two patients presenting hysterical personality.

A central objective of the monograph is to demonstrate that a modern definition of the hysterical personality can and should be formulated. The definition should go beyond previous attempts in several respects. It should not be based solely on a descriptive list of signs or symptoms or solely on a highly abstract and unidimensional concept of unconscious dynamics. It should be a definition of an underlying personality structure. This underlying structure should include a delineation of the nature and intactness of psychic structures, the dominant defenses, characteristics of the ego and superego, an infantile libidinal fixation point, the nature of perception and cognition, and the general functioning of the personality type. The definition should not be based on the presence of conversion symptoms. Conversion symptoms should be viewed as a type of symptom that may occur in the hysterical personality and during some eras was typical of it, but is not universally or basically defining of it. It will be argued that the hysterical personality can be recognized cross-culturally and historically by certain patterns of functioning that reflect its characteristic ego defense, object relations, reality testing, self-image, superego functioning, and psychosexual conflict.

While the underlying processes remain constant bases of this personality type, the overt symptoms and overt personality traits of the hysteric are culture and era specific. In fact, one of the most salient social-interpersonal aspects of the functioning of the hysterical ego is its capacity to express underlying psychic conflicts through marginal, but never completely alienating, modes of the particular culture. This characteristic of the hysteric has made defining hysteria very difficult, and has made defining hysteria by its overt symptoms even more problematic.

What, then, has been defined and explored under the label "hysteria"? Doubtless the definitional problems have led clinicians, on the basis of a superficial descriptive set of criteria, to diagnose as hysterical patients who in fact had no business to be so diagnosed. I, however, have been impressed by the fact that, although there are many diverse definitions and approaches to the disorder, and although *some* writers are clearly defining something entirely different from most of the others, there are some striking convergences among contributors to the subject. This led me to a basic set of assumptions on which this monograph rests. If these assumptions are kept in mind, the various approaches to the subject presented here will be clearer. (1) An entity that has been variously labeled hysteria, hysterical character, conversion hysteria, does exist in nature—that is, there is a regularly occurring constellation of mental processes that can be usefully defined for the clinician and researcher. (2) In spite of the inadequacy of definition of this syndrome, there has been a collective clinical sense of the syndrome called hysteria—review of previous contributions to the theory of the disorder can yield, in spite of the problems of definition, some consensual clinical judgment about what is basic and universal to the disorder. (3) The study of hysteria has been significantly hampered by the lack of both a universal, culture-free definition of the disorder and a coherent picture of the dynamics and psychic structure found in this personality type. (4) With modern psychoanalytic concepts, the hysterical personality can be defined without reliance on the occurrence of specific symptoms. Such a definition can organize and synthesize observations and theories of many earlier contributors to this subject.

1

FREUD'S THEORY OF HYSTERIA

Hysterics suffer mainly from reminiscences.
—Breuer and Freud, *Studies on Hysteria*

The most extensive approach to hysteria has been the psychoanalytic. Freud began his study of mental life through the study of hysteria, and thus the early psychoanalytic study of this disorder forms much of the early history of psychoanalysis. The original theory of the disorder and the subsequent modifications and revisions parallel the evolution of Freud's general psychology. To study hysteria without a review of the early psychoanalytic approach to it is to miss the most important chapter in the history of the study of the disorder.

Freud's work is often misread, misunderstood, and misquoted because the changes in his theory and the consequent changes in the meaning of his concepts are unrecognized. Because readers ignore the major points of transition in Freud's thought and therefore fail to view it in phases, his work seems confusing and contradictory. It is therefore to a historical overview of the development of Freud's views on hysteria that we now turn.

BREUER'S AND FREUD'S INITIAL RESEARCH

Freud first explored hysteria following a period of neuro-anatomical research pursued as a medical student under

9

Brücke and later as an assistant at the General Hospital of Vienna. After being appointed as a lecturer of neuropathology at the University of Vienna, he traveled to the Salpêtrière to study with one of the foremost neuropathologists of the day, Charcot. Freud was most impressed with Charcot's investigations of hysteria, which demonstrated the production of hysterical paralyses and contractures by hypnotic suggestion, the occurrence of hysteria in men, and the genuineness and regularity of hysterical phenomena.

Though hypnosis was considered by much of the medical community of the day to be fraudulent, Charcot demonstrated that hypnotic suggestion could produce and remove symptoms in patients suffering from nonorganically based physical difficulties. Freud's report of Charcot's techniques to the physicians of Vienna met with unreasoned opposition.

Freud proceeded to treat patients with nervous difficulties privately, soon learning that electrotherapy and the neuropathology books on it "had no more relation to reality than some 'Egyptian' dream-book, such as is sold in cheap bookshops . . ." (Freud, 1925, p. 16). So even before Moebius advanced an explanation of the success of electrotherapy as based on suggestion, Freud had put it aside, coming to rely exclusively on hypnotism as his one systematic therapeutic approach. He journeyed to Nancy, a new center for hypnosis, to perfect his therapeutic techniques. In Nancy, he saw Liébeault use hypnosis among the poor, saw Bernheim's hypnotic experiments with hospital patients, and came to discuss with the latter the therapeutic possibilities of the hypnotic method. After Bernheim failed to achieve more than only short-term results with a patient Freud had brought with him to Nancy, he frankly admitted to Freud that he achieved his great therapeutic results only with hospitalized patients, and could not duplicate them with his private patients.

From the very first Freud went beyond Bernheim's, Charcot's, and Liébeault's use of hypnosis. Apart from the use of hypnotism for suggestion, Freud questioned the hypnotized patient about the origin of his symptom, finding the patient capable of describing the onset of his symptoms, something he was able to do at best only haltingly and imperfectly while awake. Freud learned this method from Dr. Josef Breuer, an older physician he met while working in Brücke's laboratory, whom Freud respected and with whom he came to collaborate very closely. Breuer shared with Freud, both before and after the latter's trip to Nancy, a new research and treatment approach he had used with a hysterical patient: Breuer had first used hypnosis to overcome the patient's confusions, inhibitions, and physical disorders. He then employed hypnosis again in an attempt to find a link between her hysterical difficulties and other experiences in her life. This procedure revealed that all of the patient's symptoms constituted "residues or reminiscences" of emotionally moving events she had experienced while nursing her father. In most instances these reminiscences involved an impulse or a thought the patient had tried to suppress as she sat with her dying father. Under hypnosis, when these situations could be remembered and the feelings about them expressed, the symptom would vanish, at least temporarily.[1] This method not only yielded therapeutic results but was more scientifically interesting and personally appealing to Freud than the "monotonous, forcible prohibitions used in the treatment by suggestion" (Freud, 1914, p. 9).

Freud then replicated Breuer's results with his own patients, and proposed to Breuer writing two joint publications, which came out as "On the Psychical Mechanism of Hysterical Phenomena: Preliminary Communication" (Breuer and Freud, 1893) and *Studies on Hysteria* (Breuer and Freud, 1893-1895). These contributions presented a very rudimentary "theory" of the origin of hysterical symptoms and their treatment.

In the first work, Breuer and Freud (1893) considered hysterical symptoms to be brought on by the trauma of an accident or a frightening psychological event such as having a momentary hallucination or distressing feelings of shame. The theory of the origin of hysterical symptoms was expanded to include partial traumas and to take into

[1] Though the patient had recovered, Breuer was most secretive about the final stage of the treatment, for reasons Freud only later understood. See below, p. 16.

account a special sensitiveness or susceptibility to strong feelings that makes some people especially prone to develop such symptoms. For example, an association is formed in a young woman between a terrifying hallucination and her arm, which at that moment is hanging over the back of a chair and has "fallen asleep." From this hysterical anesthesia and paresis of that arm developed. In other cases there may be a more complex connection than a simple temporal association between a physical sensation and a precipitating event. The specific somatic manifestation may have a symbolic meaning, such as "healthy people form in dreams" (1893, p. 5). Hysterical vomiting, for example, may be an expression of moral disgust.

THE PATHOGENIC IMPACT OF MEMORIES

The traumatic event or cumulative partial traumas were seen as remaining alive within the hysteric long after they had occurred. They were conceived as "foreign bodies" that endure within the hysteric and produce his symptoms. On the basis of their discovery that when the hysterical patient succeeds in clearly recalling the exciting event, relating it in detail and expressing in words the feelings connected with it, the symptoms disappear, Breuer and Freud concluded that these forgotten events and suppressed feelings were the cause of the continuing symptoms. At this juncture we might note several aspects of this initial conceptualization: (1) recollections of the events need to be complete and, more important, must be accompanied by feelings in order to be therapeutically effective (implying that dammed-up feelings were basic to hysterical symptoms); (2) the hysterical symptom is conceived to be formed by processes similar to normal dream mentation; (3) a "trauma" is basically psychologically (as opposed to objectively) defined—it is what is distressing *for a particular person* (involving, for example, special sensitiveness to strong feelings); (4) several minor traumas, as well as one major one, can cause hysterical symptoms; and (5) memories provocative of hysterical symptoms may remain within the mind "for a long time with astonishing freshness and with the whole of their affective colouring" (p. 9), while not at the conscious disposal of the patient. This implies that ideas can be retained outside of conscious thought and that such thoughts are "timeless" and unchanging.

Breuer and Freud then explained *how* these hysterically exciting thoughts could remain fresh, timeless, and outside of consciousness. A theory of normal associative connection between memories, a precursor of the theory of the unconcious, was formulated to explain the endurance of hysterogenic memories. Breuer and Freud posited a psychological process in normal, healthy people by which the memory of a traumatic event is made innocuous: the memory becomes combined with other associations and ideas and thereby modified and corrected by them. For example, the feelings connected with an injury or accident are weakened by being connected with the memory of the final, fortunate outcome of the situation, by an objective evaluation of the facts, and by consideration of one's safety and over-all worth in other situations. This process dissipates the accompanying feelings and thereby prevents neurotic resolution.

The memories of such traumata are not at the disposal of the hysteric. They are absent from his memory, and thus have not undergone the process of connection with other ideas and the "effacement" that follows from it. In the hysteric the normal process of absorption of these memories and the affects connected with them fails to take place owing to one of two psychological conditions, one clearly more Breuer's explanation, the other more Freud's: the memories and feelings are denied associative connection with other thoughts either because of the patient's *intention* to exclude them from awareness (Freud), or because the psychic experiences took place during an abnormal state of consciousness, one marked by a disconnection with other content and a particularly strong emotional connection within the ideas, a *hypnoid state* (Breuer).

Ideas could also be intentionally cut off from association if the trauma concerned something the patient wished to forget and exclude from conscious thought. Thoughts, experiences, and feelings unacceptable to the patient himself or which he felt would be socially taboo were so cut off from conscious thought. Since the authors (probably primarily Freud) described this "deliberate" or "intentional" forgetting or exclusion from consciousness long before the structural theory and ego psychology, the model did *not* permit or include a notion of processes of exclusion occurring outside of consciousness. This early concept suggested simply that the patient found thoughts connected with trauma unwelcome and in some way forced them from his mind.

The major and highly significant difference between Freud's and Breuer's conceptualizations, one that has continued throughout the history of the study of hysteria, and according to Freud represented a major step in the transition from catharsis to psychoanalysis, concerns the role of wish and intent in the formation of the hysterical symptoms. The hypnoid theory (hypnoid hysteria) suggested that the hysteric was beset by an altered state of consciousness during which an experience is incompletely absorbed, dissipated, and vented. The second theory (defense hysteria) posited a process of forgetting based more on the individual patient's active wish or need to forget—a theory based on purposes, intentions, and internal conflicts.

THE HYPNOID STATE

Though the concept of the "hypnoid state" has been abandoned, it deserves some further consideration if only for historical completeness. Though Freud finally came to reject the concept, finding it an essentially "physiological theory" that failed to explain the nature of internal psychological conflicts, the concept of a hypnoid state does anticipate later concepts of hysterical *ego* functioning.[2] The concept of the hypnoid state shed little light on the mechanism of hysterical symptom formation; indeed, it served to obscure the impact of warring intentions that in *Studies on Hysteria* and the two papers on the defense neuropsychoses (Freud, 1894, 1896b) became the *basis* of the theory of neurotic symptom formation. The concept of a

---

[2] As mentioned earlier, Freud himself stated that this initial theory did not seek to establish the nature of hysteria but sought merely to explain the origin of its symptoms (1925, pp. 21-22).

hypnoid state does, however, provide a quite valid, if rudimentary, description of some aspects of hysterical character or the
hysterical ego that Abse (1959) and Shapiro (1965) later
described. The hypnoid state described a state of consciousness
in which ideas emerge with particular intensity, in which they
fail to be brought into commerce with other ideas, in which
conscious, rational, and objective processes of thought fail to be
brought to bear on the pathogenic thoughts, and, most
important, in which "narrow fields of association" occur. The
concept of a hypnoid state also seemed to imply that *any*
surprising incident, if it occurred in a hypnoid state, would lead
to a case of "acquired hysteria."

The concept, most probably Breuer's, was that something
outside enters a hysteric and literally causes the disorder, like a
germ invading a host. This formulation, of course, ignores the
wellsprings of intention in the hysteric and obscured Freud's
most profound contribution in the early phase of his work — his
understanding of the struggle to repress internal intentions.
Nevertheless, the hypnoid-state concept *does* embody later
descriptions of such cognitive, characterological, and ego-
psychological facets of the hysteric as (1) the narrowed, restricted availability of ideation and fantasy, (2) the hysteric's tendency to keep a rational and objective evaluation of troublesome
events, and (3) most of all, the hysteric's proclivity to dissociate,
repress, and forget. In sum, the concept of hypnoid state
represented an initial, albeit narrow and primitive, attempt to
describe aspects of the hysterical personality that have subsequently seemed to be quite basic — the nature of consciousness, thinking, and perception in the hysteric.

THE SHIFT FROM PHYSIOLOGICAL TO PSYCHOLOGICAL

Up to this point the study of hysteria was firmly grounded in
medicine, physiology, and neuroanatomy. The study of
hysteria was really the study of conversion symptoms, patients
being labeled hysterics because they presented such symptoms.
Perhaps owing to the medical and physiological backgrounds of
both Freud and Breuer, the study of character or personality
could not at this early stage even be contemplated. The
"research" problem, such as it was, was posed by puzzling

symptoms. Though Freud and Breuer disagreed on many important points, they both viewed the symptom, be it hysterical attack or conversion symptom, as a result of emotional excitation, arising in hypnoid, traumatic, or emotionally distressing states. Conversion was seen as a flow of this unexpressed "affect" (Freud's term for feelings *and* energies throughout these early papers) into the soma.

In the notion of "conversion" the beginning of a concept of psychic energy can be discerned. The theory includes an assumption that strong feelings, if not expressed or brought into active commerce with other ideas, will express themselves through other channels. The idea that the damming up of affect can create a symptom introduced a dynamic factor, and, with the complementary notion that the dammed-up energy can be transformed and redirected, an economic assumption was also posited. In the earliest work the nature of this dammed-up energy was not specified.

It was the specification of this "excitation" that caused Freud and Breuer to part ways, and that inaugurated the clearest transition from catharsis to psychoanalysis. Freud came to recognize clinically that not just any kind of excitation, but specifically sexual excitation, was universally found to be at the base of hysterical symptoms. When Freud began to observe the importance of sexuality in his clinical study of hysterics, informal remarks he had heard Breuer, Charcot, and others make about sexual involvement in neurotic problems coalesced for him. Other physicians had noticed the role of sexuality, discussed it informally in hospital corridors, but could not admit it publicly. Interestingly, when Freud later reminded several of these men of their remarks, they denied them.

The most fundamental cause of Breuer's break with Freud, however, went beyond this theoretical dispute, involving Breuer's countertransference reactions to one of his early patients, Anna O. As Freud reconstructed the situation, Breuer had, without realizing it, stumbled on the central role of sexuality in hysteria. The young woman patient whom Breuer had cured by catharsis had proceeded to develop romantic, highly erotic feelings toward him, culminating in a hysterical symptom which we can see today expressed her unconscious fantasy of having his baby. He had considered these feelings to be unconnected with the patient's difficulty and regarded the episode as an embarrassing near transgression, best forgotten. He had, of course, unwittingly stumbled onto, as did Freud later with more understanding, the phenomenon of "transference love."[3]

FREUD'S EARLY THEORY

In this early period Freud's major theoretical contributions appear in his two papers on the neuropsychoses of defense (1894, 1896b), in "The Aetiology of Hysteria" (1896a), and in *Studies on Hysteria* (Breuer and Freud, 1893-1895). Though still accepting the possibility of "hypnoid hysteria" or "retention hysteria," Freud pointed out in one of his contributions to *Studies on Hysteria* (p. 286) that he had been unable to find a case of hypnoid hysteria of the sort Breuer had observed in Anna O. He added that he had had no success with a case he thought was "retention hysteria," hysteria conceived as resulting simply from the blocking of an outlet of excitation. The cases he observed always revealed a psychic conflict, an internal war between repressed ideas and affects and defenses against them. He saw the patient's resistance to the cathartic method as the expression of a need to keep unacceptable ideas out of consciousness. He thus regarded the resistance as an expression of the same psychical force that had played a part in the original repression and had served to prevent such pathogenic ideas from becoming conscious. The resistance, then, was another form of the original repulsion of the traumatic or disturbing thoughts connected with the onset of the symptom. Indeed, in one case, when he found no noticeable resistance, the patient suffered a relapse and he concluded that he had not helped her find the true roots of her illness. He therefore became suspicious of the concept of hysteria without psychological conflict, and built his first systematic theory of

---

[3] Pollock (1968, 1972) has delved further into the complex motivation that underlay the Breuer-Freud-Anna O. relationships.

hysteria on a concept of intrapsychic conflict, labeling the syndrome "defense hysteria." Following a loyalty to clinical observation that endured throughout his career, Freud, in a series of papers in the late 1890's, described a mechanism of hysterical symptom formation that became the basis of his general theory of neurosis.

Freud saw hysterical symptoms (at that time conversion symptoms and hysterical attacks) emerging as the result of repression of ideas that were incompatible with the person's moral and social sensibilities. To maintain repression, to keep an unbearable idea unconscious, the affects connected with it had to be withdrawn from it. The quantity of excitation that had been connected with the idea, now detached from it, is transformed into a somatic expression that Freud called *conversion* (1894). To keep the idea repressed, to keep it weak and innocuous, the energy must continue to be channeled into the soma, and the symptom thereby endures.[4] The unconscious memory trace of the repressed idea formed the hub of a second, unconscious psychical group. Once this second psychical group is formed, usually owing to a traumatic situation or psychologically traumatic experience, later experience could reunite the weakened idea with the walled-off affect, the idea could then threaten to re-emerge, and the patient was compelled to handle the new psychic conflict in one of several ways: (1) by associative absorption (bringing the emerging memories into contact with other ideas, which helps the patient see the original situation more realistically); (2) by discharge of energy in hysterical attacks; (3) by channeling excitation into new conversions; (4) by abreaction. Thus Freud conceived the basic process as arising from psychological conflict, the conflict between an idea and the forces of resistance and defense that press to avoid it. The essential "cause" of this conflict lay in the

---

[4] This initial theory is in some ways crude, for it holds that the quantity of excitation is channeled into a "memory symbol," the conversion symptom, which often has some symbolic relationship to the repressed idea. How, it may be asked, can *energy*, which by definition cannot be an idea, create a symbol? With the "telescopic model" presented in Chapter VII of *The Interpretation of Dreams* (1900), this becomes better explained, and later, with the introduction of the structural theory (Freud, 1923), it is even better conceptualized.

incompatibility of the idea with the patient's moral standards and beliefs. It was not the content of particular ideas or traumas that lay at the root of the hysterical symptom, but the fact that the ideas were repressed, had become unconscious, and continued in conflict with conscious, moral motives. If a memory of a sexual occurrence and the feelings surrounding it were conscious, then hysterical symptoms would not arise from it (Freud, 1896b). The concept of repression (which in these early papers meant what was later called "defense") and the corollary concept of resistance (the expression of defense in the treatment situation) came to be defining aspects of psychoanalytic theory (Freud, 1914). With his recognition of the role of defense and the treatment resistance that devolved from it, Freud turned away from hypnosis toward his new free-association technique.[5] It was at this juncture that Freud felt the history of "psychoanalysis proper" had begun.

THE ROLE OF SEXUALITY AND THE SEDUCTION THEORY

Establishing the role of sexuality in hysterical symptom formation led to Freud's major detour in the development of his theory of neurosis. Through both his cathartic and later free-association methods, Freud found himself led further and further back in the patient's life to the early years of childhood and to memories which time and again centered on the sexual sphere. The patients frequently reported having been seduced by a father, uncle, or other adult. These reports led Freud in 1896 to a theory of a specific etiology of hysteria according to which it was caused by actual excitation of the genital organs before puberty (seduction theory). In this theory the hysteric during childhood had been a passive participant in sexual activity. As Freud at this stage had not yet posited a concept of infantile sexuality, he considered these seductions to be pathogenic only insofar as unconscious memories of them were reactivated and energized at puberty when, it was thought, the

---

[5] It was probably also the case, as Freud himself acknowledged, that his scientific (as opposed to clinical) interest led him to the free-association method, just as it had earlier led him away from suggestion to catharsis.

sexual drives first arose. At puberty, when the sexual feelings·
emerged, the memory of these incidents became traumatic and
then demanded repression. Later traumatic experiences,
which earlier had been considered a primary cause of hysterical
symptoms, were now regarded by Freud as precipitating the
hysterical symptoms by awakening the unconscious memory
traces of these childhood traumas. This explains how an event
which does not on its face seem traumatic (such as a sexual over-
ture in adulthood) may bring on a hysterical neurosis, for the
true cause was the memory this incident had aroused.

There is, then, a five-part process: (1) a passive sexual
seduction occurs in childhood, a memory trace of which is laid
down; (2) the memory is rendered traumatic at puberty with
the onset of sexual urges; (3) the memory is now frightening and
unacceptable, demanding repression and unconscious defenses, and a predisposition to later hysterical symptoms is
established; (4) an event in adulthood triggers a painful idea
that is unconsciously associated with both the unconscious
memory of the sexual situation and the sexual feelings that had
become attached to the memory at puberty. This reawakens the
childhood trauma, and threatens to bring up the unacceptable
sexual memories and feelings; (5) a symptom forms as a
compromise between the feelings connected with the memory
and the resistances against it.

This theory was in many respects noteworthy, in spite of the
erroneous conclusion about infantile seduction. (1) It presented
very clearly the role of sexual excitation in hysterical symptom
formation; (2) it took into account the impact of childhood and
adolescent development for the first time; (3) it posited that
an early childhood memory can be reawakened and
transformed, a concept that applies the notion of strengthening
or weakening ideas (previously discussed in hysterical symptom
formation) to childhood psychological development; (4) it
replaced the notion of a hereditary predisposition to hysteria
with a conception that stresses the role of latent conflict — a
balance between repressed ideas and repressing forces can be
maintained until a later trauma upsets it and threatens to
bring repressed thoughts back into awareness; and (5) the
symptom may be "overdetermined," that is, the product of

several unconscious memories and the defenses against them.

Though these points deal with the dynamics of hysterical symptom formation, to a limited degree Freud also addressed an issue concerning the hysteric's character style. He threw new light on what had been previously described as the hysteric's exaggerated reactions and hypersensitivity to external events. He pointed out that the hysteric is responding not to the actual event, but rather to a reactivation of a much earlier experience — a living out of a memory and the feelings connected with it in response to a contemporary situation. The concepts he generated to explain specific symptoms can also be applied to the formation of hysterical personality patterns: overdetermination, the impact of childhood experience, psychic compromise, and the consequences of repressing unacceptable thoughts, feelings, or memories.

ABANDONMENT OF THE "SEDUCTION THEORY"

Once again demonstrating his courage and scientific integrity, Freud came to see that the "seduction theory" was wrong, and that what patients had reported as memories of seductions were in fact fantasies that had been formed to cover up autoerotic activity (and associated fantasies) in childhood. With Freud's realization that these "memories" were remnants of infantile wishes came his recognition of the role of infantile sexuality.

With this recognition, Freud revised his earlier notion of an energizing at puberty of earlier incidents of seduction. He came to realize that autoerotic activity, along with the excitement and fantasies associated with it, was the primary material demanding repression. The theory was amended as follows: (1) hysteria results from a set of essentially *internal*, psychological events — psychical reality was found to be much more important than physical reality (actual events of childhood) in the genesis of hysterical predisposition; and (2) the hysterical symptom is generated by conflict over enduring, ever-fresh repressed sexual fantasies of *early childhood*.

In Freud's early work appear some significant communalities and differences between hysteria and obsessive-compulsive neurosis that have endured as essential to the definition of each. He observed the obvious differences in symptoms: in hysteria there is a conversion symptom, whereas in the obsessional neurosis a seemingly unimportant idea becomes a preoccupation. They were, however, fundamentally similar in that both were seen (1) as provoked by a passive sexual seduction (in obsessional neurosis an aggressive sexual act was seen as covering a previous passive sexual seduction), and (2) as arising from a conflict over the expression of sexual thoughts or feelings (sexuality at this point was not discriminated into oral, anal, and phallic). In the hysteric the noxious idea is weakened by the detachment of its affective charge, the idea then being repressed and a quantity of excitation being channeled into the soma. In the obsessional the same aim, repression of a past experience, is handled by the separation of thought from affect and the attachment of the affect to some innocuous, irrelevant, inconsequential thought while the original noxious thought remains conscious in weakened form. The essential differences between the two were: (1) the hysteric channels the affect that has been separated from the noxious sexual idea into the soma (conversion), whereas the obsessional attaches this affect to another, previously unimportant idea; (2) the obsessional fends off "reproaches" that are emerging from repression, whereas the hysteric is seeking to fend off reminiscences; (3) the obsessional manifests a variety of transmutations of his reproachful feelings, such as shame, dread of others, self-reproaches, and other feelings that Freud called "obsessional affects"; (4) the obsessional develops a severe, preoccupying doubt about his actions and tries to quiet these "obsessional affects" through compulsive acts, sometimes culminating in elaborate rituals (Freud, 1894).

It is apparent that in making these distinctions Freud is taking into account the nature of the personality that produces the symptoms, even though his interest at this point was mainly in the psychology of symptom formation. Though the state of Freud's theory (prestructural theory) and the direction of his research interests both prevented him from expanding on these problems of character, some important aspects of obsessional and hysterical personality functioning can be gleaned from his analyses of symptoms. The hysteric renders affect or thoughts unconscious, whereas the obsessional detaches affect from one idea and attaches it to another. Expanding this observation and using ego-psychological concepts, the hysterical personality may be said to use repression of ideas or affects and to have a generally shallow and diminished conscious fantasy life. The obsessional personality uses isolation of ideas and affect. Such a person has a parallel characterological tendency to hyper-cathect irrelevant, trivial, and useless information. A hysteric's symptom is expressed through the soma and the self feels passive in relation to it. This type of symptom choice reflects a characterological ego disposition to wishes: feeling an ego-syntonic passivity and helplessness in relation to disguised expression of such wishes. The obsessional's symptom choice reflects a characterological ego predisposition to vigilant control of hostile impulses, to maintain an active position, and an attitude that thoughts in themselves are dangerous. In Freud's observation that the obsessional is fending off "reproaches" whereas the hysteric seeks to avoid reminiscences, we see the obsessional's predisposition to struggle with the aggressive and magic power attributed to words and the absence of this tendency in the hysterical personality. The hysterical personality struggles more directly with prohibited sexual longings, whereas the obsessional also struggles with problems centering on the magic power of his words, feelings, and actions. When Freud discussed the presence of "obsessional affects," such as dread of others, shame, and self-reproaches, and their absence in hysterics, he was again implying a difference in the underlying personality organization that we would, in structural terms, conceptualize as a difference in the rigidity and harshness of the superego. These differences could be conceptualized effectively only with the advent of the structural theory, for they rest on differences in ego defenses, autonomous ego capacities, ego style, and the nature of the superego.

THE SECOND PHASE IN THE DEVELOPMENT OF FREUD'S
THEORY OF HYSTERIA: THE CASE OF DORA

Freud's theory of hysteria took its next major turn with his
report of a fragment of an analysis with a patient he called
Dora (1905a) and two theoretical papers on hysteria that
appeared around the same time (1908, 1909a). He made
several significant refinements and additions to his general
theory and technique during this phase of his work, a phase
he considered to be the beginning of psychoanalysis proper.
He had abandoned his seduction theory, recognizing that
what his patients had reported as early childhood events were
in fact fantasies that originated in infantile sexual wishes. He
had concluded his major study of dreams, describing very
systematically the specific mechanisms by which unconscious
infantile wishes were transformed into the manifest dream.
Finally, aided by his analysis of Dora, he had written his
"Three Essays on the Theory of Sexuality" (Freud, 1905c), in
which he explored more comprehensively the nature of
infantile sexuality. These investigations, along with his own
self-analysis, set the stage for a more systematic description of
hysterical fantasy, defenses, and symptom formation.

With his understanding of the role of infantile sexuality,
he came to see hysterical symptoms as the expression of
unconscious sexual fantasies (either formed in the unconscious or rendered unconscious by repression) that originate
in the sexual fantasies of early (prepubertal) childhood.
These fantasies were repressed when infantile masturbation
was given up, but threatened to re-emerge if, for one reason
or another, no channel for libido (erotic energy) was
available in adulthood. The unconscious fantasy presses for
expression and gratification and is repressed at the price of a
pathological compromise, the formation of a symptom. Thus
he came to see the hysterical process as having as its aim the
restoration of the original infantile sexual gratifications, the
release of sexual energy, and the reinstatement of a relaxed
state (constancy principle).

He now emphasized a view of the role of the symptoms
that he had partially stated in earlier papers. The symptom

was not simply the translation of an affective charge into the soma; rather, it was an expression, via conversion, of an unconscious fantasy. Though Freud had always seen the hysterical symptom as arising from conflict, he had not emphasized earlier its function as a compromise or as itself a disguised expression of an unconscious fantasy (wish).

The nature of these unconscious sexual fantasies was seen as "perverse." In contrast to the earlier notion, even agreed to by Breuer, that sexual excitation lies at the root of hysteria, Freud now reported that "perverse" unconscious sexual fantasies and wishes of all sorts, fantasies of homosexual, sadistic, and masochistic acts, existed in hysterics and were apparent both from their symptoms and from the material they produced in analysis.

The symptom was often seen to have its roots in several different sexual fantasies, and at times as a combination of both sexual and nonsexual wishes, though the sexual wishes were always considered to be the most basic. These sexual fantasies often expressed two inherent aspects of human sexuality—the masculine and the feminine. Thus, in many hysterical fantasies and their resulting symptoms, there proved to be a homosexual as well as a heterosexual trend. Hysterical fantasy was seen as expressing man's essential and universal bisexual predisposition, though Freud thought this predisposition showed itself more clearly in neurotics.

During this phase there was a rich cross-fertilization between Freud's work on the psychology of dreams and the psychology of symptom formation. Freud believed that the hysterical symptom, whether conversion symptom or hysterical attack, expressed an unconscious idea via the same processes of distortion that were used in dreams. Unconscious wishes and fantasies are expressed in disguised form in symptoms by the same processes that *transform the latent unconscious dream thoughts into manifest imagery*. Moreover, the meaning of the symptom could be understood using the same technique of analysis he had found effective in understanding dream distortion and the latent dream wishes it disguises.

The symptom, like the dream, represents several fantasies

simultaneously by the process of condensation — combining, for example, a recent wish and an infantile precursor of it. The symptom may represent a wish by a pantomimic expression of its opposite, just as a dream disguises a wish by representation of the opposite or removal of affect. The hysterical attack, like the dream, may portray and disguise the unconscious wish by symbolically expressing the parts of the fantasy as reversed or condensed.

The theory of hysterical symptoms was also elaborated during this phase by a more systematic assessment of their function.[6] Though the hysterical attack is most fundamentally generated by an unconscious complex composed of a libidinal, sexual wish and an ideational component attached to it (fantasy), it may also serve a need of the person to flee into illness as an escape from what is experienced as painful or frightening reality, and may itself be a source of gratification. The hysterical attack may be aimed at certain people in order to obtain certain comforts or supports from them. Freud adds that such attacks may be delayed until such a person is present and that the patient may therefore appear to be consciously manipulating.

Freud was adding here an important new dimension to the understanding of hysterical symptoms. A symptom, though entirely unconsciously created, may have a current *interpersonal function*. He even warns that some hysterical people, when they do not express their fantasies as symptoms, may be inclined to bring them about in action, though he does not define such behavior as a specific symptom. "We also know of cases — cases which have their practical importance as well — in which hysterics do not give expression to their phantasies in the form of symptoms but as conscious realizations, and in that way devise and stage assaults, attacks, and acts of sexual aggression" (Freud, 1908, p. 162). The conflict, in this case, may be played out in a larger, interpersonal arena as well as via the formation of a specific somatic symptom or set of symptoms.

[6] Freud is here discussing hysterical attacks, but seems to be suggesting the applicability of his observations to all hysterical symptoms.

In addition, Freud presented a new definition of hysteria in which for the first time he focused on a general character trait rather than on specific symptoms: "I should without question consider a person hysterical in whom an occasion for sexual excitement elicited feelings that were preponderantly or exclusively unpleasurable; and I should do so whether or no the person were capable of producing somatic symptoms" (Freud, 1905a, p. 28). This is the first time Freud defines hysteria not by the presence of conversion symptoms, but by a feeling of displeasure in response to a potentially sexually stimulating experience. He seems to be suggesting here that hysteria can be usefully defined by reference to the transformation of potential excitement into displeasure and pain.

This statement brings us to a most important turn in the road: here Freud was saying that hysteria is not defined by the presence of somatic symptoms, implying that these are but one form of expression of neurotic conflict in the hysteric. He was also saying that there are certain action patterns, really character patterns, that may be considered hysterical symptoms. He sidesteps the problem of defining the disorder and distinguishing it from other disorders, saying only that such people respond with unpleasure to their own sexual excitement.

The Dora case spelled out several specific defenses, most of which were expressed in some form in the patient's resistance to treatment: reversal of affect, displacement (as to body site, i.e., feeling disgust in the throat instead of feeling genital sensations), and the function of "reactive thoughts" (a thought that asserts itself in excessive and exaggerated form in consciousness and which is contrary to one that is repressed). The role of overdetermination of symptoms and associations and the defensive function of manifest dream images are further emphasized in this case. Freud also discussed the differential impact of forgetting, calling attention to the marked variations in Dora's memory and perception depending on the extent to which they approached unconscious wishes.

Though Freud presented his discovery of infantile sexuality

in both *The Interpretation of Dreams* (1900) and "Three Essays on the Theory of Sexuality" (1905c), the Dora case carefully illustrated this theory. Without yet describing regression, he described the patient's association between genital sensations and infantile feelings and experiences connected with urination and defecation. Going far beyond the cases in *Studies on Hysteria*, he now made continual references to an unconscious substratum of infantile sexual experiences and memories.

It was in the description of the Dora case that Freud discussed a change in his technique for treating hysteria: he stopped asking the patient to work on his symptoms one by one, and instead he began letting the patient talk about whatever he wished, whatever was coming to the surface at the moment. A major contribution of this case study, though not essential to our discussion of hysteria, involves Freud's recognition of both the therapeutic liability and the potential of the transference. The case ended prematurely, as Freud had not succeeded in "mastering the transference in good time" (Freud, 1905a, p. 118). He came to understand that in the transference to the analyst, the patient lives out fantasies and wishes that have been aroused and are in the process of being made conscious in the analysis. The therapist is used as a replacement in the present for someone toward whom feelings had been directed in the past.

THE THIRD PHASE OF FREUD'S THEORY OF HYSTERIA:
THE *Introductory Lectures*

The next major coalescing of Freud's thoughts on hysteria is found in his *Introductory Lectures on Psycho-Analysis* (1916-1917). The theory of hysterical symptom formation is presented in combination with a more general theory of symptom formation, based also on the analyses of obsessional symptoms. Much more than before, the theory of hysteria is in a general theory of neurotic symptom formation.

Freud continued to see the neurotic symptom, whether obsessional or hysterical, as originating in conflict between sexual urges and defenses; however, he now noted new mechanisms, and re-emphasized others that he had previously discussed. The pathology of the development of the libido, the ego instincts, regression, fantasy, and a dynamic-economic concept of psychic energy were all viewed as aspects of the neurotic symptom formation.

The nature and forms of expression of the defenses against unconscious forces, and the nature of these forces themselves, came under more systematic scrutiny at this time. Freud now clearly saw the patient's resistance as resulting from the forces of repression that keep the unconscious wishes or strivings from emerging into consciousness. The resistance, which demonstrates repression *in vivo*, was seen as taking several forms in the treatment. Intellectual resistances referred to the patient's unwillingness to believe in and accept as his own the existence of unconscious wishes. Transference resistances referred to the patient's repeating impulses and expectations from his early life instead of remembering them. These were considered extremely valuable, since they contained much important material about the patient's past, which could be used to demonstrate to him experientially the source of his neurotic difficulties. Other resistances that reflected "character traits, attitudes of the ego," which also could be demonstrated to the patient, were found to be useful. The analysis of these character and transference resistances were eventually to become the prime focus of psychoanalysis for Freud. Though at this stage Freud had no structural concept of ego, using the term to refer at times to person, social self, or self, there is nevertheless an emerging understanding of differences in people's defensive strategies. The resistance is not merely the expression of a formless, monolithic, and undifferentiated "defense," or "repression," but begins to be seen as having qualities that are specific to diagnostic groups and perhaps ultimately specific to the individual. Thus the hysteric would tend to resist by forgetting, the obsessive by doubting.

With this more differentiated concept of resistance, the general differences in functioning among patients could be better specified. This more refined concept of resistance helped build a bridge to the psychology of character. It was on the basis of the psychology of resistances and the differing resistances patients use that Wilhelm Reich formulated the first comprehensive psychoanalytic psychology of character.

Freud saw infantile sexuality as passing through phases determined by the passage of the libido through various erogenous zones of the body: through oral, anal, and phallic periods in which the mouth (and mucosa), the anus, and the genitals respectively become primary pleasure zones, each in turn being especially excitable. The unfolding of sexuality was seen as reaching its infantile culmination with the Oedipus complex, in which phallic-genital urges are primary and are directed toward the primary objects, the parents. The nature of "sexual" gratification, then, was seen as having a history that contains many types of pleasure before "genital primacy" is reached. Thus a variety of pleasures, perverse to the sensibilities of most adults, were seen as entirely *normal* aspects of infantile development.

Sexual "energy" was conceived as moving from zone to zone during development as sexuality unfolds. This energy was conceived to be, within limits, plastic, mobile, and fluid, capable of moving back to previous zones of pleasure, reviving the pleasurable aspects of these zones (regression), capable of changing its object, and capable of abandoning sexual aims altogether and becoming invested in social aims (sublimation). The inherent limitations on this mobility, coupled with the impact of frustration of sexual drives, may lead to a damming up of libido and a new channel for its expression—a substitute gratification. The libido then seeks new objects and new paths. The aims, forms, and targets of sexual energy, within limits, were seen as changeable (dynamic assumption), and the quantity of sexual energy was seen as fixed (economic assumption). Thus when drives are frustrated, by either external factors (the unavailability of an object, for example) or internal factors (the safety and preservation of the self—"ego instincts"), conflict becomes inevitable and some new path for channeling the libido must arise. This dammed-up libido may find various resolutions: one striving may be replaced by another striving, for the libido is plastic; one gratification may compensate for a frustration; the impulse may change its aim, change its object, or become "sublimated"; or the dammed-up libido may be tolerated.

One potentially pathogenic channel this blocked libido may find is that of regression, the reinvesting of an earlier pleasurable site. Regression was considered a precondition (but not a sufficient cause) for a neurosis. Under the pressure of such conflict the libido may regress to a point of earlier gratification, a point of fixation during development. The extent and nature of the fixated libido during the unfolding of infantile sexuality might predispose the person to regression of libido and therefore to neurosis. Frustration is the trigger in adult life for the libidinal regression to this point of fixation.

This regression, however, is still but a *precondition* for neurosis. An additional factor was considered necessary for frustration and regression to eventuate in a neurotic conflict: the regressive aims and object of the libido must be opposed by a part of the personality. If gratifications afforded by the regression of libido fail to encounter any internal objection, then a perversion, not a neurosis, will result. The regressive aim, object, and manner of instinctual gratification must be met by a defense for a symptom, the neurotic compromise outlet for the drive, to result. Without such symptom formation there is, by definition, no neurosis. The neurotic conflict results from a sexual striving that has been frustrated, undergone regression to an earlier point of fixation and, in regressed form, met with displeasure and repudiation by the Conscious and Preconscious systems. Though there is as yet no structural concept of ego, only a topographic concept of Conscious, Preconscious, and Unconscious, there is at this juncture a concept of strivings for control, self-preservation, and the application of energy to socially productive pursuits. The defensive side of the conflict that produces the neurotic symptom comes to comprehend more than a desire to fend off a socially or personally objectionable thought or wish. It comes to include a clash of two sorts of "instincts," the libidinal ones and those oriented toward the person's self-preservative, survival needs. These ego instincts are therefore as central to the etiology of a neurosis as the quantity of libidinal charge or the nature of the libidinal wish. Thus it is by virtue of the development of the ego instincts that a tendency to conflict arises, a tendency that is an essential ingredient in the formation of neurotic symptoms. Discussion of ego instincts opened a new avenue in psychoanalytic research on the neuroses, for it sharpened the concept of intrapsychic conflict and helped to further consideration of individual differences in ego-defensive functioning. The concept of ego instincts was a precursor of the later investigation (with the structural theory) of the neuroses, which involved systematic investigation of the nature of ego defenses, their quality, rigidity, etc., and ultimately of the psychoanalytic study of character.

Finally, the understanding of the neurotic process was augmented by an emphasis on the role of fantasy in symptom formation. Freud came to regard fantasy developmentally as a compensation that becomes necessary as pleasures are renounced or delayed in compliance with the demands of reality. Renounced wishes and their gratifications are permitted to live on as fantasies, free from the constraints of reality. Freud saw fantasy also as an intermediate stage on the path to symptom formation. When libido is dammed up, fantasy residues of earlier abandoned forms of sexual pleasure become reinvested with libido. Though these fantasies are "tolerated" in the ego, as they do not make any real demands to be lived out, they maintain a direct link with unconscious infantile fixated drives, and the libido can therefore easily flow back to these fixation points via such fantasies. However, with the surplus energy resulting from frustration, these fantasies and the unconscious drives connected to them begin to push for realization, coming into conflict with the ego, thereby demanding repression and setting the stage for symptom formation.

Though Freud discussed hysteria separately much less often in this period of his work, he did consider the nature of regression in hysteria. While regression was seen as a precondition for neurosis, the extent of regression and the points of fixation were considered to vary with the type of neurotic symptom. Hysteria was characterized as a regression to the phallic-Oedipal period of development when "genital primacy" was established, and *not* as a regression to earlier, pregenital points in development. Even though the hysteric's defense against genital strivings, expressed, for example, by a preconscious and conscious rejection of sexual wishes, may resemble a pregenital sexual adjustment, Freud conceived the hysteric as having achieved unconscious genital primacy. This formulation of the dynamics of the hysteric, though implied earlier by Freud, was more explicitly presented during this phase. The presence of a phallic-Oedipal fixation and the absence of significant pregenital regression have remained, for most authors, the essential features of the hysteric's libidinal life. This conceptualization represented a consideration of hysteria as a personality organization, for these dynamics were conceived as more enduring and basic aspects of the disorder than the presence of conversion symptoms. At this juncture, however, the personality-organization conception was limited, for the psychoanalytic theory of development consisted essentially of the development of the drives, without regard to the many distinguishing features of the hysterical personality that can be conceptualized only with the structural concepts of ego and superego.

HYSTERIA AND THE STRUCTURAL THEORY: FOURTH PHASE

It was during the early 1920's, with "Beyond the Pleasure Principle" (1920) and "The Ego and the Id" (1923) that Freud added a structural theory, a theory of intrapsychic agencies, to his topographic one. The theory of neurotic symptom formation, with the addition of the structural concept, is found most completely in "Inhibitions, Symptoms and Anxiety" (1926). The structural theory, along with refinements of some previous concepts, permitted important shifts in the conception of anxiety, symptom formation, defense, and the genesis of neurosis. The evolution of these concepts is of particular importance for our purposes, for it promoted a clearer understanding of the similarities and differences between hysteria and obsessional neurosis and introduced the conceptual tools necessary for understanding hysteria as a personality organization.

PSYCHIC STRUCTURE AND THE DIFFERENTIATION OF
THE CONCEPT OF DEFENSE

Though Freud dealt with the nature of intrapsychic conflict from his earliest works onward, with the structural theory the concept of the repressing part of the personality underwent thorough-going changes. Where earlier Freud used "defense" and "repression" more or less interchangeably and considered repression to be basic to all neuroses, he now considered repression as only one specific form of defense. Freud suggested that the nature of defensive activity may be correlated with particular neuroses, noting that repression (without regression from the earlier consolidation of genital primacy) is a basic defining feature of hysteria. "Defense" came to be considered a superordinate category, and repression, isolation, and undoing as specific defenses within it.

Freud characterized repression as a barring of exciting experiences and pathogenic thought structures from awareness or memory. These memories and wishes were rendered unconscious. The defense of repression was contrasted with the defenses found in the obsessional neurosis, which do not render conflictual thoughts unconscious. While the pathogenic thought may exist (in weakened and sometimes abbreviated or distorted form) in the obsessional's consciousness, the whole ego has succumbed to a defensive struggle in response to pressure from his unusually severe superego. Normal traits of conscientiousness, cleanliness, and pity become exaggerated to ward off the regressive anal-sadistic ideas (reaction formation). Motor activities are sometimes used magically to undo and cancel out the unacceptable wish (compulsions). The ego in the obsessional prevents connections between ideas, symbolically avoiding "touching" the ideas even though they may be entirely conscious, and magically undoing the ideas and setting them apart and away (isolation). In hysteria the ego is seen as turning away altogether from the disagreeable impulse and allowing it to follow its course in the unconscious; the ego plays no further role in the form of expression of the impulse (Freud, 1926). The hysteric was seen to rely on repression, a defense pressing for the forgetting and unknowing of unacceptable thoughts, wishes, and memories. This narrower, more specific definition of repression has continued to be a most central defining feature of the disorder. Here is another point in Freud's thinking at which hysteria is further conceptualized on the basis of enduring personality processes. When the hysteric's use of repression was combined with the phallic-Oedipal fixation point of the libido, the essence of the psychoanalytic conception of the disorder had been achieved.

More important, it was with the advent of the structural theory, and the more differentiated concept of defense that it contained, that the psychoanalytic study of total character functioning could be comprehensively explored. In short, only with the advent of the structural concept of the ego could predominant *forms* of defense, and intrapsychic compromises unique to certain patients, be defined. The psychoanalytic definition of hysteria then needed to depend less on the presence of conversion symptoms. Though Freud clearly believed the presence of conversion reactions was not a necessary or sufficient condition for defining patients as hysterical, implying only that such symptoms are common in such people, it is unfortunately the case that much of the psychoanalytic literature on this subject has fallen back on conversion reactions as definitional of the disorder. It is also unfortunate that, with the exception of Reich, Federn, and a few others to be described later, psychoanalysts have paid less theoretical attention to personality than to symptoms. Interestingly, however, in many case histories reported in the analytic literature the treatment was as much concerned with the analysis of character as with the analysis of specific symptoms.

INTERNAL ANTICATHEXIS VERSUS EXTERNAL ANTICATHEXIS: AN EARLY CONCEPT OF HYSTERICAL EGO STYLE

Freud went on to describe an essential difference in the direction and range of the defensive processes of the obsessional and the hysterical patient. Arguing that the ego must have anticathectic energy at its disposal to fend off instincts, Freud said that such anticathectic activity is quite easily observable in the obvious defensive maneuvers of the obsessional (reaction formation, excessive conscientiousness, exaggeration of other "moral" character traits, etc.) and, although harder to detect, also exist in the hysteric. In the obsessional these anticathectic defensive processes have become so widespread in the personality as to constitute character traits. In the hysteric such processes, which tend to be directed at denying ambivalence toward an object, even when they include reaction formation, are confined to particular relationships. The defense is used in relationships with a particular object and then often with considerable tenacity, but it is not so widespread as to be a general disposition or proclivity of the ego. Thus, in addition to using somewhat different defenses than the obsessional, the hysteric turns his defensive efforts toward problems in a *specific set of affectionate relationships*, whereas the obsessional can loosen his ties with the original object and replay his needs and defenses within virtually any subsequent relationship, as close or as superficial as such a relationship may be.

The direction of the anticathexis also differs in the two neuroses. As a repressed instinctual impulse may be "activated" either from within by an internal source of excitation (an arousing sexual fantasy, for example) or from without by perception of a desired object, the direction of the defense may emphasize external or internal experience.

The obsessional defensively reinforces conscious attitudes that oppose these repressed instinctual trends. The emphasis is on resisting the internal awareness of unacceptable thoughts or wishes by warding them off through an act of will or ritual. The anticathexis in the obsessional is directed, then, toward internal experience. The defensive activity is directed toward avoiding objectionable and tabooed thoughts that arise from within by limiting and constricting internal experience.

The hysteric's defenses are directed outward, against *perceptions* that might trigger unacceptable, dangerous, or tabooed wishes. The ego fends off dangerous wishes by narrowing its exposure to external situations that might excite them. Such situations are avoided or, if they occur, conscious attention and interest are withdrawn from them. This tendency reaches its most extreme form in phobias.

Thus Freud began to construct a picture of interlocking defensive patterns in hysteria, another clear move toward a more holistic definition of the disorder as a personality organization rather than as a symptom complex. The tendency to repress, a defense of "not knowing," is complemented by a tendency to avoid situations that might trigger unacceptable wishes. The hysterical mechanism permits material to be thoroughly excluded from consciousness, and the hysteric is willing to buttress this stance by seeking to avoid situations that might excite him. Though, of course, this withdrawal is itself a symptom and may become generally a problem for the patient, the hysteric often presents his problem in circumscribed form, in response to particular people or particular situations. The hysterical ego is not, like the obsessional ego, infiltrated by constant defensive activity, but may function reasonably normally outside of the specifically affect-laden contexts.

Implied in Freud's delineation of these differences is a basic characteristic of hysterical ego style that was later spelled out more fully by others. The hysteric locates the source of his feelings, the triggers of them, in the situations through which he moves. If situations can be avoided, or if other people can be coerced to change, then the hysteric is inclined to feel that the unacceptable feelings will disappear, for he does not fundamentally accept them as coming from within. The obsessional, by contrast, is all too willing to accept that such wishes come from within, even when their exact nature is distorted or masked, and he comes to reproach and castigate himself mercilessly for them.

REGRESSION RE-EMPHASIZED

At this point in Freud's work the most basic difference between the obsessional neurotic and the hysteric continues to be the instability of the obsessional's genital organization. While both neuroses were seen as resulting from a need to fend off the libidinal wishes of the Oedipus complex, the ego of the obsessional very easily throws over the recently consolidated genital primacy and regresses to the anal-sadistic stage. In the hysteric no regression was posited; rather, the libidinal developmental achievements were seen as maintained, with repression the primary defense (reaction formation and phobic avoidance were seen as used secondarily).

Regression of the libido was seen to aggravate the conflict in yet another way in the obsessional—by making the superego severe and intolerant. The superego organization was conceived as emerging primarily from the id, and therefore a regression of the libido to an anal-sadistic level and a defusion of instincts would make the superego "harsher, unkinder and more tormenting than where development has been normal" (Freud, 1926, p. 116). In obsessional neurosis, the conflict is aggravated by the regression of libido in two ways: the defensive forces become stricter and more intolerant and the drives themselves more aggressive, sadistic, and generally less acceptable (for these strivings are not erotic longings for an object, but sadistic, much more infantile wishes to reproach, torture and kill).

By contrast, the hysteric's superego is less severe, more tolerant, and less tormenting. Because the hysteric's psychic conflict is characterized by repression, without regression of the libido from genital primacy, his superego does not take on the anal-sadistic quality that it does in the obsessional. Thus, in contrast to the obsessional, the hysteric's wishes are less infantile and sadistic and the superego is less severe; the ego is capable of defending against the wishes without pervasive disruption of its functioning.

This quality of the hysterical superego has been described either directly or indirectly by later contributors in their descriptions of the manipulative and mischievous aspect of the hysteric. This sort of superego makes the hysteric more comfortable being flashy, self-involved, and daring. It is just this quality of the hysterical superego that permits him to seek loving or flattering or exciting attachments even if this means transgressing external or internal standards of what is appropriate. The hysteric, in an effort to fulfill needs, is much more willing than the obsessional to act in a way that will please the object and is less concerned about being "true" to himself (more will be said about the hysterical superego in Chapters 3, 4, and 5).

OEDIPUS COMPLEX AND CASTRATION ANXIETY

Freud clearly affirmed the genetic importance of the Oedipus complex during this period. He saw the Oedipus complex as at the heart of both obsessional and hysterical difficulties. In both disorders the Oedipal wishes toward parents have been accompanied by fears of castration and/or loss of love. In normal development, as a result of these fears and out of love for the same-sexed parent, the child to some extent puts his sexual strivings aside, forms identifications with his parents, and consolidates a superego that will protect him from his wishes and guide him in directions similar to the rival parent — all of which inaugurates the latency period. In the neurotic situation the fear of castration and/or loss of love becomes so severe that the wishes become intolerable. In the hysteric they are repressed, but continue in the unconscious without any change in intensity. In the obsessional, the superego is so severe, and the ego, having prematurely consolidated, is so strong, that there is a regression to the anal-sadistic period and further defenses against these regressed wishes develop. In the hysteric, then, the conflict remains around genital sexual wishes and unconscious fantasies. Hysterical symptoms all basically express a battle with sexual (genital) wishes toward incestuous objects. Whether this symptom takes the form of fear of a seemingly innocuous stimulus as in anxiety hysteria, or the form of a somatic symptom as in conversion hysteria, there is in the unconscious a genital wish, met by repression, which continues to seek expression. This, then, is the hallmark of the dynamic struggle in the hysteric.

ADDITIONS TO THE THEORY OF SYMPTOMS

The structural theory, along with Freud's continued psychoanalytic observations, added several new dimensions to the function of symptoms or hysterical attacks, but they continued to be viewed basically as a compromise between an unconscious infantile wish and a defense. Even after the advent of the structural theory and an expanded view of the function of symptoms, the conflict between wish and defense continued to be considered fundamental to neurotic symptom formation.

Freud described an additional process that was secondary to the initial symptom formation. The ego, having access to desexualized energy that still maintains a tendency to bind and unify, seeks to make the symptom(s) part of its own organization (an early version of the synthetic function). Freud compared the ego's adaptation to the symptom with the ego's adaptation to the external world. Because of its synthesizing tendency the ego brings the symptom into its own orbit, adapting itself to it in various ways. The ego recognizes that the symptom has to stay, and proceeds to use it to secondary advantage. Thus the original conflict between repressed wish and defense continued to be regarded as the initial process of symptom formation, which then undergoes a secondary process of amalgamation with the ego, resulting finally in a distortion of ego process. This concept has some important implications for the development of ego-characterological formations secondary to symptom formation. The adaptation to a phobic symptom, for example, could lead to an inhibition of certain ego capacities (assertive, independent, exploratory ego activity, for example), a perceptual and cognitive style inclined to not looking and not knowing, and an ego mode of relating to objects characterized by dependence on them for performing a variety of tasks (a generalizing of the mode of relating to the phobic companion).

FREUD'S THEORY OF ANXIETY HYSTERIA

Freud's major researches on the neuroses grew out of his study of conversion hysteria and the obsessional neuroses.

There was, however, a third type of symptom pattern, that of the phobia, that drew his attention. Though he reports only one case in which phobic symptoms were central (Little Hans, Freud, 1909b) and one in which such symptoms played a secondary role (the Wolf Man, 1918), he would turn to the dynamics behind phobias as illustrations of the essential aspects of the neurotic process. In one of his most extensive metapsychological works on the dynamics of neuroses, "Inhibitions, Symptoms and Anxiety" (1926), the dynamics of a phobic symptom served as one of the pivotal phenomena for his wide-ranging discussion.

In this work, Freud spelled out the constituent processes in anxiety hysteria, using the cases of Little Hans and the Wolf Man as illustrations. Upon analyzing Little Hans's fear that horses would bite him, Freud discovered that the child's murderous wishes toward his father had been displaced to the horses and then the wishes projected onto the horse. In the case of Little Hans there was also an oral regression of libido, leading to a fear of being bitten, but this was not considered essential to the phobic process. According to Freud, the displacement from the father to the horse was the essential anxiety-hysterical process.

Freud cited the two cases of anxiety hysteria, Little Hans and the Wolf Man, to demonstrate that in both the basic fear was of castration. The fear of castration and the later fear of the internalized castrator—father, the superego, together with the self-preservative strivings of the ego, were viewed as provoking repression. This repression, together with the tendency of the repressed drives to seek discharge, constituted the neurotic conflict.

Freud commented that the phobic symptom often has the effect of placing the patient in a position of being guided and assisted by another person. This childlike position helps the patient to avoid the solitude that would tempt him to masturbate and to become aware of his "unacceptable" instinctual impulses. The patient unconsciously feels that avoiding aloneness prevents the upsurge of these impulses and the castration or loss of love that he fears will result from them.

Freud uses phobias (anxiety hysteria) to epitomize the process of "anticathexis" seen in all hysterics. Yet he is careful to distinguish between hysteria and anxiety hysteria, implying that the latter is not per se to be considered hysteria and can occur in a variety of neuroses. His observations, however, *do* suggest that there would be a higher incidence of phobias in hysterics, that their defensive proclivities would make them more likely to develop such a symptom than would an obsessional's. This seems even today to be a sensible approach, and one that is suggested in the final chapter. Phobias occur in many types of personalities and are part of many psychopathologies, but the hysterical personality is particularly likely to develop neurotic phobias.

This view of phobias has relevance to conversion as well. Hysteria cannot be defined by the presence of phobias or conversion symptoms, for these symptoms appear in other types of patients. Some hysterics may present neither symptom. Nevertheless, hysterics, by virtue of their underlying dynamics and structure, are more inclined than any other single personality type to develop these types of symptoms.

HYSTERIA CONCEPTUALIZED AS A PERSONALITY STRUCTURE

Although in Freud's early work there are seeds of later conceptualizations about character, he concentrated on the psychology of symptoms at that point, largely because symptoms, along with dreams, screen memories, and parapraxes provided such clear expressions of conflicting intrapsychic forces, the nature of unconscious mental processes, and the dynamics of compromise formations. In his prestructural theoretical work he aimed at elucidating the nature of unconscious processes and impulse-defense compromises, paying relatively little attention to the nature of and individual differences in the repressing or defensive forces. It was with the advent of the structural theory and its elaboration by Hartmann and Anna Freud that many aspects of psychological functioning and individual differences of functioning could be woven into psychoanalytic theory. It was only with this integration that a psychoanalytic theory of personality became possible. The advent of the structural theory and the advances in ego psychology that followed widened the scope of psychoanalysis in several respects important for the psychoanalytic study of general personality functioning. The ego came to be seen as not merely a repressing agency, but as a combination of functions and structures (of both primary and secondary autonomy), as an unconscious defensive sector in which specific defensive mechanisms are found (Anna Freud), and as an adaptive sector. The ego was seen both as more independent of the id and as having a range of defensive and adaptive possibilities at its disposal. Its structure was also seen as significantly influenced by the environment, particularly the relationships with key early objects.

CONCLUSION

To isolate the psychoanalytic study of hysteria or anxiety hysteria from the development of psychoanalysis and Freud's own professional development is analogous to studying art with only the sketchiest understanding of the artist or his times—that is, it has some value but is artificial and misleading. The study of hysteria was for a time the whole of psychoanalysis and never ceased to be a disorder of central interest to Freud. Freud's study of the disorder parallels the general development of his thought.

Freud's discussion of hysteria laid down what have continued to be the basic tenets of a psychodynamic approach to the disorder: (1) hysteria involves an infantile conflict at the phallic-Oedipal stage; (2) the hysterical ego resorts primarily to repression, dissociation, amnesia and, less important, to reaction formation as defenses; (3) the hysterical symptom commonly shows itself as a conversion reaction, hysterical attack, or phobia, and carries with it secondary advantages; (4) the hysteric's superego tends to be relatively pliable, less severe than that of the obsessional; (5) the hysterical symptom becomes synthesized with the ego and may itself secondarily become recruited to gratify the unconscious needs that it was used to fend off; (6) the hysteric tends to fend off internal conflict by internally blocking perception of or physically withdrawing from external stimuli that promise to spark unconscious needs or their derivatives; and (7) unconscious fantasy is an essential intermediary step in the formation of the hysterical symptom.

Though Freud concerned himself with hysteria throughout his work, he seemed only partially able to conceptualize the hysteric as a distinct personality organization. He seemed always to see the obsessional's kernel conflict as more likely to infiltrate into the fabric of character. The hysteric was defined as a neurotic patient with a certain class of symptoms, and the hysterical ego style was not viewed as extensively disrupted by the neurotic conflict. Freud may have said little about the hysterical character for three reasons: the study of hysteria began as a study of hysterical symptoms; the ego activity of the obsessional shows itself in more obvious and verbal form in the patient's conscious associations in analysis; and Freud studied hysteria most intensively in the first half of his psychoanalytic career, before the advent of the structural theory. Without the structural concept of the ego, it is difficult to conceptualize regular and enduring modes of defensive or adaptive functioning, both of which are necessary to a holistic model of personality functioning. For these reasons Freud never approached the problem of the hysterical "personality" as such, though the seeds of such a conceptualization are to be found in his work on hysterical symptom formation and in his general observations of his hysterical patients.

The hysterical personality may also have eluded Freud because of one very basic feature of the hysterical ego (discussed below in Chapter 4) — its tendency to live out for ego-defensive purposes a prevalent cultural myth or identity. Freud's patients were living out a somewhat exaggerated version of the image of the Victorian woman, their personalities being therefore difficult to discriminate from the "normal." It may have been, therefore, that the nature of the hysterical personality failed to be of interest for

Freud because one of its most essential ego-characterological traits, the identification with current cultural forms, passed unnoticed.

This review of Freud's concept of hysteria takes us to the late 1920's. The subsequent psychoanalytic theory of the disorder cannot be so neatly traced. It divided into the further study of conversion, the study of character, and the study of specific defenses and defensive styles. The original findings were also amalgamated with general psychiatry, with projective-test psychology, and with offshoots of psychoanalysis (such as the work of Angyal, Sullivan, and Farber). To assess these later developments means broadening our sights and embarking on another review that will perhaps leave us as confused as enlightened.

2

DEFINITIONS OF HYSTERIA

> *Hysteria is an extraordinarily interesting disease, and a strange one. It is encountered in the earliest pages of recorded medicine and is dealt with in current psychiatric literature. Throughout all the intervening years it has been known and accepted as though it were a readily recognizable entity. And yet, except for the fact that it is a functional disorder, without concomitant organic pathological change, it defies definition and any attempt to portray it concretely. Like a globule of mercury, it escapes the grasp.*
>
> —Veith, *Hysteria*

DEFINITIONAL CONFUSION

Though it was through the treatment of hysterics that Freud made his initial discoveries of the impact of the unconscious on mental life (Breuer and Freud, 1893-1895), attempts to define and explain hysteria are beset by endless paradox and enigma. Hysteria, hysterical character, hysterical personality, conversion hysteria are in constant use among clinicians, yet each of these terms is at best loosely and at worst completely idiosyncratically, defined. The study of hysteria is so interwoven with the early development of psychoanalytic theory that it has even been suggested that the course of psychoanalysis might have been different if Freud's initial patients had not been hysterics (Rycroft, personal communication to Wisdom, 1961).[1] And yet Freud's own comments on the syndrome are "scattered, unsystematic, strangely late or non-existent" (Wisdom, 1961, p. 236 fn.). Though hysteria has been considered most responsive to traditional psychoanalytic treatment and it is usually assumed that much is known about it, upon closer scrutiny much about the theory of hysteria is obscure (Wisdom, 1961). The syndrome has been approached from so many points of view, and so rarely systematically, that a clear, shared definition has been elusive.

THE PRE-FREUDIAN HISTORY OF HYSTERIA

Problems of defining hysteria are not new. Perusal of the long history of the study of hysteria reveals that the explanations of the disorder have been extraordinarily wide-ranging. Egyptian physicians and the Greek Hippocrates believed that hysterical symptoms arose from the wandering of the uterus through the body, where it was thought to impede the functioning of other organs. Interestingly, the treatments they devised to lure the womb back to its normal position, such as using the dried excrement of men as a fumigant, or manipulating the vulva and vagina, betray an unconscious recognition of the sexual longings and conflicts of these sufferers. Later Greeks and Romans thought the impact of sexual abstinence on the physiology of the genitals led to retention and congestion of fluids in the genitals and resulted in hysterical manifestations.

To the medieval Christian, it was unthinkable that abstention from something as carnal as sexual activity could lead to disease. Hysteria was, rather, an expression of possession by the Devil himself or his messengers, such as witches.

[1] Rycroft has suggested that the theory of primary-process thinking might have been different if Freud's practice had consisted predominantly of obsessionals.

With the rebirth of secular science that followed the Middle Ages, hysteria came to be considered a disorder that arose neither from the thwarting of natural sexual urges, nor spiritual alliance with the Devil, but simply as a neurological affliction. The first truly "psychological" theory of the disorder was presented by Sydenham in the late seventeenth century.

From the middle of the eighteenth century on, virtually all of the earlier theories of the disorder burgeoned once more without satisfactory synthesis. Hysteria was concurrently considered a uterine or female pelvic disease, a neurological condition, and a condition resulting from undue stimulation or insufficient release of erotic drives. During the same period the behavioral anomalies considered to be hysterical proliferated. A theory remarkably like Freud's initial theory of hysteria was proposed by Carter (1853) in the middle of the nineteenth century. The backdrop for Freud's contributions to the study of hysteria and personality was the late nineteenth-century work of Charcot and his pupil Janet: they recognized the power of emotional trauma, the tendency of hysteria to mimic physical disease, the suggestibility of the hysteric, and emphasized the power of the unconscious mentation that develops around sexual ideas.

The confusion of terminology and theory surrounding hysteria, which began with the confluence of theoretical approaches in the eighteenth century, persists today (Veith, 1965). Indeed, the confusion in the last 20 years may be even greater than it was in the late nineteenth century.

SOURCES OF DEFINITIONAL CONFUSION

Currently it often *seems* that the very phenomenon being described differs from author to author. Part of the reason is that definitions of hysteria vary in emphasis and approach. One set of definitions is descriptive in emphasis, a second relies on dynamic constructs, a third emphasizes ego process, and a fourth approaches definition empirically. Few successfully designate criteria that are both cogent and reliably identifiable.

The descriptive approach strives to define the overt behaviors evidenced by patients with hysteria. These behaviors may include isolated symptoms or complexes of behavioral characteristics considered to distinguish hysteria from other disorders. Some descriptive approaches are limited to descriptions of symptoms, some to descriptions of personality traits found in the hysterical character; still others try to embrace both.

The descriptive approach has liabilities. First, the descriptions are often, in actuality, rather vague. Second, the omission or underemphasis of a theory of the dynamics which lie at the root of the behavior described can lead to the error of assuming that two patients who manifest the same overt behavior have the same ego structures and internal conflicts.

The second approach, in pure form, emphasizes a higher-order theoretical construct of dynamics. Definitions that refer to a particular intrapsychic constellation, to the predominance of one or two defenses or to the developmental fixation point, are prime examples. This approach does not necessarily ignore the behavioral symptoms of hysteria; rather, it considers such behavior as a secondary consequence of the defining intrapsychic situation. In this type of approach, moreover, the nature of unconscious wishes is usually emphasized far more than the nature of the ego. For example, many psychoanalytic authors define hysteria by the presence of phallic-Oedipal conflicts, repression, and other higher-order concepts connected with the struggle between incestuous wishes and the defenses against them. The overt disturbance caused by the internal state is seen as taking many forms, all of which subsequently come to be defined as "hysterical."

Several problems arise from this approach. First, the higher-order processes and conflicts, such as repression and Oedipal conflict, are ascertained according to each clinician's skill, theoretical bias, and personal understanding of these concepts. Second, owing to the complexity of these conceptions, their basically clinical origin, and the difficulty of describing the process of clinical inference, the method of inferring these dynamics has never been made explicit enough for research purposes.[2]

The third approach, in many ways the most promising of the four, rather than describing either higher-order intrapsychic processes or the overt "appearance" of the personality, seeks to understand and describe the modes of operation and structure of the hysterical ego. Unfortunately, this ego-process approach has been relatively neglected in the study of hysteria, although ego psychology has flourished in other fields of psychopathology (Hartmann, 1939).

The least frequently explored of the four approaches, the empirical approach, strives to test the reliability and validity of various definitions of hysteria. This approach has generally sought to test "descriptive" definitions.

What will emerge first from this review is that various authors have considered different sets of characteristics to be definitional of hysteria. Nevertheless, although few of them define hysteria by exactly the same set of characteristics, there are clear intersections among these sets of symptoms and behavioral traits. (There are also characteristics named by some authors that fail to intersect with those mentioned by any other authors.) While the areas of overlap do not validate the concept of hysteria, they do provide some important points of departure for further discussion. This review will resemble a factor analysis in its search for and highlighting of the trends that run through a variety of approaches.

What will emerge are two main points of intersection, two clusters of characteristics considered to be hysterical. One delineates a personality type that is by and large a mildly to moderately disturbed neurotic patient with phallic-Oedipal conflicts who functions quite well in spite of his pathology. The other describes a personality racked with more severe pathology, presenting much more disrupted functioning, oral-addictive trends, and serious personality defects.

---

[2] Chodoff (1954) noted that the description of dynamics is so imperfect and overlapping as to be inadequate even for clinical diagnostic purposes.

CHARCOT, BREUER, FREUD: SYMPTOM DEFINITION

Charcot and his contemporaries defined hysteria in terms of age-old symptoms and changes in consciousness thought to accompany them. Charcot described stages in the hysterical seizure and considered fits, paralyses, and anesthesias as primary symptoms (Charcot and Marie, 1892). Janet (1892-1894) described a "restriction of consciousness" as a prelude to the hysterical trauma state. Both the Paris and Nancy schools stressed suggestibility in their definitions, and considered lethargy, catalepsy, and somnambulism as symptoms warranting a diagnosis of hysteria.

The definition of hysteria adopted by Freud and Breuer was based on these notions. They noted the restriction of consciousness, high suggestibility, alteration of memory functions, and dissociative phenomena generally considered at the time as characteristic of hysteria, and added the concept of "splitting of the mind." Breuer and Freud (1893-1895) held that in hysteria ideas originate in hypnoid states during traumatic episodes, and remain cut off from other conscious processes. In 1905, however, Freud (1905b) publicly withdrew his earlier support of a hypnoid explanation of hysteria and, along with other reasons, broke with Breuer.

During the period of scientific investigation of hysteria just described, the metamorphosis of the concept that has led to the current confusion began. In this period, hysteria was first defined as a complex of symptoms. Though it must be said that these theories are psychological ones, hysteria was *not* defined as a personality type. With their discussion of a genetic predisposition to hypnoid states, Breuer and Freud initiated the transition from a symptom-complex definition of hysteria to a personality-configuration definition. (See Chapter 1 for a discussion of Breuer's and Freud's early work.)

ABRAHAM AND THE PSYCHOLOGY OF CHARACTER

The work of Abraham in the 1920's helped to bridge the psychoanalytic study of symptoms and the psychoanalytic study of character. He described the influence of pregenital drive fixations on character formation. He traced the character traits found in obsessional neurotic adults back to the anal eroticism of early childhood (Abraham, 1921). He also described the effect of oral eroticism on character formation (1925) and, finally, the characterological implication of attaining genital primacy during development (1924). Abraham's contributions are significant in several respects. He described in rich clinical detail orally and anally derived character traits as seen in adult patients. He showed very clearly how an adult character trait is the product of the same compromise between impulse and defense as is a symptom. He also discriminated among various characterological outcomes in the adult on the basis of the predominance of the impulse or the defense in the particular patient. For example, an anal fixation may show itself in a patient's tendency to surround himself with clutter or in an excessive orderliness. In these papers he presented a highly sophisticated conceptualization of early development, tracing character traits to particular *aspects* of the anal or oral phases. In some patients the anal-phase fixation involves the angry, obstinate retention of feces, in some the smell of the feces, in some the pleasure at passing the feces and the fear of their loss, in some the pleasure of postponing evacuation of feces, in some a wish to mess, etc. He also described the effect of very early oral eroticism on the later anal-phase development and the resultant effects of both in adult character traits.

Abraham's contributions are perhaps most noteworthy for the breadth of his consideration of the personality. He did not just consider narrowly defined character traits; instead, he described neurotic character *patterns* as seen in the adult personality. For example, he illustrated the anal character's tendency to be occupied with the reverse or opposite sides of various things or situations: making numerous mistakes between right and left, east and west, living on the back side of the hill, sitting where others stand, dressing for warm weather when others are dressing for cold, and even enjoying foods that are opposite to the general taste. His consideration of these trends ranges from the physiognomy characteristic of the anal character to the interpersonal ramifications of anal eroticism in adults.

Though Abraham's work is of less value than Wilhelm Reich's (discussed in the next section) to the study of hysterical personality, in particular because he did not discuss the hysterical or phallic character (he described genital character formation which sheds some light on the healthier aspects of the hysterical personality), his systematic study of the relationship between unconscious (infantile) impulses and defenses and character formation clearly helped to promote the psychoanalytic study of character.

REICH AND WITTELS: PSYCHOLOGY OF CHARACTER

As discussed in the previous chapter, before the advent of the structural theory it was difficult for a psychoanalytic theory of personality or character to be formulated. Once the structural theory had been presented by Freud in the 1920's, Wilhelm Reich drew on it and tried to make sense of the pervasive resistances presented by patients in analysis. He presented these resistances as part of the patient's characterological armor. He thought it was crucial for the analyst to deal with these pervasive, though often subtle, character defenses. In order to do so, the analyst must be armed with knowledge of the patient's character. ("Armed" is used advisedly, for Reich's writing gives one the impression that the analyst must assault and overcome all the resistances, tear away all the character armor, before any useful analytic work can be conducted.) Reich therefore set out to present a constellation of character formations found in analytic practice. While it is striking that relatively little was written on the psychology of character even after the inauguration of structural theory, it is likely that Reich had an impact on psychoanalysis via his role as a teacher. According to Sterba (1975), Reich's seminar was, during the 1920's, the central training seminar at the Vienna Institute.

As part of this larger effort, Reich (1933) described a "hysterical character." While Charcot and Marie in 1892 discussed a hereditary predisposition to hysteria, and Freud (1894, 1905b) the developmental accidents that promote it, it was with Reich that hysteria became a label for a distinct personality type. He described traits characteristic of the hysteric: pronounced coquettishness in women, effeminacy in men, unpredictability, suggestibility, sharp disappointment reaction, imaginativeness, lack of conviction, compliance, compulsive need to be loved, overdependence on others for approval, capacity for dramatization, somatic compliance, and evident apprehension as sexual behavior comes close to the goal. But Reich went somewhat beyond this behavioral level of description in defining hysteria and distinguishing it from other conditions. He stressed the relatively later psycho-sexual fixation point that resulted in hysteria and the conse-quent difference between hysterical and depressive or autistic states. Defining only strictly phallic-Oedipal mechanisms as hysterical, he did not consider pregenital mechanisms or attitudes as belonging to the hysterical character type. If depressive or autistic characteristics, or fundamentally oral attitudes, were present, these features were seen to modify or fundamentally rule out the diagnosis of hysterical character. Reich acknowledged regression to oral mechanisms in hysteria, but stressed the genitalization of the mouth in con-trast to the immutable orality of the depressive personality. Reich's definition of hysteria as strictly phallic-genital was later contested by Marmor (1953) and Johnston (1963).

In part as a consequence of his definition of hysteria as a disorder that occurs at a relatively late developmental period, Reich also considered a relatively mature level of object rela-tions as a defining feature of hysteria — one of the first examples, it appears, of a definition of hysteria in terms of object relations, an approach that was later greatly expanded by Fairbairn's (1954) object-relations theory of hysteria. Kernberg (1967) has recently stressed the maturity of object relations in hysteria in distinguishing it from the borderline disorders.

While Reich's accounts of the hysterical and compulsive character types have proved to be cornerstones of the psy-choanalytic study of character, his description of a third character type has been generally overlooked—the phallic-narcissistic personality. Standing between the hysterical and obsessive-compulsive personality developmentally, this character type both manifests aspects of the anal-sadistic position and approaches the object-libidinal level of the genital character. According to Reich, phallic-narcissistic personalities, in spite of their narcissistic preoccupation with themselves, have strong attachments to people and things outside, and in this respect they most closely resemble Reich's genital character (most mature, healthy character). The phallic-narcissistic personality also is given to impulsive acts of courage, exhibitionism, and openly phallic, aggressive behavior. In men, great pride is concentrated in the genital, which is felt to be more an instrument of aggression and vengeance than of love. In women the fantasy of having a penis is prominent, although Reich believed this character type was found less frequently in women.

Reich's phallic-narcissistic character was clinically distinct from the hysterical personality. As the former concept fell into relative disuse, however, the latter was broadened to include patients Reich might have labeled phallic-narcissistic (such as cases reported by Allen and Houston, 1959; Prosen, 1967). Consequently, highly exhibitionistic, aggressively demanding, narcissistic, and jealous personalities are considered hysterical, along with personalities of marked suggestibility, compliance, and absence of *overt* aggression and demandingness.

This, too, added to the definitional confusion surrounding hysteria. In retrospect, retention of the concept of a phallic-narcissistic character might have promoted a more precise, delimited definition of hysteria. Indeed, this character type resembles the oft-described male hysterical personality—the Don Juan personality.

PHALLIC NARCISSISTIC PERSONALITY CONTRASTED WITH HYSTERICAL PERSONALITY

There are clear clinical and conceptual advantages to distinguishing between the phallic-narcissistic and the hysterical character types. The former seems to be organized around wishes to exhibit and be admired, and fear of shame and humiliation. The hysteric, by contrast, seems to be struggling with guilt about internal wishes. To be laughed at or criticized leads the phallic-narcissistic character to become acutely and depressingly aware of limitations that bring to the fore his infantile sense that his body is not as large as his parent's. His character pivots on his need to prevent this experience of his own inadequacy. The hysterical character struggles to prevent the emergence of tabooed thoughts, wishes, and feelings about important objects, a struggle in which censure by others is secondary. Quite unlike the phallic-narcissistic character, the hysteric is often willing to present himself as weak, flawed, and silly if that is necessary to avoid incestuous thoughts and to hold safely onto an infantile fantasy of an important object. The phallic-narcissistic character works very hard to seem perfect and beyond criticism, whereas the hysterical character labors to expunge perverse, incestuous, or in other ways socially objectionable urges.

Both the hysterical and the phallic-narcissistic personality types present fixations at the phallic-Oedipal level, but the distinction between them is important clinically. The true hysterical personality manifests a triangular Oedipal conflict. The conflict centers primarily, though not exclusively, on issues of jealousy of the parents' relationship with each other and is, therefore, more oriented toward tabooed or unrealizable wishes that involve important family objects. The phallic-narcissistic personality struggles more with a sense of genital or body inferiority. The central conflict is, therefore, less oriented toward impulses that involve objects and remains more a pre-Oedipal (specifically phallic) concern with the intactness, size, and acceptability of the body. The central conflict revolves around a narcissistic battle to affirm the power and size of the genitals (or other body displacements from it) to ward off the unconscious, often traumatically induced idea that the genital is small, dirty, and insignificant. This defensive process often involves exhibitionistic inclinations as well as acting out directed toward quieting unconscious fears of one's vulnerability and weakness. Counterphobic, extraverted activities which flirt with danger or death are not uncommon in such personalities. The hysteric, by contrast, is less concerned with the intactness of his body and more with his forbidden wishes toward tabooed objects. The conflict in the hysteric revolves more around the wish to establish a prohibited Oedipal relationship. In contrast to the phallic-narcissistic personality, the hysteric does not seek to affirm power or bodily intactness, indeed, often invokes pseudopassivity to avoid instinctual and social pressure. The hysteric, in sum, strives more or less conflictually to establish an infantile tie with an object, whereas the phallic-narcissistic personality is more concerned with establishing phallic adequacy and superiority. While the hysteric may have a wish for a fantasy transformation of the body, such as a wish for a penis, a larger penis, or a larger body,[3] such wishes are in the service of a more primary unconscious wish for a romance with a parent.

Central to this distinction is that the hysteric is more comfortable presenting himself as weak and passive, whereas the phallic-narcissistic character strives to deny to himself and to others that he has any flaws, weaknesses, or childish longings. The hysteric's comfort with passivity, its ego syntonicity, will be seen later to be an enduring, very basic feature of the disorder. The hysteric's need to maintain a sense of his own passivity is essential to a new, more viable definition of the disorder advanced later in this monograph.

Wittels (1931), a contemporary of Reich's, reviewed the various forms of hysteria as they were then defined: conversion hysteria, spasmodic hysteria (hysterical seizures, fits, etc.), and anxiety hysteria (phobia). He also described the hysterical character. He defined the hysterical personality as more fearful and passive than did Reich, who continually stressed the energy and liveliness of the hysterical personality. Wittels also emphasized the feminine, infantile aspects of this character type. He described such personalities as unreliable, lacking the need to complete anything, given to living in

---

[3] And such derivatives as wishing for large breasts.

fantasy, blurring boundaries between the self and the external world, and impulsively using drugs and alcohol or attempting suicide. The hysterical personality depicted by Wittels is thus more primitive and impulse-ridden than the one described by Reich, who placed the hysterical personality developmentally as the closest neighbor of the "genital character." These disparate views of the hysterical personality have appeared again and again in the literature since the time of Wittels and Reich.

Though Wittels did not speak in explicitly ego-psychological terms, he conceived of the hysterical personality as racked by defects in the ego's capacity to prevent impulse from being translated into action and to maintain a subjective sense of the boundaries between thought and action. He considered penis envy and the consequent search for a substitute penis as central to the dynamics of this personality type, and also stressed its intense voraciousness and addictiveness. A search for an ecstatic, intoxicated state was, according to Wittels, a prime longing of the hysterical personality.

A major weakness of Wittels's approach is his lack of systematic examination of ego processes. He implied that there is a basic, motiveless passivity in the hysteric, a constitutional weakness. There is no attempt to make sense, from the point of view of ego adaptation or defense, of the psychological *purpose* of this character pattern, and one is left to conclude that such personalities are simply lazy.

Reich's description finds most salient the conflict between genital strivings and superego prohibitions and the consequent formation of psychological compromises and widespread use of repression. For Reich, the hysterical personality is in conflict in such approach-avoidance compromises as, for example, being sexually provocative and then unresponsive. The ego of the hysterical personality forms such compromises, according to Reich, rather than permitting the uncontrolled impulsive action described by Wittels. In contrast to Wittels, Reich defined the hysterical personality as operating on the genital level with oral regressions, but not as manifesting intense, addictive searches for primitive excitement or intoxication.

The dispute between Wittels and Reich goes to the heart of the differences in conceptions of the ego and psychosexual development of the hysterical personality. Marmor (1953) and Johnston (1963) have extended Wittels's position, whereas Fenichel's (1945), Fairbairn's (1954), and Kernberg's (1967) definitions are consistent with Reich's. The original divergence between Reich's and Wittels's views has recently widened into very different conceptions of the disorder.

FENICHEL'S DEFINITION

In his most thorough work on neurosis, *The Psychoanalytic Theory of Neurosis* (1945), Fenichel discussed hysteria as a phobic state (anxiety hysteria) or as a conversion reaction. The former he approached in terms of displacement and the latter in terms of repression and somatization. The assumption that hysterical character and conversion reactions always coexist was later challenged by Rangell (1959), and questions about the coincidence of hysteria and phobias have also been raised by Salzman (1968), who discussed phobias in the obsessive-compulsive neurosis, and by Cameron (1963), who considered phobias a form of psychopathology independent of character.

Fenichel's account of anxiety hysteria deals with the part played by primal-scene experiences and by fear of retribution for sexual thoughts and acts. He also included an area that is often neglected in the discussion of hysteria—the handling of aggressive feelings.

What Fenichel had to say about conversion (or hysteria, as he used the terms interchangeably) constitutes the dominant, classical psychoanalytic thinking on the topic. He noted two prerequisites for conversion, one psychological and one physiological. The physical prerequisite is a general erogenicity of the body which makes it possible for every organ and every function to express sexual excitement. The psychological prerequisite is a tendency to turn from reality to fantasy, to replace real sexual objects by fantasy representatives of infantile objects, a process he termed "introversion." In the hysteric, introversion takes the form of a retreat from disappointing reality to magical, wish-fulfilling daydreams. If these daydreams remain internally separate from repressed ideas and feelings, then daydreaming is pleasurable and largely conscious. If, however, as often happens in the hysteric, daydreams find connections to repressed material, they in turn must also be repressed. These fantasies can strive to return from repression, and the resulting conflict yields conversion symptoms.

According to Fenichel, the tendency toward an autoplastic (internal innervation) resolution of internal conflict is basic and unique to hysteria. This view reflects a bias found in Fenichel and other classical psychoanalytic writers, one that has particular shortcomings in the study of hysteria. He emphasized the intrapsychic function of conversion, considering it the paradigmatic autoplastic symptom, not recognizing its alloplastic intent. This bias, whether valid or not, is clear even in the terminology used to discuss the function of conversion: from Freud onward, "primary gain" has referred to the importance of the symptom for the patient's internal psychic economy, while the ego's alloplastic intent in using the symptom to manipulate other people and the current life situation is termed "secondary gain." This distinction, if taken too far, can be misleading. As Hartmann (1939) first pointed out, and as Erikson (1950) incorporated in his typology, every "act" of the ego is designed simultaneously to fit the perceived limits and possibilities of the environment and to maintain the internal emotional harmony of the organism. Thus to designate the internal formation of a symptom as "primary" and its interpersonal purpose as "secondary" is artificial and invalid.

Fenichel (1945) described the kinds of unconscious fantasies and conflicts that frequently occur in hysteria. He believed that hysterics either never get over their early object choice or return to it later in life after a major disappointment. All sexuality for the hysteric, then, comes to represent this first, infantile, incestuous love. The need to repress the Oedipus complex results in the repression of all sexuality; unconscious incestuous fantasies that derive from the Oedipal crisis are in turn converted into symptoms.

In summary, Fenichel's theory of hysteria can be reduced to three elements: (1) the hysterical tendency toward introversion; (2) the repression of Oedipal fantasies; and (3) the symbolic use of the body to express these fantasies. A shortcoming of this conception is that the first two are common to many neuroses—the retreat to fantasy, the repression of Oedipal fantasies, and the neurotic expression of unconscious fantasies are present in virtually every neurosis. Somatization or "materialization" thus remains as the only process unique to hysteria. But even this criterion has been disputed by Rangell (1959), who believes that conversion reactions occur independently of hysterical character traits.

ATTEMPTS AT DEFINITIONAL CLARIFICATION

During the 1950's several authors confronted the state of definitional confusion that had developed. Chodoff and Lyons (1958) observed that the term "hysteria" was being used in five different ways: (1) to refer to a pattern of behavior exhibited by people considered to be hysterical personalities or hysterical characters; (2) to denote a psychosomatic disorder called "conversion hysteria" or "conversion reaction"; (3) to refer to a psychoneurotic disorder characterized by phobias and/or anxiety manifestations—anxiety hysteria; (4) to describe a psychopathological pattern (a hypothesized description of internal dynamics, psychosexual development, etc.); and (5) as a term of opprobrium.

Confronting this state of definitional confusion, writers in this period tended to challenge many of the indicators earlier considered diagnostic of the disorder. Chodoff (1954), for example, questioned the usefulness and validity of Charcot's *la belle indifférence* (the hysteric's casual indifference to his symptoms). Chodoff took issue with the assumption of many writers, beginning with Charcot, that through repression and/or conversion the hysteric is free of conscious anxiety and is therefore consciously indifferent to his symptoms. All too often, according to Chodoff, *la belle indifférence* was used in the literature to classify a posteriori the patient as hysterical in the course of arguing a particular position on hysteria. He criticized H. Deutsch (1942) for defining hysteria in this monolithic, invalid fashion, and noted that in *Studies on Hysteria* Freud adopted different conceptions of the disorder with respect to different cases. The patient Elisabeth von R. was diagnosed as hysterical by virtue of *la belle indifférence*, but the others manifested conversion anxiety, tension, and sadness over their symptoms. Chodoff advanced a new explanation for *la belle indifférence*, claiming that it does *not* result from the process of conversion absorbing anxiety but is actually a secondary denial of the symptom produced by the original repression. Although some hysterics do manifest this secondary denial, such a defense is neither necessary nor sufficient to a definition of hysteria.

In 1959 Rangell claimed that the conceptual marriage between hysteria and conversion was fallacious. He traced the heretofore accepted connection to Freud's definition of conversion in *Studies on Hysteria* (Breuer and Freud, 1893-1895), "The Neuro-Psychoses of Defence" (1894), and Fenichel's (1945) later elaboration of this definition. Both Freud and Fenichel considered conversion as the somatic representation of conflictual thoughts concerning phallic and Oedipal issues. Since hysteria was also considered by both to be a disorder rooted in just such phallic-Oedipal conflicts, "conversion" came to be a term virtually interchangeable with "hysteria." Rangell agreed with the foundation of Fenichel's definition of conversion: that conversion symptoms speak symbolically via the language of the body in expressing both a forbidden wish and the defensive forces that mask it. However, he broadened the notion of conversion to include conversion reactions that express pregenital conflicts. He recommended that conversion be recognized as occurring in a broad spectrum of personality types, ranging from the hysterical patient who creates a somatic symptom in his struggle with Oedipal conflicts organized at the phallic level to the catatonic schizophrenic for whom a somatic symptom expresses a struggle that involves the most primitive, cannibalistic aggression.

Rangell cited a study by Chodoff and Lyons (1958) as support for his thesis. This study purports to demonstrate that conversion reactions do not necessarily occur in patients with hysterical personalities. Chodoff and Lyons found that only about 5% of a sample of patients with conversion symptoms manifested what they defined as hysterical personality, thus confirming Rangell's belief that conversion is not the same as hysteria.

Rangell also broadened the conception of conversion in another way. In disagreement with Grinker and Robbins (1954), who restricted conversion to the "voluntary sensory-perceptive systems," Rangell argued that conversion can take place at any level of ego or libidinal development, and consequently psychological interference with involuntary systems during infancy can lead to somatic innervation of the involuntary systems. Further clarifying this area, Rangell noted that fixations at later periods of development, when the organism's executive processes become more pervasive and efficient, tend to result in difficulties involving the voluntary systems. By virtue of the later point of developmental fixations these somatizations should be labeled "hysterical within the larger category of conversion." In this author's opinion, Rangell's paper is a significant one in the study of hysteria. Rangell's contribution is vital for the definition to hysteria to be presented here, for he considers conversion symptoms to be common in hysteria but not limited to hysterics. He is pointing, then, to the importance of assessing the nature of the personality organization that produces the symptoms. It is a central contention of this monograph that conversion has been a common symptom in hysterics, more in some eras and cultures than others, but that the only certain and reliable definition of the disorder must be based on the underlying personality structure.

By the mid-1950's there was such confusion about the concept of the hysterical personality that no such category was listed in the *Diagnostic and Statistical Manual* of the American Psychiatric Association (1952). Chodoff and Lyons (1958) generated a definition of the hysterical personality by consulting representative descriptions of it in the literature and distilling seven characteristics from them. In the short run, this proved to be a heuristically useful accomplishment. Their definition was accepted as *the* definition by several subsequent authors. This consensual definition of the hysterical personality based on Chodoff and Lyons's study consists of the following characteristics: (1) egoism, vanity, etc.; (2) exhibitionism, dramatization, lying, exaggeration; (3) unbridled display of affects, labile affect, inconsistency of reactions, etc.; (4) emotional shallowness; (5) sexualization of nonsexual situations; (6) intense fear of sexuality, frigidity; (7) demandingness and dependence. (This last characteristic is mentioned by modern writers on hysteria, whereas suggestibility was stressed by earlier ones.)

Essentially, Chodoff and Lyons investigated the intersection of the sets of traits that various authors have considered to be hysterical. Their findings do support, to some degree, the view that an enduring constellation called hysteria exists. But they did not consider what are the irreducible aspects of the personality structure of such patients.

In the 1950's the aggregation of symptoms previously relied on to define hysteria was being challenged at every turn. With conversion distinguished from hysteria, the diagnostic significance of *la belle indifférence* questioned, and such classical forms of hysteria as seizures, paralyses, and anesthesias apparently disappearing, some theorists, following Reich's lead, sought new approaches to definition, going beyond the descriptive behavioral level and relying on descriptions of characterological traits.

EASSER AND LESSER: AN INTENSIVE APPROACH

In 1965 Easser and Lesser, through a clinical study of six "hysterical" patients, offered the most extensive, subtle description of the hysterical personality so far. In addition, they formally distinguished between two types of hysterical character: the "hysterical" and the "hysteroid" personality. Their "hysterical personality" corresponds generally to Reich's description of the hysterical character, and the "hysteroid" personality is similar to Wittels's description of a more disturbed hysterical character. Easser and Lesser appraised the hysteric's fantasy life, interpersonal style, defensive use of emotion, and exhibitionistic, manipulative, and narcissistic potential. They also stressed the strengths of the "hysterical" personality. The characteristics they defined as hysterical were: (1) the use of feeling rather than thought in crises ("labile emotionality"); (2) hypersensitivity to others because of an excessive need to love and be loved, which often leads to a continual testing of the love of others through putting on shows for real or fantasied purposes (direct and active engagement with the human world); (3) responding badly to frustration, and also to internal excitement and its accompanying fantasies; (4) use of fantasies of romance and romantic sexuality to heighten and sexualize existing relations; (5) suggestibility, broadened by Easser and Lesser to include the hysteric's active encouragement of suggestive behavior in others; (6) dislike and avoidance of the exact, the rote, and the mundane; (7) denial of the unpleasant, the distasteful, the actual or fantasied transgression, through a characterological naïveté and insouciance (maintenance of a self-presentation as a "child-woman"); (8) defensive substitution of or qualitative change in emotions, so that an emotion "becomes, paradoxically, a substitute for itself. . . . an emotional reconnaissance is, as it were, sent forth in lieu of true, meaningful reactivity" (p. 398).[4]

The hysteroid personality is in many ways a caricature of the hysterical personality, though qualitatively different in certain respects. Where the hysterical personality may come to liberate impulses in a modulated fashion during or after a successful analysis, the hysteroid personality presents very erratic, impulsive behavior that seems to be governed by changes in mood. The hysterical personality, although he encounters conflicts *within* his relationships, usually does have a range of relationships in his life. The hysteroid personality has more fundamental problems in *forming and*

---

[4] Siegman (1954) had also discussed this defensive use of emotionality in hysterics (see p. 104).

maintaining relationships, and in those he does manage to form continually vacillates between idealizing the partner and completely devaluing him. These relationships often rupture suddenly and precipitate feelings of detachment, isolation, depression, and paranoialike trends. Where the hysterical personality struggles with the expression of phallic, genital urges, the hysteroid personality is subject to more primitive fears of being engulfed or overwhelmed. In the latter personality there is less ego capacity for delay of gratification, emotional control, and purposeful action. The hysteric regresses to pregenital ego states to ward off sexual feelings, whereas the hysteroid, in an effort to fend off fear of passivity and primitive orality, tends to impulsive action and reaction, including pseudo erotic behavior. Easser and Lesser also argue for their distinction on the basis of a difference in the psychological development of these two kinds of character, a matter that will be taken up later. Zetzel (1968) makes a similar distinction between the true hysteric, who tolerates anxiety and depression, distinguishes interior from exterior reality, and maintains a therapeutic alliance, and the "so-called good hysteric," who is either basically depressive or a personality with significant ego defects. (See above, p. 51.) Unfortunately, the term "hysteroid" seems currently to be repeating the history of the term "hysterical." In clinical parlance it seems to be synonymous with "hysterical" or to mean "with hysterical features."

CRITIQUE OF THE "HYSTEROID PERSONALITY"

This terminological confusion may stem in part from Easser and Lesser's unfortunate choice of a label that implies some inherent relationship between the hysteroid and the hysterical personality types. As Easser and Lesser themselves note, the hysteroid personality differs from the hysterical personality in many fundamental respects. But their attempt to clarify miscarries because their system of categorization continues, in a subtle way, to be determined by the superficial appearance of the personality: the two personality types are both labeled "hyster-" because on initial observation they both appear dramatic, romantic, sexualized, naive, and childish. The hysteroid personality is seen as a caricature of the hysterical. What Easser and Lesser fail to recognize is that the hysteroid's tendency to erratic, impulsive behavior, failure to sustain enduring relationships, feelings of detachment and isolation, paranoialike trends, primitive fear of being engulfed and overwhelmed, and limited capacity for delay of gratification reflect such profound, pervasive differences from the hysterical personality that it is confounding to consider them in any way in the same category. The differences between these two types, which I consider basic, all fundamentally involve the operation of the ego. If the capacity of the ego to regulate impulse, direct behavior, maintain differentiated object representations, delay gratification, and fend off primitive affective states is recognized, then the similarities of the two personality types are of the most superficial kind. This points up the necessity of considering adaptive and defensive style and the intrapsychic conflicts with which they are inextricably interwoven as primary to a definition of psychopathology.

When these ego aspects are carefully considered, Easser and Lesser's hysteroid personality emerges as similar to and perhaps identical with the borderline personalities described by Kernberg (1970): (1) the primitive fears are consistent with the primitive affective component of introjection described by Kernberg; (2) the continual vacillation between idolizing and completely devaluing the love object parallels Kernberg's "splitting"; and (3) the poor capacity to regulate, direct, and delay impulses is consistent with Kernberg's description of poorly differentiated ego structure. Considering the confusion of categorization implied by the term "hysteroid," it would make most sense conceptually and diagnostically to discard the term "hysteroid" in favor of Kernberg's "borderline personality-infantile type."

Some writers have rejected the idea of two types of hysteria altogether, holding that *all* hysteria is basically oral. In contrast to Easser and Lesser and Kernberg, who, as we have seen, considered it clinically valid and necessary to define the true hysteric as more *intact* than the borderline, hysteroid character, Marmor (1953) echoes Wittels's contention that the hysterical character is highly infantile and regressed. (These writers recognize only *one* hysteria.) Where Reich argued that the hysteric's concern about oral matters represents a genitalization of the mouth, Marmor argued that it reflects a basic orality. Marmor also believed that the hysteric's incestuous and perverse fantasies have oral roots. For example, in place of Fenichel's (1945) interpretation of fellatio fantasies as a displacement upward of genital wishes, as a wish for revenge and impregnation, and as an attempt at identifying with the man through a fantasy of incorporating the penis, Marmor asserted that the penis is a fantasy substitute for the breast.

EMPIRICAL DEFINITIONS OF HYSTERIA

Very little empirical research on hysteria has been carried out. An examination of a few studies will illustrate the state of this area. Purtell, Guze, and Zeigler have conducted several studies aimed at clarifying the definitional problems surrounding hysteria. Purtell, Robins, and Cohen (1951) demonstrated a stable, definable clinical syndrome called "hysteria" that is distinct from conversion reactions or other psychotic disorders. Ziegler and Paul (1954) studied the "natural history" of hysteria in hospitalized women, conducting a follow-up study on 22 patients who were hospitalized before the age of 20 with an initial diagnosis of hysteria. They found that 48% of these women had subsequently been hospitalized, all but one diagnosed as psychotic. The psychoses ranged from acute episodes in some women to chronic "back-ward" situations in others. What this study rather starkly points up is the unsatisfactoriness of basing a diagnosis of hysteria on symptoms. Noticeably absent as a criterion for diagnosing these patients as hysterical was any description of the nature of the intrapsychic conflict. Upon investigation it emerged that 14 of the 22 patients later diagnosed as psychotic had originally been diagnosed as hysterical almost exclusively because they exhibited medically unfounded somatic complaints. Others seem to have been diagnosed as hysterical partly because they exhibited a few hysterical character traits and partly by default. Specifically, they were labeled hysterical because they presented themselves as "naïve," "childish," "self-dramatizing," and did *not* exhibit any overtly psychotic behavior such as hallucinations.[5]

Guze (1967), in a more recent paper, discussed the problems surrounding the validity and usefulness of hysteria as a clinical diagnosis, and presented a study intended to demonstrate the validity of a symptom-complex definition of the disorder. He first criticized the widespread use of "conversion symptoms" and "hysteria" as synonymous, and the equally unexamined tendency to diagnose virtually any medically unfounded symptom as a conversion reaction without careful investigation for the presence of etiological factors of a psychological nature. Guze argued that for a diagnosis to be valid it should ideally meet the following requirements: (1) upon follow-up the patient should not be found to be suffering from a different illness; (2) the patient's condition at follow-up should be consistent with the prognosis implied by the original diagnosis; and (3) where family studies are available the condition should appear quite often among relatives.

Guze's own study was of 28 women who had originally been diagnosed as hysterical on the basis of a checklist. Symptoms included general somatic complaints, sexual problems, mood disturbances, and conversion symptoms. Six to eight years later, 25 were again diagnosed as hysterical on the basis of the same checklist. Guze concluded that the validity of the diagnosis had been confirmed by this demonstration of its continuity over time. Unfortunately, rampant methodological and inferential fallacies in this study make it useless. While the study demonstrates the intertest reliability of the checklist, no theoretical rationale is presented for considering this specific symptom complex as

---

[5] Ziegler and Paul (1954) believe that diseases such as hysteria should be studied over a longer period so that the course of the disorder can be understood. He also notes the difficulty of distinguishing hysteria from malingering and psychopathy.

hysterical. Indeed, several of the items seem far more definitional of depression than hysteria—such as "wanting to die" and "feeling hopeless." A second finding of the study was that 14% of the female relatives of hysterical patients suffered from hysteria as compared with 1.8% of a control population of females. But here again the criteria for hysteria are arbitrary, and the control-group findings seem to have been confounded by a class bias. As was noted earlier, "theoretical" approaches to a definition of hysteria stress the internal dynamics postulated to *be* hysteria, but fail to present an independent *description* of the phenomenon. Studies such as this one fall short in the opposite respect: the phenomenon is described with great clarity, but there is no theoretical foundation for this particular aggregation of symptoms to be considered a distinct psychological syndrome.

In 1968 Lazare and Klerman tried to establish a set of valid and reliable criteria to distinguish hysterical personalities. They compared depressed women with hysterical personality features and depressed women without such features. The study begins with a composite descriptive definition of hysteria drawn from the literature. This definition, however, stresses the self-centered, exhibitionistic, and psychopathic qualities of the hysterical personality. Other empiricists (Eysenck, 1957; Guze, 1964) have also considered hysteria as similar to psychopathy. The prevalence of a belief in such a similarity again points up the difficulties of empirical approaches to hysteria that do not employ a theoretical construct corresponding to conscience or superego. When behavior alone is evaluated, it is impossible to distinguish a flamboyant patient with a strong conscience and sense of morality from one with poorly internalized limits.

Lazare and Klerman found a variety of differences between the two groups of depressed women. Upon admission the average weight of the hysterical women was 21 pounds lower than that of the nonhysterics. The hysterics had less educaton, supporting the often-made assertion that hysteria is currently a lower-class disorder. As would be expected, fewer hysterics were employed in obsessive jobs such as bookkeeping, stitching, or scholarly pursuits, and more were employed in the women's apparel fields, reflecting the hysteric's typical exhibitionism and body emphasis. Lazare and Klerman also found that far more of the hysterical patients had fathers with alcohol problems. The hysterics had their first children earlier, supporting the common assumption that hysterics are strongly motivated to become pregnant. They also had more extramarital affairs. They had more nonpsychiatric hospitalizations, especially for gynecological surgery, reflecting both the hysterical tendency to chronic invalidism and, as observed in the history of the treatment of the disorder (Veith, 1965), their tendency to elicit medical treatments involving the genitals. In the milieu-therapy setting, the hysterical group was described by the ward staff as openly demanding, angry, bitchy, and sexually provocative with the doctors, in contrast to the nonhysterical group, who were more frequently viewed as overtly passive.

Although this study is an interesting one, the validity of generalizing from it to other kinds of hysteria is questionable for several reasons. The subjects are both hysterical and depressive, and they are hospitalized. There is no evidence that the findings would hold for less severely disturbed, nonhospitalized, nondepressed hysterics. Furthermore, demographically the data seems particularly biased by the fact that the sample consisted of hospitalized women.

Winokur and Leonard (1963) studied the sex lives of a small group of hysterics ($N = 14$) and found a marked sexual inhibition in comparison with normal performance as recorded by Kinsey. They found a striking deterioration from relatively normal sexual activity during the premarital and early marital periods to abnormal performance as marital life continued.

In a similar study with "pure hysterics" Blinder (1966) looked for common personality traits and developmental information among subjects considered hysterical on the basis of psychiatric records. Although this study is also plagued by severe methodological shortcomings such as no controls, no interviewer reliability, use of records *only* for diagnosis of hysteria, etc., Blinder found the following traits to be frequent in the sample: (1) female; (2) often the youngest children; (3) born of mothers who had scant time or talent for serving as identification models; (4) fathers even less able to provide for their daughters' emotional needs; (5) a number of persistent childhood neurotic traits, but coming to psychiatric attention only in late teens or early twenties because of depression, prolonged states of tension, attempted suicide, conversion symptoms, or a combination of these problems; (6) medical histories showing a high incidence of abdominal surgical procedures, the majority gynecological; (7) maturation apparently a slow, uneven, incomplete process, as demonstrated by the immaturity of day-to-day interests, relationships, and values; (8) sexuality inhibited and underdeveloped — little confidence in themselves as women, leading to discomfort around women, flirtatious but sharply circumscribed relationships with men characterized by avoidance of sexuality; (9) a haste to bear children, husbands often inadequate and abusive, and a high divorce rate; (10) a high incidence of alcoholism in spouse, siblings, and other family members; (11) a significant number of remarriages to older, passive, emotionally and sexually undemanding men; (12) good at school and raising children; (13) few genuine relationships; and (14) adept at using symptoms and histrionics to get their own way.

This study supports many of Lazare and Klerman's (1968) later findings, with one important difference. Lazare and Klerman emphasize the psychopathic aspects of the hysteric, whereas Blinder seems to stress the masochistic, self-destructive elements.

Some points of agreement between these two studies deserve further comment. Both found that the fathers of hysterics often suffer from some degree of alcoholism. This finding may result from a social-class bias in these studies, since both samples seem to have been composed of lower-middle-class or lower-class women. There is, however, another, more speculative, interpretation of this finding. It may be that the drunk father, who often tends to be brutal, intrusive, and sexually provocative once his superego has been diluted with alcohol, evokes within his daughter a fear of his attack and elicits in her the sorts of tabooed, incestuous wishes toward him that in his drunken state he may at times openly entertain toward her.[6]

In addition, both studies corroborate the hysteric's seeming desire to be ill, and to be the object of medical treatments that are disguised sexual gratifications, a characteristic that seems ubiquitous historically (Veith, 1965). A third finding of both studies, the tendency to be pregnant early, is an interesting one, as the hysteric's desire to be pregnant to gratify infantile Oedipal fantasies has been commented on by many psychoanalytic writers (Freud, 1905a; Fenichel, 1945; Abse, 1966). Perhaps it is the neurotic importance of being pregnant that leads hysterical women to become pregnant somewhat earlier than nonhysterical women.

Aside from the methodological weaknesses of these empirical studies, there is another, more fundamental impediment to their usefulness. It is most difficult to extrapolate from the results of such studies, which rely on descriptive definitions, because there is no description of the nature of the ego. Without such a description the results are difficult to apply to any specific clinical case.

The only comprehensive theory that has grown from experimental-empirical work is that of Eysenck (1957). He analyzed performance on tests of visual acuity, object recognition, mental speed, and accommodation, and concluded that two factors are common to all psychopathology—intro-extroversion and neuroticism-psychoticism. Using these factors as a matrix, hysteria would fall in the extroverted-neurotic quadrant. In contrast, the introverted-neurotic quadrant would contain psychasthenia, also termed dysthymia by Eysenck, a state characterized by anxiety, depression, and obsessive-compulsive features. In subsequent studies Eysenck and his students reported a variety of differences between the hysteric and the dysthymic. The

---

[6] To speculate even further, it may even be that the confused, "foggy" cognitive and perceptual style of the hysteric, commented on by Shapiro (1965) and others concerned with projective tests (Schafer, 1948; Rapaport, Gill, and Schafer, 1968), is in some cases an identification with the father's drunken, confused state.

hysteric was comparatively low in perceptual rigidity, persistence, and level of aspiration, and comparatively high in interpersonal sensitivity and the use of repression. Eysenck argued that the difficulty of conditioning hysterics is central to an understanding of the disorder. Because of their low conditionability they are poorly socialized and consequently more responsive to the immediate situation than to the enduring, internalized standards conditioned by the society. Because his theory did not include such constructs as ego or superego, however, it could not distinguish between psychopathic and hysterical personalities.

PSYCHOLOGICAL-TESTING APPROACH TO HYSTERIA

The development of psychoanalytically based psychodiagnostic testing was a major step toward a better-defined psychoanalytic theory of hysterical personality (as well as other psychoanalytically defined personality constellations). Most important, it was a systematic attempt to apply a broader view of the ego, ushered in by Anna Freud (1936) and Hartmann (1939) among others, a view that opened the way for the psychoanalytic psychology of character. Though the diagnostic-testing literature has certain shortcomings, the most severe of which is that a definition of hysteria is never really systematically presented, its emphasis on the ego makes it probably the most promising approach to diagnosis, though an all too often neglected one (Reichard, 1956).

Psychoanalytic diagnostic testing as developed by Rapaport and his students (Rapaport, Gill, and Schafer, 1968) explored the nature of the ego's cognitive functioning, capacity to maintain smooth integration of feelings and thinking, modes of handling conflict, and the nature of its contact with reality, among other features. Developing as it did at the time when psychoanalysis was discovering the importance and complexity of the ego as an organ of adaptation (Hartmann, 1939) to complement Freud's earlier discoveries of the id and psychic conflict, psychoanalytic diagnostic testing attempted to assess the ego's capacity to synthesize, control, and channel instinctual impulses, to respond to superego guidance, and to maintain adequate contact with reality. The ego continued to be viewed as the locus of defensive functioning, but defenses came to be seen as but one of the ego's interrelated functions. The psychoanalytic diagnostic-testing approach pioneered by Rapaport's group sought to describe the range of defensive operations, the conditions under which the various defenses are called into action, the stability of the defenses, and the tendency of particular defenses to fail to operate. This approach involved more than an effort to establish the predominance of a given defense; it was an attempt to assess the ego as a complex organizing agency. This work, along with that of Anna Freud and Hartmann, was central to the evolution of the psychoanalysis of symptoms into the psychoanalysis of character.

The essential axiom on which psychoanalytic diagnostic testing rests is that personality organization and psychic conflict will express themselves in concept formation, attention, concentration, and memory. In the case of psychopathology, it is therefore considered possible to find in early signs of thinking disturbance indicators of possible later maladjustment. Inferences drawn from the subject's perceptual and cognitive behavior in response to a variety of standard stimuli are viewed as registering important trends in the patient's functioning.

Major psychoanalytic indicators of hysteria as found in Rapaport, Gill, and Schafer (1968) and Schafer (1948, 1954) can be summarized as follows:

1. Hysterics tend *not* to take full advantage of their native intellectual capacities owing to the generalized effect of repression on their cognitive and intellectual functions. This tendency expresses itself throughout the test battery.

Though the Rorschach test best differentiates among the neuroses, there are a few basic Wechsler Intelligence Scale indicators:

2. Hysterics score lower on the subtest that taps routine, specific information, facts about the world (Information) than on the subtest that taps understanding of interpersonal, social functioning, facts-in-action, "facts embedded in relation-

ships" (Comprehension). These scores are seen as an expression on the level of concept formation of long-standing tendencies to repress knowledge of *specific* facts, to avoid an inner life of thought, and to be oriented outward toward the environment, toward action.

3. Scores on subtests that involve verbal thinking are generally lower than those that tap visual-motor aspects of intelligence. The lower verbal-thinking score is seen as a manifestation of a general cognitive tendency rooted in the hysterical tendency to repress verbally represented thoughts, wishes, and ideas (in contrast, for example, to the obsessional tendency to master ideas by isolation, intellectualization, magical thinking, etc.). In the hysterical personality the visual-motor areas are obviously relatively freer from this influence, for they do not draw as much on verbal thinking.

4. If the patient is assessed as neurotic on the basis of other tests *and* scores lower on Information (see 2. above) than on Vocabulary (capacity to define or give synonyms for words), hysteria is a possible diagnosis. The point here is similar to point 2.: repressive tendencies lead the patient to "forget" information. The higher score on the verbal intelligence test corroborates the dynamic, defensive basis of this forgetting or seeming ignorance, for this tends to reflect reliably the patient's basal verbal intelligence.

5. The hysteric's performance on Picture Arrangement, which requires him to put in correct order a set of pictures that tell a story, is usually *not* lower than vocabulary or the mean of the other subtests. Picture arrangement, which reflects a capacity to make sense of basic interpersonal situations reasonably quickly, is adequately or excellently performed (as measured against the vocabulary and mean score) by the externally oriented hysteric.

On the Story Recall test, which requires the subject to remember a short story and to report it immediately and then again after an interval, there are a few hysterical indicators:

6. A tendency to affectively toned, though not bizarre, distortions, reflecting a moderate cognitive disorganization in response to the affects elicited by the story. The affects tend to interfere with the memory of the actual story and to introduce

their own ideational representatives into it. This cognitive behavior reflects a larger tendency of the hysterical ego to blur the distinction between memory of reality and memory of a fantasy, especially if either is affect-laden.

7. On the well-known Word Association test, the hysteric blocks on and has longer response times on words with sexual connotations, reflecting the impact of repression on perception and cognition. Unlike the schizophrenic, the hysteric does not show signs of dereistic thinking, in which words are cathected as if they were the things they are supposed to represent.

In many respects the Rorschach is the best projective tool for the diagnosis of hysteria:

8. The hysteric tends to give exclusively form responses less often than do other types of neurotics. Form-dominated responses reflect intellectual control, and fewer such responses in the hysteric is viewed as a result of his intense affect and anxiety and diminished intellectual control.

9. Of the hysteric's form responses, a high proportion are congruent with the stimulus. This congruence reflects a basic intactness of the perceptual organization and an essentially good understanding of reality. This basic capacity is intact partly because the hysteric is not subject to the pressure of overvalent ideational content (owing to pervasive repression), which tends to interfere with an accurate, consensual appraisal of reality.

10. The hysteric tends to give few human-movement responses (which reflect internal fantasy and ideational life) owing to repression and the struggle to control impulses.

11. Hysterics give a good number of color-dominated responses. The handling of color is an indication of how the ego handles affects. Hysterics tend to create percepts that use the color of the blot, frequently respond to the chromatic before the achromatic part of the blot, and use color more often than human movement. The last of these comparisons, called by Hermann Rorschach the Experience Balance, reflects the hysteric's tendency to a labile and intense affective life at the expense of delay and ideational productivity. When both color and form are determinants, color tends to be the

predominant determinant in hysterics more often than in neurotics of other kinds. Form, however, continues to play some part in the hysteric's percepts (in contrast to those of more disturbed personalities), reflecting a weakening, not an abolition, of controls.

12. The content of the hysteric's Rorschach responses often presents rather transparent symbols of the underlying neurotic conflict over sexual urges (such as "an erect snake about to strike," an example quoted by Schafer). This reflects the hysterical ego's tendency to unconscious symbol formation, what some have called symbolization.

13. The record tends to contain a high proportion of "popular responses." This reflects the superficiality of the hysteric's experience and his tendency to a naïve, simplistic view of reality.

14. On both the TAT and the Rorschach the hysteric tends to give strong affective responses to the test stimuli, such as affectively charged explanations, affect storms (crying, anxiety, excitement) in the test session, or a distorted perception of the stimulus or idiosyncratic response to it shaped by these strong affects. On the TAT, the hysteric manifests this affective style in stories that revolve almost exclusively around the affective mood or tone of the picture, at the expense of the plot.

There are some general features of hysterical psychodiagnostic test responses that involve several tests:

15. The content of TAT, Rorschach, and other tests suggests a conflict around triangular relationships, reflecting Oedipal conflicts that are at the core of hysteria. The triangular conflict is often accompanied by an ambivalent dependence on the mother.

16. The content and over-all constriction of the protocol reflect a preference for screening, blurring, or completely closing one's eyes to external stimuli or internal thoughts. Sexually provocative test stimuli may elicit a more marked perceptual constriction. To look and to scrutinize demand very deliberate concentration, and may be a great effort for the hysteric.

17. The content of the test responses reflects several sorts of intrapsychic conflict, a few of which are the following: (a) a

conflict between establishing passive, dependent, asexual relationships with strong figures and phallic sexual relationships with them; (b) images of the phallus or phallic father are seen as the source of great strength but also as weak and impotent; (c) the body is seen as excited, beautiful, and valued by the parents, but at the same time as dirty and open to injuries from a retaliatory parent-competitor; (d) the body is seen as active, energetic, and sexually excited or as immobile, frozen, and restricted, reflecting the hysteric's conflictual experience of his own body and the excitement within it; (e) in female hysterics there are conscious images of a sexless, "innocent" self tended by foolish, demeaned men (images of deformed or little men such as dwarfs or elves reflect this neurotically compromised view of men); (f) Rorschach, TAT, and Early Memories tests responses tend to have a fairytale quality. Particularly, there are childish, fairy-talelike, pollyanna-ish images of a helpless self being saved by powerful rescuers.

Anxiety hysterics (phobics) present some special test patterns. On the Rorschach such patients give a high proportion of responses to areas that are usually small and rarely organized into a percept (*Dr*). This pattern is viewed as indicating a partial breakdown of the perceptual organization under the impact of anxiety. This anxiety, like anxiety in response to the actual feared situation, leads to a narrowed and arbitrary perception of the blot and a lessening of regard for its larger, objective reality. This process limits complex thinking, making correction of an arbitrary, idiosyncratic, and frightening experience all the more difficult.

Psychological testing has also approached the problem of hysteria indirectly, through the study of the test indicators of various defensive processes, among them repression, the dominant defense seen in hysteria. Many of the test indicators of repression are, then, of course also indices of hysteria; (a) the total number of responses (*R*) is low, reflecting over-all ideational restriction or constriction resulting from repression; (b) a low number of responses, and few human-movement percepts, indicating the dearth of available fantasy activity due to the cognitive effects of repression; (c) a high proportion of popular and animal responses, reflecting the banal experience of the world that results from the repressive restriction of thought and fantasy; (d) generally few rare responses (*Dr*) (see explanation above), and few responses that embrace the whole blot, reflecting the repressive tendency to see only the obvious and not the unusual, and to avoid synthesizing thought (necessary to make whole responses, *W*'s); (e) relatively little anxiety or emotional lability as reflected in the Rorschach determinants (low shading, low color, *FC* greater than *CF*, adequate *F%*, moderately high *F + %*). The characteristics listed under (e) are more specifically indicators of repression, and not necessarily of hysteria.

ASSETS AND LIMITATIONS OF THE
PSYCHODIAGNOSTIC-TESTING APPROACH

In the 1940's and 1950's the psychodiagnostic-testing approach had the advantage of putting into practice Rapaport's, Anna Freud's, and Hartmann's more modern view of the ego. It permitted and still permits the various ego functions to be carefully, systematically, and independently studied.

This approach facilitated the description of many features of hysteria, viewed as a personality configuration rather than as a symptom cluster. It was not restricted to a definition that centers on the diagnosis of the symptom formation, the nature of the libidinal fixation point, or the nature of the dominant defense, but permitted a view of the ego as an organ of adaptation to reality, as a locus of thought, action, and perception. With this view of the ego, psychopathology such as hysteria could be viewed not just in terms of the nature of the intrapsychic conflict, but in terms of the distortions, inhibitions, and hypertrophies of various ego functions, such as the synthetic and integrative functions and the functions of primary and secondary autonomy. It also opened the way for analysis of intrasystemic ego conflicts.

The hysterical ego could be seen to inhibit its own intellectual, synthetic, and perceptual organizing functions. The intellectual and perceptual centers of the ego could be seen to function well under certain conditions (when not under instinctual pressure or in the face of potential instinctual temptations or excitations). The hysterical tendency toward a motor expression of conflicts (conversion, acting out, phobic avoidance) could be understood as part of an internal emphasis on action functions and a de-emphasis on thought functions in the hysterical ego. This could be viewed as a general ego-functional expression of the impact of repression of thoughts. The hysterical tendency to perform better and more consistently in areas drawing on visual, nonverbal intelligence could be seen again to reflect the general impact on the ego of repression of ideas. Indeed, this approach, grounded as it was in much of Hartmann's thinking, made it possible to view these ego-defensive proclivities not just as specific expressions of repression, but as themselves a primary production of infantile development. With this new view of the ego, which opened the way for a more general psychoanalytic psychology, the areas of learning and intellectual functioning in hysteria and other personality configurations could be productively studied.

The psychodiagnostic-testing approach clarified other facets of the hysterical ego. It permitted better distinctions among different types of memory defect. A bizarre transformation of a remembered event seen in a psychotic could be distinguished from the nonbizarre misremembering of the hysteric, the latter's forgetting reflecting much more intact reality testing.

Similarly, it permitted a discrimination between the quality and quantity of disturbance of ego functions of primary and secondary autonomy seen in the hysteric and the psychotic. While the hysterical ego is viewed as being poorly able to channel affect and to synthesize it with thought and the demands of reality, certain basic thinking and perceptual processes of the ego were seen to remain much more stable than in the psychotic. As the view of the ego became more sophisticated, the hysteric could be discriminated from the psychotic also in terms of the depth, duration, and frequency of ego regression and the nature and extent of ego disruption during regression.

The impact of affect was seen to go beyond overt expression of feeling and to be a more subtle and enduring force in concept formation. It was seen to be capable of providing an affective tone or quality to the test response and, by extension, permitted a better understanding of the affective tone that the patient experiences in relationships.

The most significant contribution of the ego-psychodiagnostic approach to testing seems to this author to be in the area of investigation of the impact of psychic conflict on perceptual and cognitive processes. These autonomous ego functions could be seen to be distorted in the hysteric in the same general and expectable fashion, and the study of these distortions, apart from, yet of course related to, his symptoms, history, and life situation, became possible. In the hysteric, the blurring, screening, and tendency to fail to look at the test stimuli could be understood as a general ego pattern in which the specific defense of repression (and hysterical denial) can easily take root. This point of view paved the way for the most useful, if brief, clinical descriptions of the hysterical cognitive and ego "style" presented by Shapiro (1965).

There are nevertheless significant deficiencies in this approach, some of which are shared by other approaches to hysteria as well. Remarkably, the diagnostic-testing approach does not really present a definition of hysteria and hysterical personality. Rapaport's original diagnostic-testing research project did present a set of criteria by which hysterical patients were defined. These criteria, which stand as the only definition independent of the test indices themselves, are a mixture of the symptom-definition approach, the descriptive approach based on a simplistic assessment of the patient's overt behavior, and the dynamic approach (the latter, however, was never carefully or systematically presented).

In Rapaport et al.'s original sample of 19 cases of hysteria, 11 were so classified on the basis of conversion or phobic symptoms. (Conversion symptoms were defined by their expession of neurotic conflict, with an implication that the symbolic function of the symptom was the criterion, but the distinction between conversion symptoms and psychosomatic symptoms was not made clear). The other eight patients, who did not present discrete symptoms, showed hysterical impulsiveness and childish histrionic behavior. The authors comment that they felt justified in placing these eight cases in the group because their psychodynamics were similar and because they showed ready transference, emotional warmth, and did well in treatment. But the psychodynamics, "ready transference," "impulsiveness," and "childish histrionic behavior" are undefined and not illustrated. These descriptions run into three problems found in many attempts at defining this disorder: (1) assuming clinical description will be automatically and consensually understood; (2) assuming that phobic and conversion symptoms are synonymous with hysteria (and also neglecting to discuss the relationship between conversion hysteria and anxiety hysteria); (3) the lack of careful definition of lability and impulsiveness, making it impossible to identify the nature of the patient's activity. Specifically, it is difficult to evaluate whether these descriptions reflect a breakthrough of impulse into action, an intense (and perhaps defensive) affect state, or some combination of the two. Lability and impulsiveness in borderline cases or character-disordered patients need to be carefully distinguished before such descriptions are used as basic clinical traits of the hysterical personality.

What is unfortunate is that the psychodynamic-testing approach, capable as it was of tapping these various aspects of ego functioning, could have generated a definition of the disorder based on its *ego* characteristics. It stands to reason that this research would define its sample group initially on the basis of the clinical presentation, an area relatively independent of test performance. However, it might have been helpful to conclude the study by extrapolating from the test performance to some general features of the hysterical ego.

THE IMPORTANCE OF CONSIDERATION OF THE EGO
IN THE DEFINITION OF HYSTERIA

With the notable exception of the psychological-testing approach discussed above, the approaches to definition presented thus far in this chapter suffer from a failure to include the assessment of ego process in hysteria. This deficiency is at the root of the confusion concerning the definition of the disorder. While such writers as Wittels, Reich, and Chodoff and Lyons implicitly acknowledge a particular nature of the ego in hysteria, none of them spells out how this ego differs from that of the psychotic, psychopath, or impulse disorder. Though Marmor (1953), for example, suggests that ego psychology should be taken into account in the classification of mental disorders, his definition of hysteria rests fundamentally on his inference about the level of libidinal development. Reich (1933) also concentrated on inferences about libidinal development and never dealt with specific ego functions at all carefully. When the ego is not considered, debates concerning levels of libidinal development come to resemble the proverbial debates about the number of angels on the head of a pin. Whether the oral-dependent character structure, sexual behavior, and fantasy life of the hysterical personality represent a "genitalization of the mouth" (Reich), or an oral use of the genitals (Marmor), remains a moot point that in the end rests more on faith than on clinical inference. The following case demonstrates the pitfalls of relying too heavily on inference about libidinal fixation and paying too little attention to the nature of the ego processes.

Mr. T., a 23-year-old student, was a brilliant, affable man whose life was limited on every front by incapacitating inhibitions. His academic career had been interrupted, his relationships with women dwindled, and he came to live a lethargic, passive existence of listening to music, taking drugs, and retreating into wish-fulfilling fantasy. From the very outset of therapy he was a paradox. The core of his neurosis seemed to center on conflicts over any activity that might have phallic overtones; however, the content of his associations led time and again in the direction of enormous pleasure in oral activities and their derivatives. Though not overweight he ate and drank a good deal, and as he discussed his daily activities he characteristically located them with

reference to his meals. He became sexually excited in super-
markets, and at times when he felt unloved would go from
one food store to another. His use of drugs and "addiction"
to music had a very oral flavor. Oral associations became
more intense and frequent as therapy progressed, and it
began to seem that this patient was fixated predominantly in
the oral period. The quality of his ego functioning and object
relations was, however, very mature. Though his neurotic
conflicts had over the years encouraged a characterological
naïvete´ and massive inhibition in his relationships, his inner
experience of other people, as exhibited in extensive psychological testing and analytic therapy, was characterized by a
great deal of sensitivity and empathy concerning their feelings
and strivings.

The solution to this paradox turned out to lie in a muted,
conflict-ridden identification with and longing for a father
who had left the family when the patient was four. The
patient's mother, overwhelmingly bitter toward her ex-
husband, had taken every opportunity to paint a picture of
the father as cold, opportunistic, and self-centered. To be in
any way like the father was for this man to risk losing the
mother as well. When he entered therapy, he too had
nothing but contempt for the father, particularly for the
terrible effect of his abandonment on the mother and two
older sisters. When the patient was transferred during his
therapy to a male therapist, his unconscious identification
with his father gradually surfaced. As one would expect, it
turned out that his sexual and social inhibitions represented
for him being like his father and thus being as uncaring and
culpable as the father had been in his mother's account of
him. It was other areas of his hidden identification that
made sense of the incongruities of this case. It emerged that
the father had always taken an interest in cooking. The
patient remembered how much more he had enjoyed the
exotic, spicy food the father prepared than the "stoic," un-
seasoned food fixed by his mother. The mother had told
him, he came to remember, how bright the father was, how
much he liked music, and how much he drank. He came to
understand that his use of drugs and absorption in music

were both covert ways of maintaining an internally and externally unpopular identification and object attachment. The oral content of his associations all expressed his desire to reunite with and be like the father. Going to the supermarket, for example, was an attempt to unite with, be excited by, and be guided by the infantile fantasy of the omnipotent father. Most basically, it revolved around a negative Oedipal configuration, including a fantasy of performing fellatio on the father.

As the treatment progressed, the patient regressed to a stubborn anality, during which time in the transference and memories a stubbornness and retentiveness in food situations with the father became apparent. It turned out that battles in which the father tried to get the patient to "just taste" something which the patient continually refused to do were routine during his early years, and indeed still occurred in restaurants with the father when he occasionally saw him in his adult life. At the time he began treatment the range of his diet revealed that his tastes had ceased to expand at about age four, which was when the parents were divorced and the father left the home. With the interpretation of this material and the unearthing of his ambivalent desires to get something from the father, his lifelong food faddishness disappeared.

The prominence of oral matters in this case was deceiving, for it served to disguise the expression of conflicts concerning an abandonment at the phallic phase and earlier battles during the anal phase. One may ask if oral elements were not responsible for the choice of *what* about the father to identify with or fight about. They probably were; however, what seemed a more useful conceptualization of this case was that the patient identified with safe, passive, harmless aspects of the father in an effort both to avoid the potential wrath of the bitter, father-hating, maternal introject and to retrieve the lost father via playing a feminine, receptive role with him. The choice of oral aspects of the father served to fend off an identification with the sadistic, phallic aspects of the mother's version of the father.

A comparison of two patients will perhaps amplify the importance of assessing the ego along with the id.

Patient A., a married woman in her early thirties, came to treatment for depression and an intense, preoccupying jealousy of other women. When she sought treatment, she had grown obsessed with a woman whom she knew slightly. She would grow so angry and anxious that she began to fear she would do something violent or say something wildly inappropriate to this woman, and consequently expended much energy making sure to avoid her. She had conscious fantasies of murdering her, thought up ways to do it, and thought she would be able magically to take on her prize qualities if she did so. She measured herself against this woman, very concretely scoring herself on this or that dimension. She grew depressed and angry if she were losing the competition, and at times distrusted others' reactions to her, seeing them as critical of her, imagining slights, and exaggerating the importance to others of very minor *faux pas* of hers. At these times she grew mildly delusional, imagining her friends were discussing her qualities in a mocking way (clearly an externalization of her own systematic and preoccupying analysis of other women's qualities), and tried to attach herself symbiotically to someone she perceived as powerful and flawless, fantasying that she was borrowing strength and self-esteem. At her more conflictual times she became convinced that the therapist would mock anything she said, lost an essential and basic trust in him (she interrupted the therapy on a few occasions as a result), and experienced people as malevolent and judgmental. Her capacity to reflect on herself would disappear for weeks and she would also become very flat affectively and distant interpersonally.

Patient B., another young woman, suffered from depression and feelings of hopelessness about her life. With men she found herself in one unsatisfying relationship after another. She invariably sought men who were unavailable, and had a pattern of inquiring either directly or indirectly about other women in their current or past lives. She "inadvertent-ly" interfered with others' relationships. When this pattern was pointed out and the triangular pattern of her relationships in general was seen time and again, she eventually recognized it. The jealousy was being acted out *unconsciously*, while the patient maintained a generally warm and human feeling for the other people involved in the acting out of her unconscious fantasy. Via her dreams and free associations—in short, by inference from conscious derivatives of unconscious fantasy—it became clear that this woman unconsciously fantasied that if she had intercourse with an idealized man she would take on his qualities and those of other envied women in his life. She also revealed and could over a time recognize her unconscious fantasies of wanting to murder women perceived as more beautiful than she. Her neurosis led her to very ambivalent searches for infantile objects and also involved unconscious infantile fantasies of becoming the object's special person. In spite of these conflicts, the patient's feelings and energies remained generally appropriate in her life, indeed somewhat over-controlled. Even when she felt rebuffed or upset she could maintain trust in the therapist and her friends and a sense of the potential good will of those in her environment.

What are the similarities between these two patients? Both manifest a construction of relationships in terms of triangles, rivalries, and competition. Both show an infantile concep-tualization of how to be like the mother, conceptualizations that draw on magical thinking and pregenital stages of ego development. Both present a repetition in young adult life of an infantile fantasy of an exclusive relationship with a paternal Oedipal object and murderous wishes toward the maternal Oedipal object. Finally, both show some cannibal-istic underpinnings to these fantasies. The nature of unconscious fantasies and the psychosexual level they imply are very similar in the two patients, yet clinically their presentations are obviously very different.

The essential differences lie in the realm of ego structure and function. The defenses and the ego functions of the two patients are very different. Patient B. has a significant capacity for impulse regulation, synthetic and intellectual processes even when under the pressure of affect, and a capacity for sound reality testing and object relations under the pressure of impulse or narcissistic injury. These are not found in Patient A. A. presents consciously, in the form of delusional beliefs, what exists unconsciously in B. B. has more useful repressions, a more stable and differentiated representational world, and an ego capable of maintaining a constant and enduring affective hold on objects. A. is given to distortions of reality, primitive impulses barely under control or breaking through, primary-process thinking applied to problems of objective reality, and a sense of people as idealized or malevolent, as primitively mocking and persecutory or omnipotently benevolent. While B. unconsciously has a fantasy of gaining a phallus from a man, unconsciously associated with the Oedipal father, A. consciously believes in the magical transmission of power and the omnipotence of objects. B., even if unconsciously seeking objects for this neurotic purpose, at the same time experiences the object more broadly and realistically. A. may, at times of intense need, experience others as part objects, as need satisfiers or need frustraters, failing at those moments to be aware of any other aspects of them.

The conceptualizations that most basically reflect the essential differences in these two patients revolve around the nature of ego functioning.

Marmor based his contention that hysteria is a primitive, orally based pathology on analysis of the *content* of associations of the cases he cited. Just as the analysis of associations in the case of Mr. T. is misleading, so is Marmor's use of associative content with an oral cast to confirm the oral basis of hysteria. Only when the meaning of associations and their intrapsychic status in terms of ego processes and object ties is understood can they be used diagnostically or therapeutically.

The partial fixations at and regressions to various pregenital points found in Mr. T. are common to virtually all neurotics, and thus an attempt to diagnose strictly on the basis of the psychosexual nature of his conflicts is futile. Only by considering his pervasive use of repression, the symbolization of his conflicts, the need to maintain a myth of his own effeteness and weakness, the over-all intactness of his synthetic and intellectual processes, and the basic phallic-Oedipal nature of his conflicts, can a diagnosis of hysterical personality be made.

When the definition and theory of hysteria exclude the ego, it is impossible to specify the capacities and weaknesses of the personality, for its nature — neurotic, borderline, or psychotic — ultimately depends not on the nature of the libidinal urges or fantasy life, but on the level of ego functioning, as Knight (1953) and Reichard (1956) have pointed out. Reichard demonstrated the inadequacy of a definition of hysteria in which the nature of the ego is omitted by re-examining Freud's early work on hysteria (Breuer and Freud, 1893-1895). In this work Freud concentrated exclusively on symptoms, not yet having postulated the concept of the ego. Reichard re-examined the cases Freud reported, using current ego-psychological concepts. She argued that his patients were not a diagnostically homogeneous group and that two of the five patients were suffering from a psychosis at the time of treatment.[7] The other three could be considered hysterical according to current standards. Reichard concluded that the term "hysteria" is useless, since it has been applied to a variety of dynamically unrelated symptoms such as conversions, fugues, phobias, hallucinations, and since it takes no account of the "ego defect" involved. Only when the ego is assessed, she claimed, can a disorder such as hysteria be reliably and meaningfully distinguished from other psychopathologies and can different types of hysteria be specified. Glover (1932) had made a similar point when he suggested four approaches necessary in diagnosis: descriptive, developmental, reality testing, and ego defenses.

Just as the ego is the "organizer" of subjective experience, mediating among the internal and external pressures on it

---

[7] Others before Reichard commented on the psychotic elements in Freud's original patients (Noble, 1951; Goshen, 1952; Brill, 1954).

(Hartmann, 1950), so does it serve as a pivotal, organizing concept in psychological theory. When it is not considered, hysteria, borderline disorders of the infantile variety, the "as if" personality, psychopathy, and schizophrenia all seem similar to one another, both in superficial behavioral ways and in terms of unconscious conflicts. The conceptual boundaries which separate them become obliterated. In ignoring the ego several authors have drawn unlikely and academic parallels between hysteria and other disorders fundamentally different from it, particularly schizophrenia. For example, Marmor has noted the following areas of similarity between schizophrenia and hysteria: (1) hysterical introversion and schizophrenic autism; (2) hysterical fantasy and schizophrenia delusion; (3) hysterical materialization (Ferenczi, 1913) and schizophrenic hallucination. Eysenck (1957) has considered hysteria and psychopathy virtually identical. Jung (1936) also pointed out the resemblance of hysteria to schizophrenia: the *belle indifférence* in hysteria like the emotional indifference in schizophrenia, the presence of explosive affects in both, and the presence of "characterological abnormalities" in both. The fundamental difference lies in the hysteric's extraversion in contrast to the schizophrenic's introversion. Somewhat more to the point, Abse (1966) noted the similarity between severe hysterical dissociative states such as fugue and schizophrenic ruptures with reality. Noble (1951) described a series of patients who appear hysterical between periods when their underlying psychosis erupts. He supported the conception of a continuum between overt hysterical illness and schizophrenia, with the schizohysterical illness he describes lying in between.

CONTRIBUTION TO THE STRUCTURE AND FUNCTION OF THE HYSTERICAL EGO: ABSE, KERNBERG, SHAPIRO

Although the ego has been generally underemphasized in definitions of hysteria, some writers on hysteria have begun to take ego structure and function into account. Some (Shapiro, 1965; Farber, 1961) have dealt with general aspects of the hysterical ego, others (Abse, Kernberg) with more microscopically different aspects of ego defensive, synthetic, and attentional activity in the hysteric.

Abse (1966) dealt extensively with the ego in hysteria. He offered many types of definition, ranging from diagnostic indicators of classical hysterical convulsions and paralyses that he studied in India to very subtle accounts of the differences in ego process and states of consciousness among various neighboring psychopathologies.

Speaking generally of intrapsychic structure, Abse supported Freud's belief that in a neurosis such as hysteria, the battle is primarily between ego and id, whereas in psychosis the ego battles the external world, ruptures relations with it, and then attempts a distorted reconstruction of it (Abse, 1966; Freud, 1924). In short, the ego in hysteria is fundamentally "true" to the external world during its battle with the instincts. In comparing regression in schizophrenia and hysteria, he pointed out that the hysteric regresses to a *fantasy* of an infantile object and meets the conflicts aroused by incestuous, tabooed Oedipal wishes head on, whereas the psychotic regresses to a narcissistic level, with the ego actively involved in shutting out the external world. According to Abse, the energy consumed in the latter process is so great and the psychotic's ego resources so limited that there is neither structure nor energy to prevent primary-process material from flowing in. This in turn can lead to the development of psychotic defenses such as, for example, massive projection.

Abse discussed at length defensive processes that involve changes of consciousness; differences in these processes can be used to distinguish hysteria from schizophrenia, from other neuroses, and to differentiate among several types of hysterical reactions. For the delineation of one of these defensive processes Abse returned to the notion of the hypnoid state, a concept he considered useful but which, he believed, Freud dropped out of lack of interest in the ego. Abse described the hypnoid or dissociated state as one in which self-observation is deleted, ideation is affect-charged but vague and restricted, and the capacity for verbalization is limited, all of which are specific ego processes that fend off thoughts that are conflictual for the hysteric. In extreme hypnoid or fugue states there is even more restriction of ideation, haziness of thought, and gross affective disturbance, accompanied by a subjective exchange of the present for the past that reaches an almost complete fulfillment.[8]

Abse distinguished between the superficially similar hypnoid states and states of reverie connected with creative activity. In the latter there is a suspension of action, an emotional richness connected to the ideational activity, and open associative channels, all of which are generally in contrast to the paucity of association, diminished clarity of ideas, and tendency to action in an attempt to reduce anxiety found in the hypnoid state. In creative states the highly concentrated attention and regressive events are in the service of the ego, whereas in hypnoid states the regressive events are sequestered from normal waking consciousness by the redeployment of repression.

In conjunction with the predisposition to hypnoid states, Abse described the low attention cathexes of the hysteric and the accompanying tendency to separate instinctual representations from verbal images when under pressure from regression, depriving ideation of clarity and associative connections within the preconscious system. Along with this, the hysterical ego often cannot make use of affects as signals. In his typical foggy state, the hysteric has lost the cognitive value of emotion and awareness of its impact on others.[9]

In a state of incipient dissociation, the hysteric may begin to feel he is losing ego control and may exhibit depersonalization, another alteration in consciousness that is complementary to the original dissociation, and is motivated by an attempt to stem the dissociation. During depersonalization, according to Abse, there is a heightening of self-observation, a fixing on the external world, and a heightened capacity to describe inner experience verbally. In depersonal-

---

[8] For the hysteric in therapy, the dulling of self-observation and the exchange of the past for the present, though less extreme than in typical fugue states, can lead to intense, compelling transference distortions.

[9] Noted also by Shapiro (1965), this becomes a central characterological problem in the treatment of the hysteric.

ization the law of the superego enters the realm of the ego: the self-observation carries with it the threat of internally criticizing and negating the experience of the ego, the strangling of affect, and the reversal of pleasant into unpleasant sensations.

Abse tried to discriminate among different types of hysteria by considering the presence of a tendency of the ego to use alterations in consciousness, the types of alterations employed, and the impact of such alterations on the secondary process. For example, he used the presence of dissociation and depersonalization as one way to discriminate between two types of hysteria, the hysteriform (which corresponds closely to Easser and Lesser's hysteroid, and Kernberg's infantile, personality) and the hysteric. He asserted that in handling inner conflicts the ego of the hysteriform resorts more frequently to states of dissociation and depersonalization than does that of the hysteric. He also considered the combined presence of massive denial, a flight into activity or complete passivity, projective distortion of objects in the environment, and pathological lying as indicative of the more psychotic ego processes found in the hysteriform character. Though he included consideration of libidinal dynamics in saying that there is a fundamental oral fixation in the hysteriform, his main emphasis lay in a functional assessment of the ego of this more primitive character.

The essential differences between the hysteric and the schizophrenic, which Abse's ego-psychological approach clarified, are the hysteric's access to intact, though infantile, mental representations of objects, the ego's capacity to use fantasies of such objects, and the ego's capacity to maintain commerce with the environment, all of which are weak or nonexistent in the psychotically regressed. He also discriminated between hysteria and schizophrenia on the basis of the form of dissociation which appears in schizophrenia, as opposed to that typical of hysteria, a distinction which has been observed by no one else. In hysteria "molar" or "block" dissociation occurs. Large units of experience such as memories, fantasies, or other thoughts are separated from other units of experience, but remain in themselves basically intact. Laughlin (1956) has delineated various forms of molar dissociation: (1) side-by-side dissociation (acts and ideas that are contradictory); (2) repression (dissociated block is rendered unconscious); (3) dissociation in psychophysiological disorder (dissociation expresses itself physiologically); (4) dissociation of fragment of consciousness (part of the sensory apparatus, i.e., part of visual field, can temporarily fail to receive input that is registered consciously); (5) massive dissociation (fugues, amnesias, multiple personality). Abse added to this list a form of molar dissociation that affects the body image when a body part, because of association with forbidden wishes or impulses, is dissociated. Abse added that this kind of dissociation can be particularly disruptive to the hysterical character since such characters often imitate postural mannerisms of those with whom they identify.

In contrast, the schizophrenic exhibits "molecular dissociation"—dissociation occurs on the level of perceptual units of the environment, fundamental logical processes, and basic verbal operations. Whereas in hysterical molar dissociation the dissociated area remains intact, though rarely conflict free, in schizophrenic molecular dissociation intrapsychic conflict is distorted and denied by a dissociative process that separates words from their true referents or that reduces a meaningful, common gestalt to a chaos of colors or forms, which might then be organized around a new psychotic principle.

The notion of molar versus molecular dissociation seems to hold potential for a structural, metapsychological conception of the ego. Hinsie and Campbell (1970) included the distinction between molar and molecular dissociation in their definition of hysteria.

The nature of dissociation also distinguishes the obsessional neurosis from the hysterical. In the former there is consciousness of the dissociated system, for it either continually intrudes itself into consciousness in the form of obsessional thoughts and compulsive behavior or remains isolated in consciousness, whereas the hysteric bars the split-off system from consciousness.

In addition to his work on states of consciousness in hysteria, Abse further described the tendency of the hysterical ego to use "condensation" as found in dreams to produce a particular conversion symptom. He believed that condensation, "materialization," and symbolization, which are all part of the process of transforming verbal thoughts into nonverbal representations, tell us much about language that philosophers of language have ignored. For example, the process of conversion seems to involve a regression of the ego to a developmental period when (1) the sense mode simultaneously triggers feelings in other modes, and (2) simple sensorimotor imitation lies somewhere between identification and perception.

The ego of the conversion hysteric further manifests two processes: first, the translation of usually verbal ideation into a symbol (symbolization), and second, the symbol expressing itself through the soma.[10] Abse did not consider all psychosomatic phenomena to be hysterical conversions; some are what he termed "affect equivalents" that do not involve symbolization. Differentiating between the hysterical convulsion and hysterical symptom formation, he also noted the capacity of the ego in the latter case to "bind" energy in the symptom, whereas in the former case the energy generated by the psychic conflict temporarily abrogates the functioning of secondary process.

Finally, Abse joined Fenichel (1945) in noting the tendency of the hysterical ego to repress not only the forbidden instinct, but the superego prohibitions as well. Perhaps this is why female psychopathy has been so often confused with hysterical personality.

HYSTERIA CONTRASTED TO OBSESSIONAL NEUROSIS: FEDERN

In 1940 Federn published an article in which he examined the hysterical ego in order to distinguish between hysteria and obsessional neurosis. Although this article is rarely referred to, it is excellent, and is marred only by Federn's global use of the

---

[10] Fenichel (1945) described the same two processes.

term "ego." He uses ego to mean processes and representations of the self as well as a metapsychological concept, similar to but not quite the same as the dual use of the term "ego" found in Freud.

Federn began with a set of "rules" that form the basis of the obsessive's mental life: (1) rule of proscription—obligation to fulfill *all* proscriptives of the obsession (exactitude); (2) rule of isolation—obligation to think of nothing but the obsession; (3) rule of emptiness—obligation to have no other emotion with obsession (purity of thought); (4) rule of devotion—obligation to give his attention with the *whole ego* involved. This last rule is the most difficult for the obsessional to endure, but it is also the most compelling. This rule demands that the obsessional pursue with full devotion his rituals or obsessional patterns of thought. As he put it, "the [obsessional's] ego settles his unconscious conflicts by consciously watching his expiating processes."

These rules and the rigidity and "strength" of the ego which carries them out is contrasted with the "passivity" and "pliability" of the hysterical ego. Differing also from the obsessive's desire to avoid all internal or external distraction, the hysteric's thought or fantasies are easily interrupted by new associations. Federn described the difference as follows: "The obsessional ego keeps up the ego boundaries with great vigor. This is the main feature of the compulsive character. In hysteria the ego boundaries are weak, they are easily enlarged to include another person" (1940, p. 270).

Federn noted further that the nature of "ego splitting" also differentiates the obsessive-compulsive from the hysteric. In the hysteric, part of the ego is unconscious, whereas in the obsessive the *whole ego* must be involved. This use of the term "ego splitting" is different from Kernberg's (1967) use of it to describe a characteristic of the borderline personality.[11] Federn's use of "ego splitting" to refer to a structural aspect of the hysterical ego is confusing because the contrast is with the "whole ego" of the obsessive, which refers not to a structural or

[11] See the recent clarifying review of the concept of splitting in Lichtenberg and Slap (1973).

functional quality of the ego, but rather to a *subjective* attitude involving devotion of all of one's energies to the obsession.

Federn also observed that the hysteric, in contrast to the obsessive, is constant only as long as the "transference to the loved person is maintained." What the loved one asserts or denies, so the hysteric asserts or denies. Although this observation satisfactorily contrasts the hysteric with the obsessive, it fails to discriminate between the hysteric and more pathologically "imitative" personalities, such as the "as if" personality described by H. Deutsch (1942), or the "screen personality" of Greenson (1958), in whom there is no "core" to the personality, no enduring, fundamental sense of self. While the neurotic hysterical personality surely manifests the sort of imitative identifications with significant figures observed even in the conversion hysteric of Breuer and Freud, these are defensive maneuvers designed to repress or deny conflictual aggressive or libidinal object ties and *not*, as in the "as if" personality, to make up for a fundamental absence of a sense of self, which is a structural defect in the personality.

As noted earlier, Federn stressed the difference in "ego boundaries" of the hysteric and the obsessive, describing the ease with which the hysteric's ego boundaries can be enlarged to include important objects in contrast to the vigor with which the obsessive maintains the integrity of his boundaries. Hysterics thus have a tendency to form quick, intense, and transient identifications, as will be discussed later.

Elaborating a point made by Freud, Federn described the difference in the quality of fear in the two character styles: the hysteric fears death, a fear that pertains to the "bodily ego," whereas the obsessive has a "thinking fear" that pertains to the psychical ego. The hysteric, according to Federn, fears actual injury or physical attack, whereas the obsessive fears forbidden thoughts that might overtake him.

Federn distinguished further between hysteria and obsessive-compulsive neurosis developmentally. He described the obsessive child has having a highly developed, premature intellectual critical ability and a stubborn "willfulness" during the anal period; the hysterical character he traced back to a basic weakness and passivity. The obsessive uses his prematurely developed ego to deal consciously and actively with threatening ideas, without repression. In the hysteric, whose critical capacities do not develop precociously, the ego passively "capitulates" to threatening ideas or feelings and the reactions are repressed.[12] With this repression the reacting state of the organism is also rendered unconscious and, according to Federn, the hysteric's ego finally becomes diminished and split.

HYSTERIA CONTRASTED TO INFANTILE PERSONALITY: KERNBERG

Kernberg (1967) considered the interface between the hysterical personality and his carefully defined infantile personality (a type of borderline personality), again with an ego-psychological emphasis. Structurally, he distinguished between "high"- and "low"-level character pathology, the former characterized by more mature repressive mechanisms and the latter more primitive "splitting" mechanisms. He defined "splitting" as the process in which libidinal and aggressive versions of the internal self and of object representations are separated, a central and defining ego-defensive process of borderline personalities. According to Kernberg, the borderline has relatively intact ego boundaries and a related capacity for reality testing, but the lack of synthesis of contradictory self- and object images has numerous pathological consequences. The borderline presents primitive mental representations, primitive and poorly modulated affects, and defenses characteristic of early development. In normal development primitive defenses such as projection and splitting are replaced by higher-level defensive operations of the ego: repression and related mechanisms such as reaction formation, isolation, and undoing. In all these the ego banishes from consciousness drive derivatives and/or ideational representations that might generate intrapsychic conflict. The borderline infantile personality uses the more

---

[12] Here Federn is in sharp disagreement with Farber, who describes hysterics as basically very willful. See below, p. 118.

primitive mechanism and a variety of secondary borderline defensive strategies that result from it. The hysterical personality, on the other hand, maintains internal representations in which the libidinal and aggressive representations of self and object are fused: it is only the *drive* concerning ambivalently regarded objects that is defensively distorted and negotiated by the ego. In other words, the hysterical personality struggles with ambivalence by repressing urges, fantasies, and thoughts toward others or self, whereas the borderline personality retreats to a preambivalent state by splitting the internal representations into "good" and "bad" self or object.

Writing less structurally, Kernberg went on to delineate the crucial differences between aspects of the infantile and hysterical personalities which superficially appear similar. (1) Emotional lability—the hysterical personality manifests pseudo hyperemotionality more markedly in *specific* areas of conflict in order to bolster repression, whereas in other areas affect is genuine and focused. The emotional lability of the infantile personality, in contrast, is generalized and diffuse. The hysterical personality may temporarily lose control of impulse at the height of a crisis, whereas the infantile personality manifests a permanent inability to modulate or control impulses. (2) Overinvolvement—in the hysteric there develops a childish clinging, especially as a regressive defense in heterosexual relationships, accompanied by overidentification with the partner. All this occurs, however, in the framework of solid, secondary-process thinking and relatively accurate evaluation of reality. In the infantile personality the overidentification is more desperate and inappropriate to long-term involvements, and such personalities show a regressed, childish oral-aggressive demandingness, not typical of the hysterical patient. Kernberg went on to make similar differentiations concerning the dependence, exhibitionism, pseudo sexuality, competitiveness, and masochism present in both personalities, stressing the differences in the capacity for object relations of the two types of personality. The hysterical personality has a greater capacity to empathize with the motives of others, to perceive subtleties of feeling in others and, finally, to maintain a lasting relationship with someone if certain neurotic preconditions are met. Earlier, Hendrick (1936) had also distinguished the neurotic from the borderline on the basis of ego capacities, noting that the borderline ego cannot bind its aggressive impulses with much success, an observation consistent with Kernberg's argument.

Though Kernberg said that sophisticated psychological testing is indispensable in evaluating the qualities of the ego that are at the basis of the diagnostic distinctions he proposed, he later asserted (Kernberg, 1970) that sure confirmation of the diagnostic differentiation demands knowledge of the effect of interpretation over a period of time. In the hysteric, interpretation of narcissistic defenses will open up feelings of shame and inferiority and usher in an Oedipal transference. In a narcissistic or infantile personality this will not happen, at least not in the short run. (See also Kohut, 1971).

Kernberg has made a valuable contribution to a definition of hysteria in differentiating it from its various neighbors in the borderline realm in terms of ego process, impulse life, and object relations. He goes beyond Easser and Lesser in clearly identifying the strengths of the hysterical personality which distinguish it from the more ego-regressed, orally fixated borderline personalities that, at first glance, resemble hysterics. In his distinction he emphasizes the specificity and delimited nature of the hysteric's conflicts, his generally accurate reality testing, the essentially secondary-process quality of his thinking, the capacity for relatively mature, differentiated object relations, and the capacity to experience more modulated affects and impulses. Rather than relying exclusively on fixation point, as does Marmor (1953), or on overt behavior, as do Chodoff and Lyons (1958), Kernberg looks to much more basic adaptive and defensive modes in his efforts at definition.

HYSTERICAL EGO STYLE: SHAPIRO

Shapiro discussed neuroses in general as maladaptive styles of cognitive, affective, and intellectual functioning. Growing out of the psychological-testing approach, Hartmann's (1939) work, Erikson's contributions (1950), and G. S. Klein's (1958) research into cognitive functioning, Shapiro's theory is essentially an ego psychology of various character types. His subtle descriptions of character are reminiscent of Reich's. Reich, however, viewed character as a set of neurotic compromises resulting from drive-defense crises, much as Freud had viewed the hysterical symptom. Shapiro conceived of ego styles as continuous modes of functioning, present at birth, and subject to transformation during development.

Shapiro described a "foggy," impressionistic, nontechnical, nonfactual cognitive style as characteristic, indeed definitional, of the hysterical mode. He directly attributed the poor memory of the hysteric, which most have explained as simply the result of widespread repression, to this vague cognitive style. The hysteric remembers poorly because, he claimed, the initial cognition was vague and nonspecific. In contrast to the obsessive, whose cognitive style compels him to be aware of the details of a situation and therefore allows him to remember it far more "objectively" later, the hysteric, who was more concerned at the time with an impression in response to the situation, has no clear memory of it to refer to later.

The hysteric typically attempts to solve problems on the basis of "hunches," rather than through orderly intellectual processes. Thus, though the hysteric may solve a problem correctly, he often cannot trace the cognitive steps. This passive, impressionistic cognitive style leads the hysteric's attention to be easily captured. Thus he appears distractible, with a paucity of knowledge of specific facts, and lacking a sustained, compelling curiosity.

While at times Shapiro seems to be saying that this conception of ego style *replaces* the earlier theory of repression, this does not seem to be his consistent position. Rather, his theory seems to be that this cognitive style *favors* the use of repression. Thus "hysterical" becomes a description of a cognitive ego style, not itself psychopathology—a style that favors, when a neurosis occurs, the use of traditionally recognized hysterical defenses.

PASSIVITY AS AN EGO STRATEGY

Shapiro made a vital contribution in elucidating *how* the hysterical character is passive. Rather than referring in a vague or stereotyped way to the passivity of the hysteric, Shapiro described the *purpose* of the hysteric's apparent helplessness and ignorance. The hysteric avoids recognizing the purposes and motives behind his actions or the actions of others by feeling that he could not have known what the outcome would be. Shapiro noted that when pushed, however, the hysteric does know what to expect in response to his acts. The point is that his cognitive style leads him to avoid serious questions about his motives by enabling him to feel unsure of the consequences of his behavior. When this kind of pattern is pervasive, including feelings of incompetence about money or other realities of life, the result is what has been described as hysterical immaturity and pseudo innocence. In this way the hysteric can disown his feelings, and the thoughts or motives that generated them, by experiencing them as visited upon him from outside.

In contrast to Wittels (1931), who implied some inherent laziness and sloth in the hysteric's passivity, Shapiro makes clear that the hysteric is inclined to maintain, for both public and personal consumption, the *myth* that he is helpless, naïve, and unable to exert any control over his environment. Shapiro makes clear that this myth, which expresses itself in such ego realms as cognition, interpersonal style, and self-concept, serves a psychological *function*. This will be seen later to be a dynamic common to hysteria throughout its history and, as such, is probably its central defining quality.

Shapiro went on to describe the lack of integration of affect with thought, the "passivity" of hysterical awareness, and the transient, explosive quality of hysterical affects. What is unique about Shapiro's approach is that he presented a picture of many sides of the hysterical ego and proposed a unified conceptualization of it—integrating an understanding of cognitive style with the more traditional accounts of the hysterical ego's handling of affect, fantasy, and intellectual processes.

HYSTERICAL USE OF EMOTIONALITY

Siegman (1954) examined a specific character defense of the hysterical personality—the use of emotionality. In this well-thought-out article Siegman partially agreed with the classical psychoanalytic position that dissociation of affect and its expression through derivatives accounts for the "emotionality" observed in the hysterical personality. He believed, however, that the major part of this emotionality serves a defensive function. Though these "hysterical emotions" seem similar to others derived from more primary affect, their superficiality and shallowness distinguish them from more directly experienced feelings. They nevertheless have the insistent, compelling force of any character defense and are neither fraudulent nor subject to conscious influences. The hysteric experiences these affects as carrying him away, whether they are ego alien or not.

Siegman noted that patients often report an "ought-to-ness" about such affects, as if the emotions were in some sense "proper" in a particular situation, even though they are, of course, fundamentally designed not to impress others, but to impress an "internalized observer." At the same time, the same patients report a certain pleasure in experiencing these feelings. Siegman proposed a theory which explains both experiences. He argued that affectivity is important in the battle between the ego and the superego. To avoid guilt the ego may either obey the injunctions of the superego and repress certain libidinal impulses, or it may present certain conciliatory attitudes to the superego in return for limited gratification. The latter is the case in hysterical emotionality. One aspect of the emotionality is to demonstrate to the superego that the ego is "well-behaved," "proper," and experiencing the "correct emotions." The desire to be the "good girl" or "good boy" reflects an effort to maintain the benevolent attention of the parents and/or repent for libidinal and aggressive strivings toward them, strivings which are omnipresent in the hysteric (Cameron, 1963; Easser and Lesser, 1965; Farber, 1961). This explains the "ought to" feeling so frequently reported by these patients.

At the same time that the ego goes through the motions of meeting the demands of the superego, it is able to smuggle in, so to speak, certain libidinal gratifications, under the cover of a noisy demonstration of the "proper" emotion. This accounts for the "put on" or shallow quality of hysterical affects. It also accounts, according to Siegman, for the deep material often seen prematurely in the analyses of hysterics, as this material is offered up as a defense against impulses that are truly forbidden and remain repressed. This process gives the early phases of therapy with hysterical personalities their "confessional" quality—the attempt is to persuade the therapist, as the embodiment of the superego, that the ego is experiencing proper discomfort at such "bad" thoughts.

The defensive use of emotionality can then be secondarily cathected. Siegman agreed with Fenichel that, beyond this secondary narcissistic gain, there is sexualized excitement in the "show" itself. Because of this, Siegman criticized theories of hysteria that describe a basic passivity as fundamental to it and portray the hysteric as the passive victim of affects within him pressing for discharge. He asserted that the hysteric actively seeks out stimuli which will evoke his hysterical emotions because the experience of these feelings is neurotically gratifying.

EGO (SELF-) BOUNDARIES

Several authors have described the nature of the hysteric's ego boundaries, which in many ways is related to identification processes in the hysterical personality. Federn described the hysteric's ego boundaries as "weak" and changing. He proposed that the hysteric, in response to threat, may suspend ego boundaries in order to include someone perceived as a protecting adult, to feel enlarged and comforted by him. This process of opening and enlarging ego boundaries and including an image of someone else within them gives the hysteric who is in the midst of internal crisis a most chameleonlike appearance.

This conceptualization is a problematic one because it lacks specificity. Ego (self-) boundaries refer to several types of boundaries on very different levels of psychological functioning: (1) the internal discrimination between the self's and the object's thoughts and wishes; (2) the sense of strictly *physical* separation between self and object; (3) the sense of distinction between affects originating from the self and from the object; (4) the sense of emotional, personal distance and autonomy from objects. If there is a breakdown of self-boundary (except in dreams) in the first sense, a psychotic experience of reality results. The lack of a sense of distinction between the boundedness and impact of thoughts and wishes of self and object leads directly to a psychotic sense that one's thoughts are continually obvious to others and are omnipotent. It may also lead to a paranoid, psychotic panic that the thoughts of others are powerful and potentially destructive. Though not as seriously pathological, a rupture of self-boundaries in the second sense (physical separation) may lead to acute experiences of depersonalization, transient, severe interference with reality testing, and a serious threat to self-integrity. This can lead to a psychotic sense of being continuous with the physicality and will of others, which may lead to psychotic anxiety, a primitive imbalance of narcissism, disturbances of the cornerstone of the self-body ego, a sense of fragmentation of the self, and hypochondriacal preoccupations.

Ego boundaries in the third and fourth senses are of a very different order. Suspension of these boundaries, while boundaries in the first two senses remain intact, results in an overinvolvement with and identification with the object, not in a loss of the most basic sense of physical and psychic distinction between self and object. In his discussion of the suspension of ego boundaries, Federn did not clarify which sort of boundaries he meant. The hysteric's tendency to enlarge his boundaries to include a comforting and protecting object can be explained most validly and parsimoniously by considering self-boundaries in the third and fourth senses. The hysteric defensively strives to maintain an illusion of being protected, usually from his own active aggressive and sexual wishes, by generating a sense of being one with, or the same as, a protecting parental object. Though the hysteric strives to maintain an internal sense of being merged with the object, he fails to lose his sense of physical and psychical separateness by virtue of the structural integrity of his boundaries in the first and second senses.

Whether the hysteric's attempt to promote an internal sense of being at one with, close to, and never at odds with important objects should be viewed as a suspension of self-boundaries, or as a process of identification and over-identification, is probably moot. If the former conceptualization is chosen, however, it is necessary to limit the meaning of ego boundaries, lest unlikely and invalid parallels be drawn between schizophrenia and hysterical ego processes. I would prefer to conceive of the hysterical overinvolvement with objects as a process of identification. To consider it as a problem of ego (self-) boundaries implies that there is a structural, and therefore enduring, only slowly changing, character fault. This implies that the hysteric's suspension of self-boundaries involves a structural defect which will not change with resolution of intersystemic conflict or with external circumstances.

The defensive (adaptive) use of identification,[13] on the other hand, implies an active ego process. This is a more useful conceptualization for the hysteric because: (1) It counters the common reflex to see the hysteric as lacking or deficient psychically. (2) It more fully connotes that the hysteric manifests this process under particular, usually definable, intrapsychic conditions (for example, under the press of aggressive or sexual feelings toward an unconsciously incestuously perceived object), and that there are many areas of functioning in which the process is not invoked. (3) It avoids the liability that "ego boundary" will be misinterpreted to mean a fundamental confusion of self- and object representations (as is present in the psychotic).

If, however, the hysteric's relationship pattern is viewed as an identification process, identification must also be carefully

[13] The concept of identification too is confounded by the fact that it is used to describe a process of internalization during early childhood as well as a defensive process. It is used here to refer to a defensive process which, of course, plays a major role in the pattern of object relations.

and consensually defined. Schafer (1968), reviewing and synthesizing work on internalization, has discriminated several modes of internalization: incorporation, introjection, and identification. Incorporation refers to a psychotic idea that one has completely swallowed an object which lives on inside, controlling and directing behavior and experience. Introjection involves an internalization of an object which is poorly integrated into either ego or ego ideal. Identification is a more differentiated, developmentally advanced form of internalization. It involves an internalization of aspects of the object. It does not completely take over control of the self as the agent and does not become master of the person's acts and plans. The hysterical personality can be considered to identify in this restricted sense. He does not fundamentally lose his core sense of self, for he often has more of a core identity than he will publicly or personally acknowledge. The transient *defensive* identifications are an attempt to escape longings and the responsibilities (guilts) for such wishes, and to seem to be in the hands of someone else. The identification serves to avoid facing one's wishes, and in this sense is defensive. Furthermore, such identification is often in the service of re-enacting a longed-for infantile communion with a libidinal object. The hysterical personality, then, may shift his convictions with each new actual love object, but a more fundamental, enduring core remains untouched. The identification may be, for a short time, a wholesale one, but because there is a more enduring core, the identification is not psychodynamically vital and therefore may disappear as suddenly as it developed.

Angyal (1965) described this process without using the term "identification" in his description of the "pattern of vicarious living." He wrote: "This method implies, on the one hand, a systematic repression of one's genuine personality characteristics and, on the other, an attempt to assume a substitute personality" (p. 138). The kind of repression Angyal had in mind "is a . . . sweeping process, a wholesale indiscriminate discarding of not just some tabooed areas but of all one's genuine feelings, thoughts, and impulses" (p. 138). Thus, according to Angyal, the hysteric represses much of the self and replaces it with vicarious, unreal roles borrowed from salient people in their fantasies in the hope of filling "the inner emptiness, the assumed nothingness" (p. 144).

FANTASY IN HYSTERIA

Basic to an assessment of the ego "style" of the hysteric is an assessment of the status of unconscious and conscious fantasy in the hysterical personality. There is a general consensus that, owing to the hysteric's cognitive style and the predominance of repression, he experiences little conscious fantasy, and what there is is stereotyped, vague, laden with diffuse affect, and sequestered from unconscious ideas. Unconscious fantasy, on the other hand, has a powerful impact on perceptions of objects and the self, and on life choices.

According to Fenichel, the hysteric represses idle conscious fantasy when it touches on Oedipal content. It is the subsequent unconscious fantasy that is central to the development of the conversion symptom which, for Fenichel, *is* the defining attribute of hysteria. In a severe case of hysteria, then, one would expect to find little conscious fantasy. The projective-test data findings of little fantasy life (particularly reflected in low movement scores on the Rorschach) in hysterical personalities (Rapaport, Gill, and Schafer, 1968) are consistent with this expectation.

Easser and Lesser (1965) noted that when the hysteric inhibits or represses physical sexuality, romance invades every area of functioning. They agreed with Freud's notion that the labile affects remain conscious following the repression of the ideas with which they are associated, adding that a wish for "romance," the desexualized trappings of the sexual wishes, remains conscious as well.

Shapiro (1965), in discussing the hysterical cognitive style, carefully described the different states of hysterical fantasy. He observed that the fantasy lives of hysterics are "meager," though their whole attitude toward reality is "influenced by their romantic outlook," as in the idealization of the love partner through an impressionistic cognitive style oblivious to his flaws. Consistent with Fenichel's view and the projective-test evidence, Shapiro also believed that there is little conscious fantasy life in the hysteric.

Farber (1961) described the hysteric's diminished conscious fantasy life when he talked of the hysteric willing illusions about herself with such determination that "it [hysteria] abhors wit, discrimination, imagination, humor, and judgment . . " (p. 117). Again the illusions thrive while conscious fantasy life is strangled.

Referring to more severe hysterical alterations of consciousness, Abse (1966) pointed out the same kind of wish-fulfilling transformation of reality and restricted fantasy life noted by Shapiro (1965) and Schafer (1948), including "restricted ideation" and haziness of thought, at times approaching a complete exchange of the present for a wished-for past. Again, idle conscious fantasy is seen as restricted, but unrealistic regressive ego states distort reality. Agreeing with Fenichel's view of fantasy in hysteria, Abse noted that the kind of daydreaming in the beginning of a hysterical hypnoid state might resemble creative reverie, but in the former the regressive fantasy is soon cut off from normal waking consciousness by the redeployment of repression.

The hysterical personality, then, is characterized by minimal access to fantasy, while much conscious experience, owing to the diffuse split-off affects that remain in consciousness and the indirect impact of the unconscious thoughts, takes on a wish-fulfilling, fairy-talelike, romantic quality. What is considered romantic fantasy or daydream in the hysteric consists of meager, usually stereotyped ideation. It consists predominantly of a dreamy, mildly dissociative feeling or mood, rather than an actual daydream with any appreciable content.

Unconscious fantasy in the hysterical personality shows itself in several ways. It causes the hysterical personality to select, edit, and emphasize what happens around him to conform to his unconscious needs. As Shapiro put it, the world is experienced through the "rose-colored glasses" of unconscious longings. Such unconscious wishes and their defense may lead to the formation of specific neurotic symptoms (phobias, psychosomatic symptoms, conversion symptoms). They may also have significant impact on the hysterical personality's over-all pattern of life choices, including libidinal object choices, career decisions, and interpersonal habits. H. Deutsch (1930) described the "hysterical fate neurosis," in which neurotic conflict based on unconscious fantasy leads not to circumscribed symptoms, but to a neurotically restricted molar pattern of behavior. To illustrate, she presented a case of a woman whose central genetic conflict concerned her disappointment that her father never loved her as much as he loved her brother. Penis envy, guilt about competitive strivings with respect to her brother, and a masochistic attachment to her father through an identification with the slavish mother all resulted. These conflicts expressed themselves in unconsciously motivated object choices, specifically the choice of men who fulfilled infantile needs unmet by her father and who were sure to disappoint her every time. The objects were chosen largely to resemble her father and mother, but also had to differ from the parents in certain wish-fulfilling ways.

LIMITED CONSCIOUS FANTASY CONTRASTED WITH
VIRTUAL ABSENCE OF CONSCIOUS FANTASY:
THE HYSTERICAL CHARACTER DISORDER

Though almost all writers describe the hysterical personality as, in general, restricted in conscious fantasy and ideation, there are clearly differences in degree which are important diagnostically and therapeutically. Freud's observations on the role of fantasy will clarify this dimension.

Freud (1924) observed a difference between neurotic and psychotic fantasies. He noted that in neurosis the attempt is to avoid particular realities of the world that bring about fears and temptations by editing reality through such defenses as denial or repression. In psychosis, there is an attempt to remodel reality, to reconstruct it in accord with the psychotic's conflicts. The capacity for fantasy is crucial in distinguishing neurosis from psychosis. In the former it is the central intervening factor, whereas in the latter there is little capacity to distinguish thought from reality. For the neurotic, who is able to separate fantasy and reality, fantasy can be either a source of gratification or, as noted by Fenichel in discussing hysteria, a seat of conflict. For the psychotic, reality itself must be remodeled because the world of fantasy, as a realm separate from reality, is severely limited or non-existent.[14]

When unconscious wishes are very pressing and conscious ideation and fantasy severely restricted in the hysteric, there may develop a tendency to "remodel" reality in some rather flagrant ways. The result is a monolithic, completely un-reflective attempt to make the external world conform to wishes. Going beyond the basic modal hysterical pattern of differentially perceiving and responding to reality in accord with unconscious wishes, there is an endless manipulation and coercion of others to behave in certain fixed ways. At this end of the spectrum, there is an unrelenting demand that reality be as it is wished to be. The restricted ideation of this sort of person prevents him from stepping back from his experience and making sense of it. In psychotherapy, such patients are often unable to achieve enough distance from their feelings toward the therapist to recognize them as trans-ferences from other people in their early or current lives. For such patients, introspection, even over a period of time, may fail to transform the desire for the therapist into "as if" experiences (Tarachow, 1963). They tenaciously demand of their therapist what can never be realized—that he actually *be* the same as the father, that he actually be a lover, etc. The clinical situation for such patients ceases completely (for periods of time) to be an arena for self-understanding or self-exploration, as they attempt to remodel it so the therapist will actually respond to particular libidinal urges (Greenson, 1958; Tarachow, 1963). These patients differ from border-

---

[14] Freud made developmental sense of this difference as follows: during development a mental phenomenon, fantasy, develops which provides partial fulfill-ment of wishes and escape from pain. At the completion of normal development, this area of gratification is subjectively separable from reality.

line patients who develop a transference psychosis in that this transference situation is transient.

It is for patients such as these that the term *hysterical character disorder* should be reserved. Neurotic conflicts are so woven into the personality that awareness of conflict is absent. Conflicts have harnessed so many ego resources that the psychopathology is indistinguishable from personality characteristics. The maladaptive and often highly self-defeating patterns in such patients are ego syntonic. It may well be that a crucial factor distinguishing the hysterical character disorder from the hysteric, whose symptoms are ego dystonic, is the former's incapacity for conscious fantasy, ideation, and self-reflection. This incapacity prevents self-reflection and also interferes with recognition of the essential "as if" quality of transference feelings. In such hysterical character disorders the possibility of true borderline psychopathology should be carefully investigated.

Neurotic difficulties in the hysteric, in contrast, are ego dystonic, be they circumscribed somatic symptoms, a neurosis of life choices, or a hysterical fate neurosis. For example, a young woman in her late 20's had a history of choosing and twice marrying men who, in their basic weakness and superficial bravado, represented the patient's conflicting, infantile perceptions of her father, who had seemed at times very reliable and at other times indifferent and weak. She sought men similar to her infantile perception of her father, quickly became disappointed in them, and left them. No one could live up to her image of the strong, protecting father. Though she repeated this pattern time and again throughout her adult life, it never seemed "right" to her. It was the fundamental ego dystonicity of this pattern of life that eventually led to the understanding and end of this repetition compulsion.

Such a neurosis should not be considered a character disorder, but a form of hysteria, a hysterical neurosis (an ego-dystonic, neurotic conflict within a hysterical personality). What distinguishes the hysterical character disorder is not the expression of neurotic difficulties in life choices, but the absence of conscious fantasy, the syntonicity of maladaptive life patterns, the imperative, unreflective demand for gratification of infantile needs from important objects, and the diffuse, pervasive interweaving of conflicts with coping and defensive ego activity.

ZETZEL'S TRUE HYSTERIC: EGO CONSIDERATIONS

Zetzel (1968) made a very similar distinction between truly analyzable hysterics and the "so-called 'good' hysteric." She pointed out that many female patients with hysterical symptoms or character structure suggestive of an unresolved Oedipal situation fail to be analyzable and seem to contradict the psychoanalytic assumption that hysterics present the most intact egos and are therefore most amenable to psychoanalytic treatment. She pointed out that there are four different types of patients that present seemingly hysterical symptoms, and are often initially considered analyzable hysterics. Two of these groups, the "good hysteric" and the "potential good hysteric," have ego resources not present in the two groups of "so-called good hysterics." True hysterics (and latently, the potential good hysterics), according to Zetzel, have experienced a true "triangular conflict," and have been able to retain significant object relationships with both parents. They can recognize and tolerate internal reality, its wishes and conflicts, and are capable of distinguishing it from external reality. Affectively, they can sustain anxiety and depression and can, without extreme, desperate bitterness or self-devaluation, give up unavailable objects and gratifications. The capacity to distinguish between internal-external reality and to give up unattainable objects permits such patients to distinguish between the therapeutic alliance and the transference neurosis and to tolerate this duality. This is a major criterion for analyzability.

The two groups of "so-called good hysterics" manifest hysterical symptoms and character structure suggestive of Oedipal fixation.[15] Zetzel pointed out how deceptive such

---

[15] A weakness of Zetzel's otherwise very significant paper is her failure to describe how hysterical symptoms or hysterical character traits actually appear. Is she referring to conversion symptoms, a general tendency to somatization, or

overt aspects of the patient can be. Some of these patients turn out to be basically depressives. They have extremely negative feelings about themselves, tend to devalue their femininity, and tend to be compulsively self-critical and self-blaming. They develop intense transference neuroses and, in contrast to the true hysteric, are capable of little working alliance. The transference is characterized by extreme dependence, a sense of utter rejection, and is punctuated by outbursts of anxiety.

The second type of "so-called good hysteric" that Zetzel described is similar to Easser and Lesser's "hysteroid." (This type is similar to the hysterical character disorders described above.) Such patients are incapable of making a meaningful distinction between internal and external reality and incapable of tolerating a genuine triangular situation. They present few areas of conflict-free or autonomous ego function, past or present. Such patients have a poor capacity to distinguish between transference and reality and thus are, according to Zetzel, unanalyzable. The histories of these patients tend to include serious or prolonged physical illness in childhood, serious psychopathology in the parents, a hostile, dependent relationship with the mother, and an absence of meaningful, sustained object relationships with either sex.

Both dynamic and ego-psychological considerations are central to Zetzel's definition of the true hysteric. Dynamically, the true hysteric must manifest a triangular, Oedipal conflict, reflecting an Oedipal fixation. Second, the hysteric must manifest a variety of ego capacities: good reality testing and self-boundaries, capacity for sublimated, conflict-free activity, tolerance of anxiety, depression, and transference wishes, and the presence of enduring, actual object ties. For Zetzel, in many ways the best diagnostic test of these areas is the patient's capacity for psychoanalysis. Her major thesis is that hysterical symptoms and overt character patterns are not conclusive evidence of a relatively unmodified ego, which can best respond to psychoanalysis.

---

what? Is she referring to hysterical indifference, coquettishness, shallowness, as traits suggestive of unresolved Oedipal conflicts?

Several authors have made contributions to the study of hysteria that do not fall easily into the definitional approaches outlined thus far. These contributors offer sensitive and incisive observations about the hysterical personality, but fail to elaborate them into systematic, more extensive theories of the disorder. Each of these contributions will be drawn on significantly in the approach to hysteria set forth in the final section.

HYSTERICAL PSEUDO SELF

Angyal (1965), writing from a "holistic" standpoint all his own, dealt with psychopathology in terms of over-all patterns of living. What he considered central to the hysteric is a sweeping, general repression of the whole gamut of thoughts and feelings, the resulting gap being filled through a process of "vicarious living." The hysteric lives out a substitute personality, because she has so completely banished her genuine self. The hysterical solution, then, is an attempt to escape an inner feeling of vacuousness by fleeing to a pseudo personality. In milder forms, the hysterical pattern is conducive to empathy, sensitivity to human problems, and, owing to the hysteric's need to try to live through someone else, a tendency to attach herself to others in an effort to adopt a substitute personality.

Angyal delineated three types of hysterical personality. Unlike Kernberg and Shapiro, he believed that the three types are closely related. Simple hysteria is the fundamental form characterized by what Angyal called a "pattern of vicarious living," a pattern of taking on aspects of others to fill the emptiness left after repressing large aspects of self. "Hysteria with negativistic defenses" denotes a pattern essentially the same as the "simple hysteric" with the addition of outer layers of defense consisting mainly of negativistic reactions. In this second type the negative reactions have developed as a secondary defense against the suggestibility that is part and parcel of the hysteric's hunger for vicarious symbiotic ties. Finally there is the "borderline hysteric," who is again seen as fundamentally similar to the "simple hysteric," but who has wholeheartedly abandoned himself to vicarious living. This personality can lose himself so completely in the role with which he has identified that his fantasies about himself can resemble delusions. Angyal's *clinical* description of the "borderline hysteric" sounds very much like H. Deutsch's "as if" personality (1942), Kernberg's borderline (1967), and Easser and Lesser's hysteroid (1965). While these authors emphasized the fundamental difference between these hystericlike personalities and the true hysteric, however, Angyal did not.

Wolowitz (1971) has presented a description of hysteria that also stresses the other-directedness of such personalities. The hysteric is pictured as socialized to seek approving emotional reactions from people around him. Like Angyal, Wolowitz described the development of a pseudo self, an artifice consisting of phony, socially pleasing qualities, leading to a sense of artificiality. This pseudo self, designed to elicit reactions from others, becomes elaborated, while a more basic sense of emptiness remains. Being incapable of genuine and direct self-experience, the hysteric instead develops "qualities" to exhibit to others. There is little intrinsic self-gratification, as most of existence evolves into a pursuit of acclaim from others. For example, brilliance substitutes for the enjoyment of thinking; being sexy substitutes for feeling sexual; and being interesting substitutes for feeling interested. The hysteric, according to Wolowitz, often avoids being alone, for she does not know how to exist in the absence of others. He saw this trend as directly related to a type of involvement with objects encouraged in little girls by family and society.

Basic to Wolowitz's work is a partial, though oversimplified, truth: that the hysterical personality is organized around a fundamental motive to be approved by and to draw emotional reactions from people around him. Fitzgerald (1948) made a similar observation when he noted the hysteric's essential craving for love. Angyal, Wolowitz, and Fitzgerald join in observing the hysteric's overwhelming need to affirm his identity through objects' reactions to him, and his consequent tendency to form a facade based more on the social and interpersonal climate than on his directly experienced affects and wishes.

Farber (1961) contributed a single, highly articulate essay on the theory of hysteria. The central dynamic in hysteria for Farber is the willful maintenance of an illusion. In stark contrast to so many authors, who have considered passivity, in one form or another, as central to the disorder, Farber considered willfulness to be basic to the hysteric. The hysteric is so stubbornly bent on maintaining illusions about himself and others that wit, imagination, and intellect are threats to the illusion and consequently must be restricted. Any intellectual process that permits distance to be taken from the illusion, such as critical thought, humor, doubt, threatens to undermine its validity and reality.

Farber, Angyal, and Wolowitz were all addressing the same quality of the hysterical ego — its capacity and its need to sustain an internal sense of being something it is not, something it wishes to be or feels it should be.

Sullivan (1956) considered the hysteric's basic dynamic to be the seeking of a "happy idea" in an effort to escape blame. This search sounds similar to the stubborn maintenance of an illusion described by Farber and the pursuit of "emotional reactivity" described by Wolowitz. Usually raised by a highly self-absorbed parent who uses the child as "a plaything — a decoration of the parent's personality — rather than as a growing personality," the hysteric, too, becomes self-absorbed, can think of himself only in superlatives, and is continually railing against the inadequacies of reality. Differing from Angyal, Sullivan believed that the hysteric's self-absorption leads him to feel that others simply do not matter. Since Sullivan believed hysteria is related to the dissociative personality, he stressed the ease with which the hysteric can avoid realizing what he is expressing through conversion, dreams, or associations in psychoanalysis. He also emphasized the conventionality of the hysterical personality and his proclivity to be caught up in a cliche or dramatized performance that has no firm roots in motives or feelings.

Like many other writers, he noted the emotional lability of the hysteric, the intensity and clarity of the Oedipus complex, and the persistence of juvenile fantasy into adulthood.

Angyal, Farber, and Wolowitz all stress the hysteric's lack of a cohesive sense of self and the basic narcissistic vulnerabilities (the emptiness) rather than the Oedipal basis of the conflicts. Conflicts over sexual and aggressive wishes toward incestuous objects are barely mentioned. They therefore do not view the exhibitionism, overidentification (pattern of vicarious living), or willful maintenance of an illusion or "happy idea" as resulting from a conflict over incestuous wishes and fears of retribution (from the parent or superego) for them. Rather, they imply an essential absence of identity or a unifying core.

Farber, Angyal, and Wolowitz stressed some important ego-psychological dimensions of the hysterical personality, I believe, but they largely ignored questions about the unconscious dynamics generally found in the disorder.

BRITISH OBJECT-RELATIONS APPROACH TO HYSTERIA

Fairbairn's (1954) over-all mission in his writing was to bridge the gap he saw in Freudian psychology between impulse and ego theory. He argued that a unitary conception of ego structure can be achieved only by conceptualizing intrapsychic functioning in terms of personal relationships with early objects — an object-relations theory of personality. Fairbairn claimed that two aspects of early introjected objects are repressed. These two aspects, the "libidinal ego" and the "antilibidinal ego,"[16] represent respectively the exciting aspects and the rejecting aspects of the early object. There is left the "ego nucleus," which stands as the ego ideal. In addition, Fairbairn postulated that the "antilibidinal ego" represses the "libidinal ego," a process he called indirect (or later) repression. Thus he believed that repression and

[16] These terms are somewhat confusing in a strictly Freudian context. They involve concepts of the "ego" both as a set of functions and as a set of object and self-representations.

splitting are twin processes that occur in the normal development of children. Fairbairn's approach to psychopathology was to explain the differences in mental disorders in terms of differing techniques used to regulate the internal object relationships established early in life.

Fairbairn believed that in the hysteric's development the exciting and rejecting objects are exaggerated — the exciting object is too exciting and the rejecting object too rejecting. From this it follows that the libidinal ego is excessively libidinal and the antilibidinal ego excessively prohibitive. As noted earlier, Fairbairn observed that in the hysteric the rejecting and exciting objects do not appear in consciousness, but appear only in dreams, while conversely the ideal pervades conscious daydreams. The unconscious persecution of the libidinal ego by the antilibidinal ego leads the hysteric compulsively to sacrifice sexual pleasure and to bring suffering upon herself in other spheres. This is consistent with Fenichel's and Freud's assertion that the hysteric represses both libidinal ideas and superego prohibitions.

Fairbairn offered an alternative in the controversy about the fixation point in hysteria. As we have seen, Marmor (1953) argued that the hysteric is libidinally fixated at the oral level, while Fenichel (1945) and Reich (1933) and others located the fixation point at the phallic-Oedipal level. Fairbairn opposed the fixation-point approach of classical psychoanalytic theory and asserted, with case illustrations, that the hysteric's *genital* urges have been prematurely stimulated, sometimes as early as the oral phase. He phrased it paradoxically: " . . . whereas the sexuality of the hysteric is at bottom extremely oral, his (or her) basic orality is, so to speak, extremely genital" (p. 108). Genetically, he proposed that this premature genital excitement results from the early infantile genital masturbation, considered a symptom, that follows upon unsatisfactory object relationships. Here he drew on his approach to erogenous zones and conversion, which differed greatly from the standard psychoanalytic view. Fairbairn believed that the child is not inherently auto-erotic, but rather is object seeking (alloerotic). It is only when the object is frustrating, rejecting, etc., that a body zone takes its place. Fairbairn even claimed that erogenous zones are not part of the natural unfolding of sexuality, but are themselves conversion reactions. Conversion reactions, for Fairbairn, were thus one of many defensive techniques for repressing a problem with current or early internalized objects. Thus hysteria, like much of psychopathology for Fairbairn, is basically due to a turning away from objects to the self, a process that results in what he called the "schizoid" resolution (see also Guntrip, 1971).

Fairbairn also contended that the Oedipal conflict is not the cause of hysterical conflicts, but is rather an end product of earlier vicissitudes of infantile dependence. In contrast to Freud's conception of the structures id, ego, and superego, Fairbairn framed the struggle in terms of the original relationship of the child to the mother. Oedipal strivings, for Fairbairn, are first oriented toward the mother. The first triangle, so to speak, involves the child, the exciting object, and the rejecting object, the latter two being different internal representations of the mother. Only later does the exciting object become identified with the opposite-sexed parent.

Handelsman (1965) also theorized about the role of early object relations in personality formation. Writing about the impact of early object relations on sexual development, he observed that developmentally primitive people often have orgasms, whereas more advanced types (hysterics falling in this category) at times do not. He explained this by claiming that the orgasm itself is not indicative of how primitive or mature the sexual experience is, and went on to describe how problems during the three early stages described by Mahler (1958) can lead to various modes of sexual pleasure. While very severe problems during the autistic (0 to 3 months), symbiotic (3 to 12-18 months), and separation-individuation (12-18 months to 3 years) stages could lead to very severe personality problems, Handelsman believed that less severe problems during these periods could also have later specific consequences in the nature of neurotic adaptation. For example, problems during the symbiotic phase might lead to a symbiotic sexual adaptation in which the person unconsciously wishes to merge with the parent in order to make himself whole again. This could take the form of promiscuity, or compulsive activity in which the person talks of a desire to merge with and lose himself in the partner. Problems during the autistic and separation-individuation periods are manifested in characteristic ways which Handelsman spelled out.

Like Fairbairn's theory and the ego-psychological approaches, Handelsman's approach can help to clarify the psychoanalytic theory of sexual behavior and consequently aid in understanding the hysteric. The assumption of the possible autistic or symbiotic use of sexual behavior allows for a more subtle definition of "genitality." In this context, the sexually unresponsive hysteric can be seen as far closer to the true genitality with which he struggles than the sexually responsive character disordered person for whom sexuality is one of few sources in a desperate search for a feeling of wholeness through symbiotic union. According to this approach, the hysteric can paradoxically afford to repress his sexuality and severely limit his sexual activity because the foundation of his personality does not depend on such activity. In contrast, sexual activity for the types of people Handelsman described maintains a necessary self-affirming sense of rapport with early internalized objects.

SYNTHESIS AND A BASIC DEFINITION

In this chapter I have stressed the debates, contradictions, and inconsistencies in the definition of hysteria. Some common themes, however, run through many discussions, themes that can serve as the basis of an enduring, parsimonious, clinically usable "ideal type." What follows is my own synthesis and definition, which draws on areas of strong agreement among previous authors, but is by no means an attempt to be representative or completely consensual. My intention is to outline the points of intersection among the sets of characteristics presented by the contributors to the field, excluding views presented by only one author. The resulting subset of a larger set of characteristics of hysteria will lay the groundwork for the more comprehensive formulation of the concept of hysterical personality to be presented in Chapter 5.

The Hysterical Personality as a Constellation of Psychological Traits and Processes

In this definition, and in its more elaborated version in Chapter 5, hysterical personality refers to a personality style, not necessarily implying psychopathology. Hysteria or hysterical neurosis refers specifically to *neurotic* conflicts within a hysterical personality.[17] Hysterical character disorder refers to a hysterical personality beset with neurotic conflict, the expressions of which are ego syntonic and appear in many realms of functioning. "Hysterical" describes a constellation of character traits and psychological processes, including a skewing of ego functions, relationship modes, affective organization, and developmental accomplishments. Hysteria refers to mild to moderately severe psychopathological reaction, and excludes massive dissociation, a complete breakdown of reality testing, and the uncontrolled, explosive expression of impulse. Thus hysteria refers to a psychopathology that may interfere with living, but that does not completely prevent basic independent functioning.[18]

The Ego in the Hysterical Personality

The hysterical personality should be defined primarily on the basis of the nature of the ego. These ego qualities are: (1) A tendency toward repression of ideational content. (2) A general cognitive style that facilitates a vague and global experience of reality, a turning away from the specific and detailed, particularly in affectively and sexually arousing situations. (3) An experience of reality continually shaded by thoroughly repressed, though highly active, unconscious wishes; perceptions of self and object distorted by long-

---

[17] Such conflicts may be expressed as anxiety reaction, phobic reaction, conversion, or any other neurotic reaction. A psychotic reaction in a hysterical personality should be considered just that—a transient psychotic episode within a hysterical personality.

[18] Independent functioning refers to the minimum capacity to live by oneself, to care for one's needs, not to require custodial care.

standing illusions—some unconscious, some preconscious; little conscious fantasy; however, the hysteric's life decisions and experience are often the slaves of unconscious fantasies. (4) Thinking often fails to be directed, logical, and deductive; rather, it is impressionistic and given to ruptures in the face of strong feelings; intellectual problems are approached using "hunches" rather than a clear, logical sequence. (5) Under the impact of tabooed thoughts or strivings, consciousness and attention can be altered, leading to blocking, mild dissociation, and "fogging" of internal and external experience.

The General Integrity of the Hysterical Ego

Though there is debate about the hysteric's "impulsiveness," "passivity," and "emotional lability," the dominant outlook in the literature, which seems to be the most sensible, is that the hysterical ego generally mediates impulses well and is capable of delay of gratification, secondary-process thinking, and a generally accurate appraisal of reality. Except during regression from conflict aroused by sexual or other conflictual encounters, thought and action are adequately integrated. The ego seems to function less well than its potential when specific, delimited areas of conflict are triggered, in contrast to more disturbed personalities whose conflicts are so diffuse and whose psychic structure is so poorly established that the ego is chronically overtaxed and failing. In the hysterical ego both synthetic and integrative functions are *potentially* effective.

Hysteria Distinct from Other Psychopathologies

As an "ideal type," hysteria should be clearly distinguished from the borderline personality described by Kernberg, the "as if" personality of Deutsch, the screen personality of Greenson, and the psychoses. "Hysterical" should refer to a character structure, and "hysteria" to a neurosis within such a character. Following Rangell and Saltzman, hysteria should be distinguished from "conversion symptoms," which clearly occur in the context of virtually any character structure.

Crucial to an ego-oriented definition of hysteria or hysterical personality is consideration of strengths. As a diagnosis, hysteria seems to be most useful if it includes such aspects as solid, secondary-process thinking, relatively realistic evaluation of reality, general capacity to regulate the expression of impulse, basic capacity to sustain relationships (albeit conflictual ones), and a capacity for conflict-free areas of functioning. Only if such relatively enduring aspects of ego functioning form the basis for a personality diagnosis will that diagnosis be clinically useful. If the hysterical personality or hysteria is, in a sloppy fashion, considered to be the same as the infantile personality or the "as if" personality, very central, clinically vital dimensions will be obscured, for the differentiation of ego structures in the former is so much more extensive and intact.

The Role of Passivity in Hysteria

Though some imply that the hysteric is passive, babyish, or lazy, several authors have recently implied more sensibly that the passivity is a pervasive character and ego defense. The hysterical personality's passivity, rather than implying a *lack* of psychic structure or energy, serves a psychological function, and is part of a structuralized ego process. The hysterical personality commonly invokes passivity defensively, and in the process fails to actualize his intellectual, creative, or occupational potential. In many areas of his life the hysterical personality accepts an illusion or personal myth that he is passive, helpless, and in need of aid. This myth, which is highly syntonic to the hysterical personality, often serves as a means to avoid active sexual and aggressive strivings which are experienced as taboo. In spite of this "myth," the hysterical personality paradoxically manages subtly to exert a very significant control over those around him. Moreover, in circumstances in which the myth of passivity is unnecessary, the hysteric may be surprisingly self-confident and autonomous.

Severity of and Nature of Intrapsychic Conflict

Though there are exceptions (Marmor, 1953; Wittels, 1931), there is a consensus that "hysteria" and "hysterical personality" be reserved for relatively mild or moderate forms of neurotic and/or character disturbance, characterized by a relatively intact ego, mild to moderate incapacity to handle life responsibilities, and phallic-Oedipal (as opposed to pregenital) levels of fixation. The recent contributions on the borderline personality strongly suggest that such terms as "hysteroid" (Easser and Lesser, 1965) and "hysterioform" (Abse, 1966) be discarded, and that such patients be considered as borderline personalities.

The intrapsychic conflicts are essentially organized at the phallic-Oedipal level, predominantly at the Oedipal. Some defensive regression to oral levels commonly occurs, but such regressions are transient and rarely involve substantial ego regression. In female hysterical personalities there tends to be a classical, unresolved Oedipal conflict, revolving predominantly around a wish for a powerful father, a penis from him, or a baby by him. An identification with the mother through neutralization and sublimation is not achieved; rather, the longing for the father is repressed, and the Oedipal father is unrelinquished. In male hysterical personalities there tends to be a negative Oedipal constellation, involving a fear of the father and a defensive wish to appease and disarm him. These are, however, only trends; the particular nature of the Oedipal conflict varies immensely among individual hysterical personalities. What is basic is that these conflicts are genuinely triangular, not dyadic. Moreover, they are conflicts concerning impulses toward people who, at the point of fixation, were experienced as discrete objects toward whose representations predominantly object libido (as opposed to narcissistic libido) was directed. Though the hysteric may seek a dependent, protective relationship in which he experiences himself as childlike and helpless, these characteristics do not reflect an oral fixation. Rather, they are part and parcel of the hysteric's illusion of his own helplessness, incompetence, and powerlessness, commonly representing a partial oral regression and, more important, a *fantasy* of a pregenital paradise based on wish-fulfilling memories of its bliss. To feel active or competent leads the hysteric to fear his potential to act out prohibited, polymorphous-perverse, or incestuous Oedipal strivings, and the image of himself as childlike and innocent serves to protect him from these internal dangers.

Severity of Symptoms

In applying the term "hysteric," the over-all severity of symptoms as well as their quality should be considered. Hysteria should modally refer to patients whose behavior or symptoms interfere with, but do not make impossible, the handling of work and domestic responsibilities. The performance of hysterics in work situations is often remarkably good, in contrast to their conflictual heterosexual relationships (Zetzel, 1968). If a patient proves completely incapable of handling family or work responsibilities, and seems to have chronic, diffuse problems in all work or personal encounters, even if he has some superficial *resemblance* to the hysteric, the possibility that there are profound and pervasive ego faults and primitive experience of objects ought to be considered.

The Hysteric's Relationships

The hysteric is able to form and maintain more than short, tumultuous relationships. His relationships are characterized by an idealization of and overinvolvement with the partner, and his expectations of the relationship are romanticized and fairy-talelike. The hysteric establishes strong, intense, at times transient ties. In his relationships, he readily feels for, feels with, and feels through the partner to experience accomplishments and pleasures as if they were his own. Through the partner, he vicariously lives out his own private, often unconscious fantasies. For this reason, the hysteric's choice of love object often involves the potential for living out his own personally prohibited strivings. Though the hysteric is characterized by a dearth of conscious fantasy, he perceives his relationships through the rose-colored glasses of unconscious fantasy and preconscious illusion. The hysteric's relentless, unconsciously dominated search for an object that will live up to an unconscious infantile prototype may culminate in a "neurosis of destiny" or "hysterical fate neurosis"

(H. Deutsch, 1930) in which the neurotic search expresses itself in faulty, disappointing, and ultimately abortive life choices.

Though the hysteric may need to maintain a wish-fulfilling illusion about the object as all-loving, he is more fundamentally capable of maintaining an ambivalent, differentiated image of objects. Unlike the borderline's "splitting," which drastically obscures the actual qualities of objects, the hysteric's distortions tend to be restricted to significant objects, leaving him capable of much more realistic, subtle, and differentiated perceptions of nonlibidinal objects. Most important, the hysteric is, with therapeutic help, capable of recognizing at some level that an object cannot realistically meet an infantile need. This permits him to take distance from his needs of objects and insures an essential autonomy from them. This all makes it possible for the hysteric to distinguish between a transference neurosis and a therapeutic alliance, a major prerequisite for psychoanalysis or psychoanalytic therapy.

3

ETIOLOGY OF HYSTERIA

Consistent with much that has been written on hysteria, etiological formulations about it are often impressionistic and scattered. They also suffer from a deficiency common to much theory of psychopathology in often being based on reconstructions made with adult hysterics. Systematic longitudinal research, unfortunately, does not exist.

Investigating the specific etiology of hysteria by drawing on previous studies and case reports is beset with exactly the problems described in Chapter 2: What are the authors describing the etiology of? Some approach hysteria as a syndrome based on symptoms; for others it is a set of character traits, etc. The differing approaches to definition, coupled with the differing approaches to the study of etiology (demographic assessment, history of illness among family members, developmental patterns, etc.), make matters even more problematic.

Are these studies then of any value? In my opinion, they are of limited value. As will be seen in the next chapter, the form hysteria takes has changed with time. Many observers and clinicians have sensed that something called hysteria has continued to exist from the late nineteenth century to the present, though the symptomatic expression has changed. It has been unfortunate and misleading that a symptom (conversion reaction) remained the most central defining feature of the syndrome. It is, however, the case that during a certain period (from the mid-nineteenth century to the mid-twentieth) *many* patients presenting conversion reactions were in fact people with an underlying hysterical personality organization. Many of these reports were, therefore, in fact of people presenting a hysterical personality organization.

The studies were defining the hysteric on the basis of a culture-specific mode of hysterical expression. They were nonetheless often discussing patients we would now, from a more sophisticated ego-psychological point of view, consider to be hysterics. Obviously some were studying patients who, if they were evaluated today, would turn out to be presenting other types of personality organization.

Investigation of studies of etiology of hysteria, like the study of the definitions of hysteria, reveals that this has been an area of study in which clinicians have unsystematically sensed the existence of an entity called hysteria. It has been an area of study in which clinical impressions, sometimes real clinical wisdom, have been brought to bear on this entity, but these observations have floundered because there has been no definition of the underlying constant personality features of this character type. It is my hypothesis that, from as far back as the Egyptian physicians' practice of fumigating the genitals as a cure for hysteria to the present, there has been a core of collective wisdom about some important features of this entity called hysteria. In a sense many of the contributors to its study have had a hold on some part of the proverbial elephant; but without a theory of how these different aspects fit together and how certain overt traits change with era and culture, there was no way of seeing the full picture.

The real limitation of this review of studies is that, while these general tendencies can be useful, there are surely instances in which the definitional problems have led to the study of patients who in no way conform to the hysterical personality as described here. On the whole, it seems to me that the lack of a consistent definition among these studies limits them, but that to ignore them completely on this account would exclude some accurate, collective observations about the hysterical personality. Though these different approaches often lead nowhere because the definition and explanatory concepts are inadequate, there are some modal directions, certain general tendencies in these clinical papers and studies, that can help us begin to explore questions of etiology.

The most extensive formulations about etiology are embedded in the psychoanalytic theory of neurosis, as this theory is, at bottom, a theory of etiology. As for the childhood determinants of later neurotic pathology, psychoanalytic theory, following Freud, views development in terms of a complemental series of internal maturational factors and environmental pressures. Except for considering conflict at the Oedipal phase of development (without significant pregenital fixation or regression) to be the essential childhood determinant of later hysterical difficulties, there is very little further attempt in the psychoanalytic literature to specify genetic constellations specific to particular neuroses.

The concept of an interaction of environment and constitution in the formation of psychic structure and conflict makes eminent sense to many behavioral and biological scientists of human psychology. According to the psychoanalytic point of view, the interaction of environmental and constitutional forces is an extremely complex process and therefore few general statements about childhood environmental determinants of neurosis can be posited for all or even most children. The child's drive endowment, ego endowments, and other constitutionally based temperamental proclivities lead him to be more or less vulnerable, at this or that developmental stage, to the forces of his environment. Though certain environmental events can in virtually all cases be assumed to interfere with development (death of or loss of parent, adoption, depression in the mother in first two years, being subject to or witness of brutal behavior in parents), there are many other much more subtle interweavings of maturational and environmental factors that lead to development that has a pathogenic potential in adulthood. The best and most careful description of this process, from a psychoanalytic point of view, is Nagera's monograph (1966).

It may well be that the complexity of this process, together with the definitional confusion that has beset this area, have been major sources of interference in designing a study that will effectively demonstrate longitudinally the exact nature of this process as it relates to specific neuroses or neurotic constellations. At this point, therefore, we must content ourselves with the formulation of hypotheses, some all too speculative, using mostly impressionistic clinical data as a foundation.

With these disclaimers, several areas will be touched on: the family interaction pattern, personality style and behavior of parents, the impact of loss, constitutional factors, and the effect of differences in personality development and socialization.

Any consideration of the etiology of hysteria has embedded in it the age-old "nature-nurture" controversy — whether environment or constitution or some interaction of the two is responsible for neurosis in general and hysteria in particular. Just as particular objects of psychiatric study go in and out of fashion, as Harms (1945) observed, so too there seem to have been periods during this century when either nature or nurture theories were in vogue. Freud's final conception of the etiology of neurosis turned out to be a theory of interaction among constitutional proclivity, psychologically problematic experiences over a period of time (birth of a sibling, for example), and a fortuitous traumatic incident acting to crystallize the neurosis. The 1950's was a decade in which "nurture" theories of psychopathology reached their apex, culminating in Bateson et al.'s (1956) interaction theory of schizophrenia, Ackerman's (1958) family interaction approach to neurosis, behaviorist approaches, and Harlow's research (Harlow and Harlow, 1965; Harlow and Suomi, 1970) on attachment in primates.

There are now a few indications, on both empirical and strictly theoretical grounds, that the study of the etiology of mental disorder is beginning again to emphasize the role of constitutional factors. I will first discuss the environmental theories and then those that rely more heavily on constitutional factors.

FAMILY INFLUENCES

Most psychoanalytic theorists consider the Oedipal period as crucial in the genesis of hysteria (Reich, 1933; Fenichel,

1945). Fantasies of violating incest taboos are met with fear, guilt, and the prospect of losing love from primary objects. Hysteria is an attempt to compromise between these incestuous impulses and the internalized taboos. With this placement of the genesis of hysteria in the Oedipal period, the question arises whether particularly conflictual, intense Oedipal struggles are fostered by certain patterns of parent-child interaction. Easser and Lesser (1965) found that most of the hysterics they studied were profoundly involved with their fathers, who, whether in fantasy or actuality, were seductive, dominant, arbitrary, excitable, volatile, imaginative, and at the same time controlling. The seductive stance of these fathers changed abruptly when their daughters, the patients, reached puberty. They found, further, that charm and seductiveness were admired and elicited by the parents of these patients "as long as their physical aspects could be held in oblivion," leading, according to Easser and Lesser, to the repression of sexuality and the development of the romantic trappings of femininity.

The patients' mothers encouraged their daughters to live out their own frustrated, romantic fantasies, spending a great deal of time "prettying" their daughters and making clothes for them. At the same time the mothers themselves continued to lead mundane, conventional lives. This was also the case in Elisabeth von R.'s family background (Breuer and Freud, 1893-1895). She came into especially intimate contact with her father, whom she admired and emulated, because of her mother's recurrent illness.

Reichard (1956) summarized the features common to the backgrounds of the patients in *Studies on Hysteria* who would be considered hysterical by current standards. With the exception of Katharina, about whom little is known, those of Breuer and Freud's patients Reichard considered to be hysterics differed from those she considered schizophrenic by the absence of psychosis or serious psychopathology among males of their families and by the genuine affection and devotion in the hysterics' families as opposed to the cold, compulsive atmosphere found in the schizophrenics' families.

Thus the covert encouragement by both parents of the

daughter's sexuality and the simultaneous condemnation of her conscious sexual feelings is the central bind the hysteric is caught in. Hysteria is the outcome of a situation in which incestuous acts, and even fantasies of such acts, are consciously forbidden but are unconsciously promoted by the close, sometimes seductive, ties with parents. The tendency toward dissociation is an understandable result of such a situation, a neurotic adaptation to a neurotogenic environment. The conflict engendered by the contradictions in the parents' libidinal behavior is resolved by dissociating the conflicting perceptions of and reactions to the parents. The contradictory messages of hysterogenic parents are more circumscribed in scope and arise later in development than the double binds and fundamentally contradictory messages from the mother which Bateson has described as typical of schizophrenogenic families. For the hysteric, they center on childhood genital sexual activity, and probably emerge when the child begins to engage in the masturbation and exhibitionistic behavior common to the phallic stage of psychosexual development. Such parents generally respond less ambivalently and more perceptively to their children as infants than do schizophrenogenic parents, for the child during these earliest years does little to dispel the parents' fantasy that it is sexually (genitally) innocent. After the Oedipal period, a second hurdle occurs for these parents, as Easser and Lesser's results suggest, when their children reach puberty and their sexuality becomes more exciting and more difficult to deny.

Fenichel (1945) offered another set of sources for the intensity of the Oedipal struggle in hysterogenic families. He delineated a variety of specific traumatic events which could intensify the Oedipal conflict and thereby, according to his dynamic definition, encourage hysteria. These events are consistent with Easser and Lesser's findings in that they involve a premature and sudden exposure to sexual experiences: being seduced, primal-scene experiences, sudden sight of the genitals. Fenichel also concluded that the birth of a sibling during the Oedipal period might intensify the Oedipal crisis.

On a more theoretical level, Fenichel described several family constellations that encourage a particularly conflictual Oedipal struggle: (1) reverse Oedipus complex—the parents, out of their own unresolved conflicts, act out sexual urges toward children; (2) the family with one child—the only child does not have siblings to use as "doubles" to displace and work through the conflicts with the parents; (3) death of a parent. The death of the same-sexed parent can lead to excessive guilt about having achieved the Oedipal fantasy. The death of the opposite-sexed parent can lead to the idealization of the parent as well as a sexualization of death.

A universally accepted character trait of hysterics is the tendency to "play act" some conventional stereotype, in our culture usually a caricature of femininity. Related to this play acting is the potential for hysterical characters to form intense identifications and object attachments which result in apparent changes in their sense of identity. Angyal has referred to these characteristics as the hysteric's "pattern of vicarious living." He presented some observations on the kinds of parent-child interaction that could result in this kind of functioning. Going beyond the classical Freudian conception that specific thoughts, feelings, or fantasies are repressed, Angyal believed that in hysteria there is a sweeping "wholesale indiscriminate discarding" of feelings, tabooed or otherwise. In the early history of such patients, he reported, the parents convey to the child the sense that "the way he really is, the way in which he feels and thinks, is not good" (Angyal, 1965, p. 139). Such parents typically belittle and disregard the child, fostering in him a sense of insignificance. Angyal cautioned that the neurosis itself may often lead the patient to exaggerate and overemphasize such situations, and that they are not specific to hysteria.

Another attitude that Angyal discovered in the background of such patients is parental oversolicitude. The parent is often anxious about the child's health, and overeager to protect it from possible dangers. "A real or spurious overefficiency of the parent may have similar results," he added (p. 140). This also promotes the feeling in the child that the parent knows and can do everything, while he can do nothing. Taken to a greater extreme, the child begins to feel that he is weaker than other children and that he is not competent to cope with a dangerous world, and must turn to the parents for protection and safety.

Finally, Angyal has found that hysterical patients were often forced into roles unnatural for their age and temperament, such as the premature burden of adult responsibilities, or having to submit to parental demands to be serious and sober instead of expressing their natural impulses. Angyal concluded from his observations that parental demands that the child live out an existence fundamentally alien to his genuine feelings are far more productive of hysterical neurosis than are isolated traumatic experiences.

Thus, according to Angyal, the child comes to feel weak, insignificant, and not acceptable as he is. He also learns that he fares better if he cultivates a false role, playing out something that is more acceptable to the primary persons in his life. This paves the way for the pattern of vicarious living and the development of a substitute personality, virtually always one that has the universal endorsement of society, to fill the emptiness left by the widespread repression of the original personality. Approached from a more ego-psychological point of view, this kind of parent-child relationship makes identification with a parent or parent's fantasy a means of escape from the rejection and conflict encountered when genuine feelings are acknowledged or genuine action taken. The chameleonlike identifications and transient attachments of the hysterical personality can thus be seen to be no more than adult versions of the childhood patterns described by Angyal. Siegman (1954) wrote of the hysteric's displaying emotions which are demanded by parents, first the real parents, and then their internalized representations, in order to maintain their approval and love. Angyal also implied that these vicarious identities are psychological maneuvers to avoid rejection. Both descriptions are consistent with the generally mature picture of the hysterical ego that emerges from the ego-psychological literature. In contrast, the identities assumed by the "as if" personalities do not take the place of a genuine personality unacceptable to parents, but constitute a flimsy sense of self which is all such people are capable of.

Sullivan (1956) observed that hysterics were typically used by their parents as adornments, or as playthings by very narcissistic parents. Time and again the hysteric as a child is fated to live out the parents' ambivalently regarded fantasy of themselves. It is because the fantasy has such regressive roots that the kinds of identities adopted by the hysterical personality characteristically have such a childlike, overdone, unrealistic flavor.

Fitzgerald (1948), who held that a craving for love is the central dynamic in hysteria, proposed childhood situations which he believed involve a sudden loss of love to the child, and consequently encourage the development of hysteria: death of parent, parental strife, chronically sick parent, prolonged illness of the child, uninterested parent. In the case of parental strife, when the child is forced to "take sides," he is continually losing the love of one parent in order to maintain the love of the other. Fitzgerald believed that the child loses the nurturance of a parent who is chronically ill and often in addition loses the attention of the well parent whose energies are expended in caring for the sick one.

Harms (1945) described a hysterical personality similar to that later described by Farber (1961). He stressed the role of willful behavior, such as manipulating temper tantrums, in laying the groundwork for later hysterical resolution of conflict. Also like Farber, he stressed the strength of the ego in the hysteric. Harms viewed the second period of juvenile development (from four or five to eight or nine years) as crucial to the development of this personality, for it is during this stage that strong resistance to unwelcome influence from the outside becomes obvious. It is out of the negative emotions of this stage that hysteria is made. Indeed, hysteria may sometimes break out with "great violence" during this period. Thus Harms, as early as 1945, was calling for more attention to the development of the hysterical ego and less to the prohibition of specific sexual wishes and acts in attempts to understand the development of the disorder.

Only a small body of research exists on the impact of

parental attitudes and behavior in producing neurosis, and most of what scant literature there is sheds little light on the etiology of hysteria because the syndrome has been so difficult to define. Longitudinal research on neurosis in general is also strikingly sparse, especially compared to the quantity of longitudinal work on the etiology of schizophrenic and delinquent personalities. The studies on the development of neurosis that have been done have produced conflicting conclusions. Friedlander (1949) found striking differences in the family backgrounds of neurotic children (anxiety hysterics, obsessional neuroses, etc.) as compared to antisocial, delinquent children. She could not, however, identify characteristics of the homes of the neurotic children that adequately distinguished them from the homes of normal children. Her results were therefore suggestive of an innate, neurosis-producing sensitivity to routine life events. For example, one patient, a girl, experienced intense feelings of penis envy on seeing a penis for the first time — feelings of an intensity that did not seem attributable to past experience and that made sublimation difficult. Renaud and Estess (1961) also found that the normals they interviewed reported as many pathogenic influences in their childhoods as did psychotic populations, which again suggests that environmental factors alone cannot produce neurosis.

On the other hand, some very convincing research by Henry (1951) and Henry and Warson (1951) demonstrates the social transmission of neurosis within the family and its communication over several generations of the same family. Singer and Wynne (1963) found significant differences on projective tests among parents of children with different sorts of psychopathology, further strengthening the environmental position.

LOSS AND IDENTIFICATION IN HYSTERIA

Several authors have mentioned in passing an etiological factor that seems to me to deserve far greater attention: the loss of a loved one by death or separation during the phallic-Oedipal period or during adolescence. It is the crucial role of loss in later childhood that seems to lead identification to be such a frequent and pervasive defense of the hysterical personality.

Fitzgerald considered the death or illness of a parent to be important in fostering a craving for love. Fenichel commented that the death of a parent can intensify the Oedipal struggle. F. Deutsch and his co-workers (1959) considered conversion, in their broadened conception of it, as serving primarily to replace a lost object. They believed that through a process of symbolization, a sensory sphere, organ, or organ system comes to represent objects during normal development by a continuous process toward retrojection. Upon the loss of the object, conversion reaction of a particular body part acts as a restitution. Ludwig (1959) added that the conversion reaction would be more intense the earlier the object was lost and the more ambivalently it was experienced. Though Abse did not consider loss basic to hysteria, he did think that, owing to the hysteric's overdependence on parents, separation from the family might precipitate the neurotic difficulties. Allen and Houston (1959) proposed that the fear of losing internalized love objects, usually parents, is dynamically central to the conflicts of the acting-out hysterical patient. Thus, although none has treated this as the central, fundamental factor, many theories of the etiology of hysteria suggest that the loss of a love object plays some role in the development of the disorder. Further, an inspection of the classical cases of hysteria in the literature, current clinical evidence, and cross-cultural data reveals that the neurotic response to loss of an object through death is a common denominator and crucial factor in producing hysteria.

Seidenberg and Papathomopoulos (1962) pointed out that all of Freud's classical hysterics nursed their fathers for substantial periods of time. Nursing a very ill or dying relative, a duty demanded of daughters by Victorian culture, has a variety of emotional and interpersonal consequences: close contact with the father stirs up repressed Oedipal fantasies concerning him, anger and consequent guilt develop toward the father whose illness prevents the daughter from leading her own life, and there is often little opportunity for recognition of the ambivalent nature of these feelings. Moreover, other features concerning loss are common to all these cases. In all of them the hysterical neurosis developed around the time of the death of a close loved one; in all a concern about death is prominent.

Review of other case studies of hysterical disorders reveals the importance of an actual death or a concern with death in these patients as well. Death was also the element that precipitated the severe hysterical dissociation in Janet's classical study of "Irene." Kretschmer (1923) believed that all hysterical paralysis reduced to imitations of death, "sham-death," a point he illustrated with case examples. H. Deutsch's case of "hysterical fate neurosis" (1930) involved a woman who chose men who loved women who had died. Prosen (1967), in a paper on sexuality in hysterical females, found that the unmourned death of a father is central to a neurotic pattern of object choice.

These examples are of course only suggestive, and call for both a more extensive review of the literature and psychoanalytic investigation, but the importance of loss, usually by death, in the neurotic constellations of hysteria might best be further supported by case examples familiar to this writer.

Miss F., a student in her mid-20's, presented a character style conforming almost exactly to Easser and Lesser's description of the hysterical personality. In therapy she manifested the two strivings Farber considered basic to hysteria—to be smart and to be beautiful. Indeed, she sought therapy, at least in part, for "cosmetic" reasons—seeking the guidance of the therapist in developing a more "attractive" personality, and the therapist's approval when she was successful in this endeavor. Her attempts to be the "good daughter," acceptable to the therapist, led her to try to imitate, both unconsciously and consciously, what she felt her therapist-parent wished for her. The shifts in her sense of herself were so marked that she appeared, at first, to be a more primitive "as if" character. Competitiveness and the consequent guilt over it proved to be this patient's central character trait. At the root of her great need to be the best lay an intense rivalry with her brothers. Her hysterical neurosis crystallized after the death of one of those brothers.

Mrs. P., a secretary in her late 20's, presented a hysterical personality with a variety of psychophysiological complaints. She conformed most closely to H. Deutsch's "hysterical fate neurosis," for her neurotic difficulties mapped themselves out by her involving herself with men who appeared at first to personify her pre-Oedipal fantasy of an invincible father, but who all turned out to be disappointingly weak, just as she later felt her father to be. She also manifested many of the traits the "descriptive authors" (see Chapter 2) have defined as hysterical, including an emotional lability and a manipulative use of histrionics. Although neither parent died in her childhood, at the age of five she contracted polio, which meant that for a three-week period her parents could see her only through a window in the hospital. Occurring as this did in the midst of an especially intense Oedipal crisis, she experienced a sudden and painful disappointment in her father when he could not cure her disease. In conjunction with this disappointment, the physical separation imposed by the quarantine led to a profound sense of having been abandoned by both parents. In this case, a traumatic period during childhood led to the abrupt destruction of a fantasy of a powerful, all-caring phallic father. Though the parents were not actually dead, they were dead for her. This acute sense of loss, particularly of the father, lay at the very core of the hysterical patient's conflicts.

In another case a 32-year-old woman from a rural area manifested some strikingly classical hysterical alterations of consciousness, in connection with other hysterical features. Upon examination of the history of her symptoms, it turned out that her difficulties had begun recently, upon the death of her child.

Cross-culturally too, there is evidence that suggests the

importance of loss of objects, usually by death, in hysterical disorders. Transient attacks which appear to be hysterical, observed among the Bena and Puerto Ricans, have been precipitated by a stressful event, usually the death of a close relative (Fernández-Marina, 1961). D. Gutmann (personal communication) similarly reported that the hysterical illness, "ghost sickness," believed by the Navajos to be inflicted by the spirits, often occurs in the Navajo culture after the victim has lost a close relative or walked over a grave.

Assuming, as is proposed here, that death and loss do play a pivotal role in hysterical disorders, the hysteric's tendency to choose somatization, conversion, and identification to resolve psychic conflict becomes more understandable. These are all psychic devices that, at least in part, serve to deny or undo a loss. Thus they are common hysterical defenses because the denial of a loss is a common hysterical issue.

If death plays any role in the development of hysterical neurosis, whether as simply a trigger or as a fundamental cause, it follows that a common classical hysterical symptom, physical illness, imitates the augur of death. Imitating the disease of the lost loved one can serve a variety of psychological functions in the neurotic mourning process: it can be an attempt to reunite with the object, an attempt to punish oneself out of guilt for death wishes toward the lost object, or a plea for nurturance from the lost object ("You nurse me now as I nursed you").

The recognition of the role of phallic-phase and later loss in hysteria clarifies an often contested diagnostic differentiation—the generally knotty but important diagnostic problem concerning female patients who present both depressive and hysterical qualities. For example, Mrs. P., just described, was a very angry, demanding woman, given to intense depressions. Her search for relationships had such a desperate, addictive quality that it seemed that she was fending off a severe depression which originated in early anaclitic depressions. Indeed the patient's mother proved to be a very erratic, psychotic woman whose unreliability might have been conducive to repeated anaclitic depressions during the patient's first year. Striking inconsistencies, however, marked

Mrs. P.'s object relations. She had succeeded in many areas of her life, and her neurotic behavior took the form of compulsions to repeat what seemed like Oedipal, rather than oral, paradigms. The question that rose early in Mrs. P.'s therapy was whether she was fundamentally a depressive with major oral conflicts (a "so-called 'good' hysteric" in Zetzel's terms) or a hysterical character. Such a diagnostic decision was important in the treatment of this woman. If Mrs. P. was essentially hysterical, other conditions being met (time, money, intellectual ability, motivation), psychoanalytically oriented therapy would be recommended and the hysterical resistances interpreted. If, however, she was fundamentally depressive, the therapist might wish to work more supportively and ego-synthetically with the patient and, as Knight (1953) has suggested, leave the most mature defense processes, i.e., the hysterical ones, intact.

In many cases, female patients who present both hysterical and depressive characteristics turn out to have had developmental problems in both the oral and the phallic-Oedipal periods. In Mrs. P.'s case, however, and possibly in others too, the problems turned out to be almost exclusively Oedipal, with loss at the Oedipal period being of primary psychodynamic importance. As reported earlier, she experienced an intense sense of loss of her parents when she was hospitalized at five years with polio. Her search for relationships, though desperate and apparently "hungry," was thus in fact a repetition of an Oedipal fantasy of reuniting with the father and of his taking her out of the hospital. What was crucial in understanding this woman and designing a treatment plan for her was the realization that her desperate, "depressive" longings for people had to do with a loss—of a traumatic sort, to be sure—that occurred many years *after* the oral phase, the phase to which depression over loss is often ascribed. In this case the depression was not the result of a rift with the mother during the symbiotic or the separation-individuation phase of the oral period, but the result of a much later loss and thus more available to analytic treatment. Indeed, according to many people, the patient's mother, in spite of her psychosis, was very sensitive with, and tolerant of, infants and small children. It was when the patient ceased to depend on her that the mother behaved in more overtly psychotic ways with her daughter. Indeed, the mother was at her most bizarre around her daughter's phallic period and again at puberty. This would corroborate the research reported earlier on typical family patterns that promote the development of hysterical personalities.

Actual loss, death, and separations foster hysterical neurosis by reviving the losses that are part and parcel of the Oedipus complex and its resolution. In response to these actual losses the hysteric commonly uses identification, the same solution to loss and conflict that develops to resolve the original Oedipal situation. Thus when the issue of loss appears in an essentially hysterical patient, it is more likely that a fantasied or actual loss of an object at the Oedipal period or thereafter is responsible, rather than a rift with objects in the earlier phases of life when separation may lead to profound difficulties in consolidating coherent and enduring mental representations, self-boundaries, and basic ego structures.

CONSTITUTIONAL FACTORS IN THE DEVELOPMENT OF HYSTERIA

Several authors have dealt with innate factors, either alone or in conjunction with environmental ones, in their theories of the etiology of neuroses and character style. Freud (1896a), for example, stated that it is a mistake to look for the cause of hysteria either solely in constitutional, inherited factors or in "accidental modifications undergone by sexuality during life."

As hysteria has come to be considered more a total personality style than a circumscribed disease entity, traumatic events have ceased to seem as important etiologically. Pervasive modes of interaction or constitutional factors or both become the only reasonable alternatives to explain such a character style. Siegman (1954), Federn (1940), and Shapiro (1965), all of whom approached hysteria as a character style, laid great emphasis on the innate proclivities of an organism in developing its personality style. Federn believed it is the constitutional nature of the ego reaction, strong or weak, in response to danger that is fundamentally responsible for later choice of neurosis. In the hysteric the fundamental passivity of the ego leads to traits considered hysterical—suggestibility, distractibility, lack of enduring conviction, etc. Shapiro also considered the choice of neurosis as growing directly out of character style, the hysterical style being one which promotes repression and therefore fosters a neurosis that makes use of repression.

The obsessive has a constitutionally "strong" ego, according to Federn, as shown in the intense and precocious intellectual criticism, logical thought, and stubbornness characteristic of the obsessive. The hysterical ego, in contrast, grows from an infantile weakness and passivity. Here Federn's somewhat narrow definition of ego process is clear—he seems to consider only intellectual, cognitive modes of functioning as ego processes. The pervasiveness of such processes in the obsessive as compared to the hysteric led Federn to maintain that the former has a "strong" ego and the latter a weak one. Because of his narrow definition of ego process he saw the hysterical character as passive, and failed to understand the strength behind apparently passive ego maneuvers that Fairbairn and Shapiro pointed out.

Shapiro, following Hartmann, assumed innate cognitive proclivities. The infant, according to Shapiro, has an initial organizing configuration which is continually modified through encounters with the world. These configurations mold the subjective experience of inner tension, external stimulation, and memories of both. While general tendencies in personality style are determined by these innate configurations, specific aspects of adult ego style arise out of the specific transformations of the innate style through development. In contrast to Reich's view of character style as an elaboration of a defense against conflict, Shapiro viewed it as the organism's lifelong attempt to understand and to act. In the hysteric, the base character style is one that promotes repression, and thus fosters a neurosis that makes use of repression.

Support for this approach is beginning to come from

observational research on infants. Though no correlations have yet been discovered between initial perceptual patterns of infants and later personality styles, Escalona (1968) has observed differences in perceptual and kinesthetic behavior among infants soon after birth. She has found that the prime perceptual modality — auditory, visual, or tactile — also varies with children. Kagan and Lewis (1965) have similarly found differences in the pattern of attention in infants. Though these observations are a long way from explaining the process by which these early proclivities become woven into later personality, they do begin to suggest the importance of the sort of innate cognitive "configurations" that Shapiro proposed.

THE INCIDENCE OF HYSTERICAL PERSONALITIES
IN MEN AND WOMEN

The common use of the pronoun "she" to refer to the hysteric reflects just how basic is the belief that hysteria is more prevalent among women. Moreover, the original meaning of the term "hysteria," "wandering uterus," indicates that the disorder has historically been considered primarily a female malady. Veith (1965) found that hysteria had been treated historically as basically a feminine disorder. Wittels (1931), Fitzgerald (1948), and Michaels (1959) are just a few of the writers on hysteria who have explicitly contended that hysteria occurs more frequently in women. Easser and Lesser (1965) and Zetzel (1968) limited their discussion of hysteria to females, though Zetzel believed that hysteria does exist in men. Chodoff and Lyons (1958) reported empirical evidence for a higher incidence of hysterical disorders in women. Wisdom (1961), the exception, discussed only male hysteria.

STUDY OF MALE HYSTERIA COMPLICATED BY
DEFINITIONAL PROBLEMS

Attempts to elucidate the incidence and nature of male hysteria are met, once again, with the problem of definition discussed earlier. Easser and Lesser noted that in Western culture hysteria is associated with effeminate characteristics. Zetzel, however, observes that men with overt hysterical character traits (effeminate traits) often turn out to be more seriously disturbed than women with these same traits. These patients are often depressive characters or, at worst, "so-called 'good' hysterics" (essentially unanalyzable patients with serious ego distortion). Problems in defining and exploring male hysteria arise when hysteria is identified by overt style and manner. When hysteria is defined solely on the basis of an unconscious Oedipal conflict, equally serious definitional problems arise, for most analyzable men, even those who are obsessional and present work inhibitions without heterosexual difficulties, reveal in analysis an unresolved Oedipal situation (Zetzel, 1968). This points up once again the pitfalls of definitions that rely exclusively on specific overt behavior or exclusively on unconscious dynamics.

A definition of the syndrome, as described at the end of Chapter 2 and expanded in the final chapter, which considers ego capacities, over-all severity of disturbance, object relations, and the nature of unconscious conflict will include males as easily as females. Among other characteristics, the definition involves a triangular conflict, a particular use of emotionality, a dearth of conscious fantasy, and an ego-defensive use of passivity and other directedness, all of which are as applicable to males as to females. With such a definition, if the syndrome is more common in women, the task becomes to explain why these factors would occur more commonly in women.

Explanations of the assumed higher incidence of hysteria in women have been several. First, if one views hysteria as a personality configuration, an integrated defensive, cognitive, adaptive neurotic style, as does Shapiro, one can speculate on differences in basic cognitive orientation developing very early in life. If it could be shown that there are sex differences in innate or early environmentally induced patterns of organizing stimuli from the internal or external worlds, then it would follow that the sexes would tend to develop different cognitive formations later. Second, there may be differences in the nature of self-boundaries in men and women that grow from different early psychosexual experience of one's anatomy. Erikson (1950) has suggested differences in the experience of internal and external space which result from both anatomical and social modes as they emerge during the child's development. Third, when hysteria is defined strictly on the basis of overt character traits or symptoms, it may be considered little more than hyper-femininity, the normal female character with particular features hypertrophied by parental or social reinforcements. Fourth, if hysteria is defined on the basis of unconscious dynamics, the presumed higher incidence of hysteria in women could be understood in terms of the tendency toward differences in unconscious conflicts in men and women rooted in psychosexual differences between them.

If hysteria is considered according to the definition elaborated at the end of Chapter 2, then the presumed higher incidence of hysteria could be investigated empirically and the roots of any sex skewing could be more clearly traced to a particular aspect of the personality configuration. Such a difference in incidence might well involve several of the four factors sketched above and elaborated below.

Shapiro saw the tendency for women to present the hysterical and men the obsessive cognitive configuration as an expression of the sexual difference in "initial organizing configurations." Differences in activity and cognitive styles have been found in boy and girl infants, providing some at present scanty evidence for Shapiro's theory. Kagan and Lewis (1965) found that female infants at both six and 13 months display more sustained attention to novel music than males of the same ages, who prefer to listen to a simple, repetitive tune. While both male and female infants manifested longer fixations and greater motor quieting to humanoid patterns, there were suggestions that girls tend to fixate more reliably on such patterns than do boys. These results permit some speculations about the later tendency for neurotic men to be obsessive and neurotic women to be hysterical in personality style. The rudiments of an obsessive interest in order and regularity might be reflected in the male infants' preference for auditory regularity and repetition rather than novelty. The lower attention to visual stimuli in boys might be the beginnings of the introverted, ruminative style characteristic of the obsessive personality. Conversely, the sustained attention to visual stimulation and humanoid patterns may reflect the importance of real objects in the environment, a characteristic basic to the hysterical personality. The attention to visual stimuli might also reflect the more intense responsiveness to the environment which takes a variety of forms in the hysteric: (1) a tendency to react with intense feelings to changes in the environment; (2) a greater susceptibility to traumatic response to environmental events; (3) a high sensitivity to cues in the environment which permits the hysteric to act out conventional stereotypes; and (4) the eye for color and style reputed to be common in the hysterical personality. Finally, in the female infants' greater interest in novel stimuli perhaps we may be seeing the seeds of the hysterical personality's disdain for the mundane, and a taste for the flamboyant and exciting (Easser and Lesser, 1965).

Kagan and Lewis's results are also congruent with the concern of all sorts of neurotic women with the success of their "relationships," in contrast to neurotic men whose concerns center less on their object ties and more on issues of living up to their expectations, issues of instrumental strivings, and conflicts about their urges.

SEX DIFFERENCES IN EGO STYLE

Theories of sex differences in ego style suggest that the hysterical ego style can more naturally evolve from the feminine ego than from the masculine. Erikson (1950) found sex differences in children's play, the play tending to reflect the anatomical and social modes of each sex. Brenneis (1967) found sex differences in the ego style reflected in adult dreams. Gutmann (1965) argued that the concept of ego strength, in both theory and TAT inference techniques, has to do with the male ego, with qualities that are adaptive in a man's world. The man's world, the allocentric (other-centered) world, is one of challenge and achievement, the impersonal world outside the home. Objectivity, which demands a clear sense of ego boundaries and good, impulse-free, secondary-process cognitive skills, is one of several qualities that constitute masculine ego strength, according to Gutmann. In contrast, the woman's world is an "autocentric" world, a world that radiates from the self, that is expectable and routine. The ego that develops to adapt to this social ecology personalizes the world. He added that abolishing the self-other boundaries is important in providing the infant with the closeness he needs. Mothers who treat their infants like impersonal objects, the mode which is effective for the male ego to adapt to his geometric, technical world, cannot respond to their infants' needs. Moreover, to maintain the close, necessary relationships with family members and neighbors on a day-to-day basis, the female ego adaptively suspends objectivity, whereas a man must methodically apply such objectivity in his world to reach instrumentally defined goals.

Gutmann's description of the neurotic extreme of the feminine ego style captures some aspects of the hysterical ego, just as the neurotic extreme of the masculine ego style captures some facets of the ego of the obsessive, schizoid, or anxiety neurotic character. The tendency of the hysterical personality, as described by Federn, to open, enlarge, and include someone else within ego boundaries would seem to be facilitated by an ego that can, when necessary, interrupt self-other boundaries. The egocentrism of the hysterical personality could evolve far more easily out of an ego fashioned to cope with an autocentric world than one oriented toward an allocentric world. The impressionistic "personal" cognitive style of the hysterical personality as described by Shapiro might be one specific form of this ego-centric outlook.

It stands to reason that the lack of objectivity necessitated by the importance for the woman of maintaining vital rela-tionships with family and community becomes transformed, in the neurotic extreme, into more pervasive kinds of de-fenses designed to avoid acknowledging what is objectively true. The result is repression, dissociation, and denial, the set of defenses associated with the hysterical personality.

Gutmann, Erikson, and Brenneis all found a passive ego style (not to be confused with the pejorative general description of someone's behavior as "passive") basic to the feminine personality. The hysterical personality, as we have seen, uses the illusion of passivity to disarm inner conflict and draw guidance and nurturance from others.[1]

HYSTERIA IN WOMEN

Wolowitz (1971) has argued that hysteria is predominantly a female syndrome because its basic defining property, "the search for emotional reactivity," is merely an outgrowth of the culture's emphasis on female children's use of emotional responsiveness to define their own involvements. Wolowitz sees hysterical character and normal female identity as having "common antecedent determinants and consequent functions." He sees hysterical character as a skewed, caricatured version of normal female personality. The hysteric has been socialized too well to define herself through the reactions of others to her and grows further away from her capacity to experience and enjoy her reactions and urges directly.

Along similar lines, Marmor (1953) held that the traits of the hysterical personality are regarded by society as feminine and are more acceptable in women than in men. This observation raises more questions than it answers, for it raises the issue of whether hysterical traits are only "accidentally" feminine or are feminine because hysteria is basically a female disorder.

Chodoff and Lyons (1958) suggested that part of this phenomenon results from the fact of male clinicians diagnosing female patients. The hysterical personality is essentially a caricature of femininity, an "objective" description of women in the words of men. When behavior which is

[1] The "myth of passivity" is, in fact, the single omnipresent feature of the many disorders labeled hysteria, as will be argued in Chapter 4.

considered socially appropriate for either sex is reduced to a list of traits, the essence of the "style" is lost. Thus Chodoff and Lyons suggest that male clinicians may have constructed a concept of psychopathology which consists of those characteristics of women which men dislike most in them.

When hysteria was considered interchangeable with conversion, the higher incidence of the disorder could be partly understood culturally. Women through the Victorian period and into the early twentieth century were considered to be fragile creatures, far more vulnerable to disease, fatigue, and injury than men (Sinclair, 1965). The channeling of emotional, interpersonal conflicts into the soma was thus natural and understandable in this context. The higher incidence of hysteria in women, as well as the disappearance of the nineteenth-century variety of conversion hysteria, both seem to involve social and cultural influences. In Chapter 4 a new historical, cross-cultural perspective will help elucidate this process.

A SYNTHESIS

Several common themes emerge from this review, all quite speculative:

Family Influences

The family that tends to encourage the development of hysterical personality or hysteria in its children promotes an overdependence on parents, restricts masturbation and other sexual activities, and emphasizes politeness, decorum, and seriousness. While there is an essential warmth and protective order in these families, and especially a satisfactory, if somewhat overprotective, bond with the mother in the pre-genital years, there is in the parents both an unconscious sexualization of interactions and a conscious discouragement or condemnation of infantile sexual interest or activity. The mothers in these families seem to be anxious about sexuality, yet overemphasize the sex-specific behavior of their children. They take great pleasure in how "cute" their daughters look dressed in pretty clothes or in how masculine their little boys look in boyish play, but become very anxious whenever either exhibits sexual curiosity or sex play. They emphasize superficial sex-specific trappings, but grow anxious and withdraw when sexual behavior becomes undeniable. Often, of course, this sexual behavior is unconsciously encouraged by the parent. This situation naturally encourages the child to repress sexual interests and to emphasize instead the appearance of sexuality—to play in a self-consciously childish way at being sexual rather than actually acknowledging sexual urges toward objects.

In addition, the parent who promotes a hysterical personality in his child makes one or more of several types of excessive demands on the child: to assume responsibilities appropriate for an adult, to be a plaything or an adornment for the parent, to remain excessively dependent on or pampered by the parent.

Loss and Death

The family trends just described are exacerbated in only children and when there has been a death or a loss of a parent (or other significant person) during or following the Oedipal period. Such death or loss tends to represent unconsciously to the child the fulfillment of and/or punishment for an Oedipal competitive wish. Of course, the role of discrete trauma, originally considered by psychoanalysis to be the cause of hysteria, should still be considered, in specific cases, as significant in crystallizing a hysterical neurosis.

Loss or death of a significant person during the phallic-Oedipal period, or later in childhood or in adolescence, seems to be a major factor in producing hysteria or hysterical personality. The hysterical personality usually handles such loss by identification with the lost object or an unconscious, continuous, sometimes lifelong search for it.

Constitutional Influences on Ego-Organizing Modes

Several authors (Shapiro, 1965; Federn, 1940) suggest that a constitutional inheritance may have an impact on the nature of the ego's development. They suggest that, in addition to differences in intellectual endowment, there are characteristic modes of ego adaptation, synthesis, and cognition—"initial organizing configurations." Hysterics would be seen as having inherited an ego mode that underemphasizes extensive and complex conscious thinking, that fosters the development of cognitive states that have a repressive quality, etc. According to this view sex differences in the prevalence of hysterical personality can be partly attributed to constitutionally based sex differences in these initial patterns of ego operation. Others who refer to differences in these ego patterns attribute them more to the impact of social, familial, and cultural influences (Erikson, 1950; Gutmann, 1965; Wolowitz, 1971).

Complemental, Phase-Specific Vulnerablities

There is probably ultimately a set of vulnerabilities in development that depends on the nature of the drives, the child's intellectual and coping resources, the nature of his object attachments, and a multitude of other factors (some innate, some fixed during very early development, some much more open to later modification). The timing of an influence in terms of the dominant psychosexual modality, the balance between self- and object cathexis, and the flexibility of the ego all work together to determine whether this or that trauma, this or that set of regular environmental pressures, will prove to be pathogenic. From a research point of view, we are not much further along in the understanding of these issues than was Freud when he said: ". . . we have once more come unawares upon the riddle which has so often confronted us: whence does neurosis come—what is its ultimate, its own peculiar, *raison d'être?* After ten years of psychoanalytic labours, we are as much in the dark about this problem as we were at the start" (Freud, 1926, pp. 148-149).

One important area of psychoanalytic research, supported by a promising psychoanalytic instrument, may in the future help us to assess better the essential longitudinal and pathogenic-process questions. The Developmental Profile, based on Anna Freud's concept of developmental lines, permits the careful description of a variety of developmental processes, firmly rooted in the observed phenomenological data of the child or adult patient (A. Freud, Nagera, and Freud, 1965). The profile rests on a concept of developmental lines: these lines refer to a history of various developing behaviors in the child which reflect the interaction of drive development and ego resources (superego development, as applicable). In the hands of a skilled clinician-researcher, this profile holds the promise of making possible much more sophisticated and relevant observations of childhood activity for use in longitudinal studies of pathogenesis. (See also Nagera, 1966.)

4

HISTORICAL AND
CROSS-CULTURAL
PERSPECTIVES ON HYSTERIA

> *I wished to establish the thesis*
> *that in hysteria paralyses and*
> *anaesthesias of the various parts*
> *of the body are demarcated*
> *according to the popular idea of*
> *their limits and not according to*
> *anatomical facts.*
> —Freud, *An Autobiographical*
> *Study*

IS HYSTERIA A THING OF THE PAST?

Thus far my primary goal has been analysis. The various definitions and implicit theories of hysteria have been compared and contrasted. A preliminary synthesis was presented at the conclusion of Chapter 1. In the present chapter I will step back from the specifics of the hysterical patient in clinical practice to view this syndrome from the broader perspectives of culture and history. It is my conviction that hysteria, hysterical personality, and conversion hysteria have remained poorly defined, confusing, and enigmatic partly because the presenting symptoms or surface character traits which have been the basis of definition are strongly subject to cultural changes. The thesis to be argued here is that one of the most enduring, defining features of the syndrome is its responsiveness to cultural and social currents. Only when one steps back from the many culture- and era-specific manifestations of the syndrome does a larger gestalt become clear.

When hysteria is defined on the basis of specific symptoms, surface character traits, or symptom constellations, it can be concluded that the syndrome is rapidly moving toward extinction. At a recent case conference, an eminent clinician commented that with the disappearance of virginity and a certain type of prescientific naïveté in young women, hysteria had disappeared too. He pointed essentially to the disappearance of conversion symptoms and the decrease in the hyper-feminine character traits previously found in young hysterical women. His explanation of this trend was that as the society came to accept sexuality more openly, repression of sexual urges became less psychologically necessary and consequently hysterical disorders (defined predominantly as conversion hysteria) have declined and are destined in the near future to disappear in Western society. What is quite obviously neglected in this argument is a prime psychoanalytic discovery concerning hysteria and other neurotic disorders: that the neurotic conflict is not simply a conflict over sexual impulses, but a conflict over libidinal and aggressive drives *directed at incestuous objects*, which is the essence of infantile sexuality. Though the nature of Oedipal conflicts surely is influenced by parental behavior, family interaction patterns, and the society's definition of and expectations of the family unit, there are no indications that children have any less developmental difficulty in handling and overcoming their Oedipal conflicts. Indeed, it may well be that the American trend toward permissive child rearing, less rigidly defined roles of parent and child, and increased emphasis on openness and chumminess between parents and children promote greater Oedipal temptations for the child, and that consequently a stormier Oedipal struggle may result. My own work with early adolescents suggests that adolescence is becoming increasingly tumultuous and chaotic, due in part to a greater fear of instinctual urges that results from the greater difficulty in resolving the Oedipal conflicts in the "open" American family. This may also be an important factor in understanding the alarming increase in such regressive solutions among adolescents as drug use, sexual promiscuity, and flight from the Oedipal objects themselves. In any case, it seems clear that conflicts over libidinal drives directed toward incestuous objects, which virtually all contributors consider the central unconscious conflict in hysteria, are as common as ever. It is my contention that a review of the history of this syndrome will demonstrate that the disorder is still very much with us, but its form has evolved in ways congruent with the changing social arena.

CULTURAL CURRENTS AND THE MYTH OF PASSIVITY

When considered within a particular culture the definition of hysteria remains elusive because the definition itself rests largely on the *way* in which the disorder uses cultural forms, regardless of the culture-specific content of those forms. The hysteric uses the dominant forms of his culture in a particular way in an attempt to resolve conflict. Hysteria, therefore, assumes as wide a variety of forms as there are variations among cultures. Only when the disorder is viewed in its many specific manifestations across cultures do its common, basic structural features emerge. *The thesis to be argued here is that hysteria can be viably defined as a disorder which plays out dominant current cultural identities, often to a marginal but never to a socially alienating extreme, in an attempt to promote a "myth of passivity."* Though its overt form has evolved, its essential structural properties and unconscious conflicts have endured through a variety of cultural contexts.

The myth of passivity refers to an attempt to disown, both internally and interpersonally, responsibility in the broadest sense for thoughts, acts, and impulses. The overweening willfulness with which the hysteric strives to maintain an illusion about himself is central to Farber's (1961) definition of the hysterical personality. Shapiro (1965) observed that the hysterical personality handles unacceptable thoughts and feelings by feeling himself as the victim upon whom these thoughts have been visited. These two authors understood the paradox of the hysterical ego: it actively strives to sustain the illusion of its own passivity.

The hysteric, for a wide variety of social and intrapsychic reasons, promotes a sense within himself that he did not actively choose to have certain feelings, to make certain alliances, or to entertain certain thoughts. Each culture fosters its own myths of passivity. For example, in many cultures spiritual forces, not the personal will, are considered responsible for personal acts. In other cultures, notably most modern Western ones, the play of physical-chemical or psychological forces through the individual is used to explain a wish or an act. This observation forms part of the foundation of a treatise proposed by Szasz (1961). An unfortunate shortcoming in Szasz's work, however, is that he seems so caught up in a mission bearing on the contemporary relation of psychiatry to society that he fails to realize just how universal are the "myths" he so vehemently attacks. In addition, his position does not seem to allow for any explanation, on a personal level, of why some resort to hysteria and others do not, beyond implying that hysterics are malingerers at heart.

The point to be made here is that there are a wide variety of personal motivations for wishing to disavow the sense of intent behind psychic events. Much of the clinical literature has considered just such personal motivations underlying hysteria. The need to avoid guilt and anxiety over incestuous wishes (Fenichel, 1945) and return to a less conflictual, dependent, pregenital paradise (Abse, 1966) are two aspects of the psychoanalytic theory of personal dynamics behind hysteria. The fear of loss of love (Fitzgerald, 1948), the fear of surpassing the father (Chasseguet-Smirgel, 1970), and a fundamental sense of being unacceptable (Angyal, 1965) are other personal motivations considered basic to the genesis of hysteria.

Attempts to define hysteria strictly on the level of individual conflict are limited because hysteria represents a *mode of resolution* of conflict, along with a particular set of unconscious conflicts. This is the limitation of the purely intrapsychic dynamic approaches to definition discussed in Chapter 2. What persists as central to hysteria is that it plays out the myths of passivity supported by the cultural milieu in its efforts to resolve individual conflicts, the roots of such conflicts reflecting a passive resolution to a genuine triangular Oedipal conflict.

What is being suggested, then, is that an appraisal of several processes is necessary to arrive at an understanding of hysteria: (1) the intrapsychic, interpersonal, and social pressures that constitute the individual's internal conflict; (2) the qualities of the ego that permit a hysterical resolution of conflict; and (3) the social forces that yield each culture's characteristic hysterical alternative.

THE HYSTERIC'S USE OF DOMINANT CULTURAL FORMS:
AN EGO RESOURCE

Hysteria makes use of the dominant myths, assumptions, and identities of the culture in which it appears. The hysteric may play out a somewhat caricatured version of an accepted role in an effort to enlist caring, attention, help, or to satisfy other needs; however, he rarely goes far enough to be considered substantially deviant. As Sullivan (1956) observed, the hysteric characteristically forms his sense of himself around an identity granted a high degree of approval in the culture. Wolowitz (1971) has stressed the hysteric's search for approval and emotional reaction from others through the development of behaviors pleasing to them. This identity, be it Apache shaman, medieval witchcraft victim, or modern psychiatric patient, though seldom overlooked and often flamboyant, remains within the bounds of convention. Indeed, this flamboyance, rarely iconoclastic, resides in novel, fashion-setting modifications of what is *in vogue*. While the psychotic doubtless uses the forms of the culture in his psychotic process, he is usually considered explicitly insane by those of his culture. The hysteric, in contrast, is often hard to distinguish from the "normal." Using Western society as an example, Reich's (1933), Kernberg's (1967), and Wolowitz's (1971) descriptions of the hysterical personality sound remarkably like a somewhat exaggerated picture of the normal Western woman.

This essential conventionality of the hysteric presents a fundamental problem in defining hysteria, for living out an illusion about the self, consistent with the norms of the culture, is basic to its nature. The confusion over definition arises when the *content* of social stereotypes is considered definitional of the disorder. The "descriptive" definitions of the hysterical personality that consist of catalogues of behavior traits (Chodoff and Lyons, 1958) suffer most from this error, and often amount to no more than a description of the social stereotype, i.e., the naïve, helpless, sexy woman, of a particular culture during a particular period. Such lists are not without some immediate clinical usefulness and, as we shall see, may reflect something about the sociology, ethos, and mood of a particular culture. But no general theory of hysteria can be built on lists that constitute *only* the contemporary and culturally specific stereotypes with which the hysteric identifies.

Farber (1961) considered the willful maintenance of an illusion about the self and others to be the essence of hysteria. The hysteric's search for a "happy idea" seems to have been Sullivan's understanding of the same phenomenon. Many have commented on the hysterical tendency to mimic either an organic disease or a mannerism of a loved one (Abse, 1966) in the formation of conversion symptoms. Angyal (1965), defining hysteria completely nonsymptomatically, expanded the concept of hysterical imitation, discussing the hysteric's tendency to live out vicariously molar aspects of others' personalities in many spheres, not just in the formation of symptoms. To neglect the tendency of this disorder to masquerade in an essentially "acceptable" conventional social role, at the expense of personal anxiety and conflict to be sure, is to miss what is basic to this disorder. This neglect has contributed to the definitional confusion surrounding hysteria.

The facility with which the hysteric can utilize roles considered acceptable by his culture attests to his sensitivity to the norms of the culture, the limits of acceptability, interpersonal resourcefulness—in short, his capacity for good reality testing, impulse control, and interpersonal sensitivity. The capacity to use the socially sponsored myth of passivity requires a high sensitivity to the environment and often a resourceful use of the opportunities it offers. The sensitivity of the hysterical personality to the "atmosphere" of situations (Shapiro, 1965), his capacity to mimic and imitate (Abse, 1966; Sullivan, 1956), and the ease with which he shifts identifications (Federn, 1940; Abse, 1966) reflect other capacities of the hysterical ego that promote easy adoption of cultural stereotypes. The capacity to regress and to be flamboyant within the bounds of convention, along with the above, reflects the resiliency and advanced development and differentiation definitional of the hysterical ego. Though the defensive strategies may vary among hysterics of different cultures, the capacity to regress within culturally accepted modes, to live within the limits of acceptability, and to adopt identities in vogue in the culture are properties common to the hysterical ego wherever it is found.

It should be stressed that hysterics are not faking, playing games, or simply seeking attention, as Szasz (1961) suggests. The hysteric is neither a malingerer nor a psychopath in that the sorts of parts he plays, feelings he experiences, and actions he undertakes have predominantly unconscious roots—he is usually not aware of trying to fool or deceive. When the hysteric uses cultural myths or lives out a cultural stereotype, he is usually not making a conscious choice of identity, as would be more characteristic of a ruminating obsessional or paranoid character. Rather, the unconscious portions of the hysterical ego are able to translate unconscious conflicts into cultural modes, which, owing to the well-developed sense of reality, such an ego knows are acceptable. Indeed, the hysteric's behavior is genuinely, though transiently, regressive. The hysterical ego is marked by its capacity to dip back at appropriate moments into regressive feeling states, ideation, and wishes, while seldom transgressing the boundaries of conventionality. As will be seen, neither the shaman (Apache hysteric) nor the Victorian hysteric during their altered states of consciousness behaved in ways considered overtly objectionable in the culture, though, of course, in both cases symbolically, tabooed strivings were being expressed.

This quality of hysteria also creates problems in its cross-cultural study, for the hysteric is labeled neither insane nor appreciably deviant by members of the culture. It is probably for this reason that most of the mental illness documented in non-Western cultures is comparable to Western accounts of acute or chronic psychosis (Langness, 1967; Yap, 1951; M. K. Opler, 1959). In fact Latah, amok, and other such cultural patterns labeled hysteria sound far more like acute psychosis than anything comparable to Western conceptions of neurosis. Hysteria exists, to be sure, both historically and in a variety of cultures; however, it is often called by other names and embedded in subtle ways in the fabric of the culture. The victims of witchcraft during the Middle Ages, the American Indian shamans, many middle-class Victorian women, and many contemporary patients represent the many forms hysteria can assume. These instances will now be called upon to demonstrate the approach to hysteria being presented.

THE MANY FACES OF HYSTERIA: WITCHCRAFT VICTIMS

According to the present approach, victims of witchcraft in the Middle Ages and thereafter clearly qualify as hysterics. In a fascinating work, amply documented with transcripts from the Salem witch trials, Hansen (1969) contended that the Salem witches and those who claimed to be their victims were hysterics. Veith (1965) argued that during the Middle Ages these same groups were hysterics. Hansen's definition of hysteria rests on the occurrence of fits, hysterical hallucinations, skin anesthesias, and high suggestibility, all common in the hysterics Charcot studied at the Salpêtrière. The point of the work, argued somewhat dramatically, is that witchcraft was really practiced in Salem, because the culture believed in it. Hansen assumed that the behavioral traits found in Salem and in the Salpêtrière constituted a valid definition of hysteria. Up to a point, he was correct, for the behaviors he described were the culture- and era-specific expressions of the hysterical personality. However, his definition, based as it is on the specific expression of hysteria, does not comprehend the underlying structural and dynamic properties of this type of person.

What, it may be asked, is the relationship between the Salem hysterics and current nonsymptomatic hysterical personalities? Hansen's approach to definition would find suggestibility the only common trait, whereas the sort of historical perspective being proposed here reveals thoroughgoing similarities between them. The victims of witchcraft in both New England and earlier in Europe participated in the myths of their cultures, myths that the Devil or a witch could wrest control of the body and use it for its own purposes. The bewitched thus was not to be held accountable for his behavior, for he was but the unwilling victim of the will of another. The fits, anesthesias, and hallucinations of the victims of witchcraft were then not the victim's but the Devil's doing. These people were hysterics in that they called upon the culture's myth of the Devil working his evil through innocent victims in their effort to disown the intent behind their own acts and thoughts.

While the victims of witchcraft clearly represented examples of hysteria according to the model delineated here, the witches themselves usually did not. Women who, as Hansen described, performed private rituals or in other ways consciously willed death, illness, or bad times on others would be totally different from those who claimed to be their victims. While those accused of being witches at times claimed to be the helpless victims of the Devil's powerful seduction, such pleas probably were desperate attempts at self-justification before their accusers. The fact that so many alleged witches were ostracized, tortured, or killed further attests to their failure to live out identities considered conventional or appropriate by their culture.

While those bewitched were consciously fleeing responsibility for power and evil and enjoying, if not reveling in, their passive victimization at the hands of great and illicit powers, the witches secretly, but quite consciously, felt themselves to be the source of such power and were deliberately setting about to use it. While the bewitched were striving to feel themselves at the mercy of externalized editions of their own unconscious wishes, the witches seem within themselves to have been seeking control, revenge, and power. Where the victims probably felt special in being chosen to be the objects of the witch's evil-doing, the witch's narcissism went far beyond this to an unabashed conviction of her own omnipotence, including the immense power of her thoughts, deeds, and rituals.

Typical of the hysteric, the victim enjoyed her weakness, helplessness, and support from those around her, while the witch seems to have sought affirmations of her grandiose feelings about herself by watching the results of her powers without support from anyone else. Though the witch and her victim complemented each other, and in a sociological sense "needed" each other, psychologically they seem to be cut from very different cloth.

This discussion affords us the opportunity to clarify a criticism of the theory of hysteria being proposed. It may be argued that every personality uses forms of the culture and that every form of psychopathology can be, in part, understood by considering the cultural and social background from which it emerges and against which it exists. What, then, it may be asked, makes this a theory of just one personality configuration?

The heightening of religious zeal during the Reformation and the Christian image of woman as Satan's agent were two obvious cultural prerequisites for the flourishing of witchcraft in the sixteenth and seventeenth centuries. From a more social-historical point of view, it may be that the changes in the character of the family and the growing recognition of childhood (Aries, 1962) provide keys to psychological motives for older women to become witches: it was during the middle of the sixteenth century, at the very climax of witchcraft in England, that the family was separating itself as a distinct institution and beginning to define a private domain, separate from the life of the church and village. Perhaps witches were women whose lives became diminished and limited by the growing isolation of the family from other institutions of society. The simultaneous discovery of childhood also promoted a generational conflict in which young girls, who most frequently proclaimed themselves victims of witchcraft, accused older women of being witches (Demos, 1970; Caro Baroja, 1964; Higham, personal communication).

Such sociohistorical speculations are plausible and worthwhile, but they do not deal with the dimension crucial to the definition of hysteria. We can *understand* the existence of both the witch and her victim by such analysis, but to determine whether each is hysterical demands an understanding of *how* each uses the forms of the culture. The definition of hysteria presented here rests on the hysteric's capacity to use the cultural currency, so to speak, in a fluent, convincing. normative fashion, not simply on demonstrating that the hysteric can be seen to be the product of her particular cultural milieu. While the witch and her victim were participating in the same cultural beliefs, the witch clung to any aspect that guaranteed her omnipotence and risked persecution from her fellows, whereas her victim lived out a myth of her own submission, helplessness, and victimization which assured the support of those around her.

THE APACHE SHAMAN

The Apache shaman demonstrates how adaptive the hysterical resolution can be. Several have observed the hysterical features of these shamans. Boyer (1962) observed that shamans often display characteristics of the opposite sex and are early marked as moderately deviant by such neurotic traits as excitability, seizures, and a tendency to solitude. He considered the presence of trances, hallucinations, conversions, and phobias in shamans to be indications of hysteria. Klopfer and Boyer (1961) supported this view with Rorschach research, which found shamans to be hysterical in character.

The duties of the Apache shaman include making contact with ghosts, ghost chasing, and disposition of spirits for others in the culture. It is thought that shamans are recruited and indoctrinated into their role by a homeless spirit which has come to reside within them in times of emotional turmoil during their adolescence. The shaman then sees himself as an emissary to the spirit world, capable of calling upon and mediating between sources of awesome and frightening power, but paradoxically is himself a relatively powerless usher of such wonders. Similar to the witchcraft victim, the shaman is not himself responsible for the power that works through him. Though he may command awe and respect for being the vessel which can hold these spiritual forces, the forces themselves are not his.

In animistic Apache experience, to eat the meat of an animal brings both power and the possibility of danger. The power of a strong animal can be acquired by eating it but, at the same time, to eat such an animal increases the risk of illness and early death. Each plant and animal species has a "boss" who must be entreated to prevent retribution. For example, in collecting plants to be used in rites, the Apache collector argues aloud to the boss of the species why the plant must be picked. Boyer noted the oral and phallic symbolism that pervades Apache experience. Though the shamans are considered best qualified to seek out and be acted on by spirits, the oral-animistic beliefs are so deeply ingrained in Apache life that all people are considered more or less able to partake in the power and danger of spirits. M. E. Opler (1935; cited by Boyer, 1962) has consequently called the Apaches a civilization of shamans. In such a culture as this, it is understandable that the shaman, whose duty it is to deal with this ever-present, phallic spirit world, can attain a position of respect and sometimes leadership.

Boyer, like Veith and Hansen, used the occurrence of seizures and trances along with the presence of opposite-sex characteristics and the oral-phallic symbolism of the Apache shaman rites in arguing that the shamans are hysterics. Such features are *part and parcel* of the specific hysterical alternative possible in Apache culture, but again the features of the shaman that make him hysterical lie elsewhere—the same features that manifest themselves in cultures in which hysterics do not present such discrete symptoms as trances or seizures. The shaman uses the animistic and spiritual myths of the Apache culture, as the witch used Christian demonology, to maintain a sense of himself as the relatively passive mediator for essentially phallic forces emanating from the spirit world. The thoughts and feelings are not his, but visited on him. Typical of the hysteric as defined here, the shaman displays such high-level ego functions as good reality testing, intelligence, facility in interpersonal relations, all of which permit him to play out his identity in a conventional, convincing manner. This makes it possible for the shaman, far more adaptively than the witch, to use the most prominent, acceptable forms of his culture. Klopfer and Boyer (1961) defined the shaman as "an individual who is considered to possess supernatural powers *which support and are supported by* the common values of his culture" (my emphasis).

The shaman, Boyer observed (1962), is not as disturbed as previously thought. He has progressed to the genital level of development and may appear transiently disturbed by observers outside Apache culture because of his use of "regression in the service of the ego" (Kris, 1932-1952). The shaman serves an important function for the culture in regressing for those who call on him for help. His own personal capacity to regress and recover to a secondary-process level becomes regression in the service of the social ego—that is to say, regression sponsored by the culture, which its members can vicariously and safely take part in. The capacity to dip back into regressive ego states seems to be a feature common to the many manifestations of the hysterical ego.

As for the shaman's personal motivation for resorting to this hysterical identity, one can only speculate. The Apache culture seems to be one that would promote conflicts about confronting awesome powers. The daintiest flowers have a "boss" one may have to answer to. Seeking power by oral incorporation is coupled with great danger. Phobias are explicitly introduced very early in life to crystallize ambivalent strivings for power ingrained in the culture. For the male Apache a passive retreat from male assertiveness is one response to the immense castration anxiety promoted by the culture. A folk tale related by Boyer (1962) tells of a man who, after being derided for being "soft" by a woman, leaves the security of camp and fights off attackers. Returning to camp he boasts of what "that of a woman's breeches was able to procure for you." This story illustrates the concern with passivity and effeminacy rampant in Apache men. Boyer pointed out the obvious possibility that the man in the story is a transvestite or homosexual and noted that his fear is homosexual attack, which he resists with phallic means. When it is remembered that the Apache shaman often displays characteristics of the opposite sex, the possibility arises that the passivity of the shaman's role is sought by many Apache men as a flight from masculinity, as a type of homosexual surrender to the great power—to the "bosses." In the sense that Nunberg (1936) discussed homosexuality, the shaman submits out of intense castration anxiety and fear of his own aggression to these powers in an effort to appease them, disarm them, secretly castrate them, and incorporate some of their power. Thus this may be a common intrapsychic dynamic that leads Apache men to choose the Apache form of hysteria—shamanism.

Klopfer and Boyer's Rorschach research (1961) on the Apache shaman corroborates the picture of the hysterical ego considered basic to our definition of hysteria, as well as supporting the speculations about the dynamics behind the shaman's choice of the hysterical alternative. On the Rorschach test, the shaman subjects gave repetitive "magical" percepts, which at first blush sounded like schizophrenic Rorschach records. These percepts revolved around the magical power of the stars, and such natural occurrences as thunder, lightning, and floods. Further examination, however, revealed that the percepts were responses not infrequently given to particular cards, which, according to Rorschach interpretive theory, reflect the shaman's capacity to test reality in an accurate, consensual fashion, including a capacity to appraise accurately the social realities within which he must operate. It is exactly these ego capacities that permit the shaman convincingly to make use of the myths of passivity of his culture and consequently to be the hysteric of Apache culture. The perseveration of magical percepts is, of course, also a reflection of the medicine man's frame of reference, for the magical impact of nature constitutes the shaman's stock in trade.

Two other aspects of the shaman's Rorschachs cited by Klopfer and Boyer show them to be basically neurotic, not psychotic, and, more specifically, hysterical according to the definition presented here. Their high responsiveness to the color of the cards, which reflects the availability of emotion in consciousness, is in stark contrast to the paucity of color in chronic schizophrenic Rorschach responses indicative of affective flatness. The emotional responsiveness of the shaman would seem to be a necessity for picking up both the emotional atmosphere of a specific situation into which he has been summoned for assistance, and the "mood" of a whole culture in which he is operating at a particular time. The inability of the schizophrenic to resonate with such moods and atmospheres on other than an idiosyncratic level makes him incapable of the empathy required of the shaman. The shamans' Rorschachs showed such use of undifferentiated shading and "magical motion," both of which seemed initially to be indicators of psychosis, but again a more cogent explanation emerged. The shaman subjects were using the color to identify the source of their feelings as part of the magic mandate of shamanism. Under this mandate, Klopfer and Boyer observed, the shaman locates the source of his feelings outside himself, thus avoiding ego responsibility for his actions and feelings. The Rorschach record reflects, then, a quality central to the hysterical ego—the disowning of thoughts and feelings, particularly active phallic ones, by maintaining an ego-syntonic sense of the self as the passive victim of such inner experiences.

The Rorschach records support the speculations about the nature of the dynamics that lead the individual Apache to shamanism. The percepts reflected the shaman's struggle to avoid being the victim of uncontrollable phallic impulses, impulses usually experienced as coming from others. This supports the possibility that the Apache who resorts to shamanism does so out of fear of the "bosses," the Apache culture's omnipresent image of the dangerous, castrating father. More generally, the records reflect the absence of ego responsibility for phallic aggression. In addition, problems in accepting, and confusion about, sex roles were both common features of the shamans' Rorschachs. This suggests that the shaman retreats from masculinity out of fear of the response to his phallic-aggressive strivings. When such a retreat begins early in life, the deepest strata of the personality may be marked by feminine identifications, resulting in the feminine traits observed in male shamans.

The conflicts with which Apache shamans seem to be struggling are those with which the hysterical personalities in all cultures struggle — phallic-Oedipal conflicts. From these reports of Apache shamans, it seems that they also present the ego-adaptive and ego-defensive modes characteristic of the hysterical personality.

Shamans in other cultures often prove to be hysterics, presenting recurrent features which teach us much about the hysterical process. J. Murphy (1964) reported the process of shamanization and the status of the shaman among the Alaskan Eskimos. The shaman is first called by a vision and must then go through a rigorous trial alone in the arctic until his "familiar" (totemic animal, usually an arctic animal like a polar bear) comes to him. People report that the shaman seems "crazy" for several days during this recruitment; however, typical of the hysteric, this craziness proves to be transient, expectable, and specific to the initiation rite. The Alaskan shaman is called on to retrieve lost souls, mollify the spirit world after the violation of a tribal taboo, hunt for witches, and extract an object or spirit that has intruded itself into the sufferer.

The duties of the Alaskan shaman, like those of the Apache, involve searching for and guiding powerful external forces, again building his identity around a culturally salient myth of passivity. There are other similarities between the shamans of these two cultures: (1) They manifest "exceptional" or mildly deviant characteristics which are culturally accepted as cues to accord them great power and prestige. (2) Their spirits often call on them to be like the opposite sex, either by claiming to feel pregnant or by wearing for periods of time clothes appropriate to the opposite sex. Murphy reported that in the past homosexuality and transvestitism occurred among the Alaskan shamans and were not condemned by the society. (3) They succumb to seizures as part of their ritual "cures" of others.

During the ceremony the Alaskan shaman, after bringing those present to a high emotional pitch, with dancing and singing, often collapses into a seizure in which his "familiar" is said to be acting through him. Just as the victim of the witch feels himself to be, for the moment, only the vessel for the witch's powers, so the shaman seems able to give himself up totally to the spirit of his totemic animal.

SHAMAN: HYSTERIC OR PSYCHOTIC?

There is a subtle but important conflict in Murphy's account of the degree of disturbance of the shaman, a conflict that runs throughout the literature on shamanism in many cultures. She commented that from the reports of shamans many sounded substantially disturbed psychologically, adding that, owing to the waning of shamanism, these reports could not be documented and evaluated. At another point she remarked that in spite of the shaman's loss of control during a seizure of possession by the familiar, they also evidence a great deal of responsibility, self-control, and capacity to manage the social powers accorded them. Whether the shaman is schizophrenic, warding off a psychotic break through socially useful adaptation (Ackerknecht, 1943), epileptic, or hysterical is a question that recurs throughout the literature on the subject. Murphy's difficulty in documenting severe psychological abnormality among the Alaskan shamans may reflect the regressive qualities unique to hysteria: the capacity to allow himself to slip into regressive modes, including such dramatic behavior as epileptiform fits, while maintaining the strength and capability to retrieve himself from the experience relatively quickly and completely. Moreover, such episodes are like invited, if somewhat intemperate, guests; never unwelcome, unexpected intruders. This kind of regression will be seen to show itself in the hysterics of all the cultures and eras considered here—it is, as it were, hysteria's signature on the ego.

Self-induced, transiently regressive alterations of consciousness have been documented by Fuchs (1964) among the *barwa* (Balahis shamans of central India). In what Fuchs called a self-hypnotic trance promoted by drinking liquor and smoking marijuana, the *barwa* begins speaking in an unnatural voice and loses consciousness. Consistent with the observations put forward here, Fuchs considered these trances to be hysterical, not psychotic. He supported this view by pointing out that the *barwa* choose to have the hypnotic seizure experience, unlike someone more disturbed who would be unexpectedly overtaken and overwhelmed by a seizure or alteration of consciousness. Gelfand (1964) made a similar observation among the shamans of the Shana, Rhodesian blacks.

In all of these cultures the shamans become the foci of their communities through their capacity for the transient hysterical regression as described here. They are at the spiritual and social crossroads of their cultures, for their personal identities rest on the most valued myths of their societies. In each case they enact a role generated by current myths that insures their sense of passivity in relation to great, illicit, and dangerous forces.

Throughout all these accounts is the shamans' experience of themselves as passive guiders of or potential victims of phallic forces located in spirits outside themselves. This functions as a defense against recognizing their own active, phallic wishes. In characteristic hysterical fashion, this overt subjective sense of passivity in relation to spiritual powers masks the substantial social power their position enables them to exert. This striving for active phallic control and mastery, covered by a subjective, conscious sense of passivity, is the hallmark of all hysterics, including the Victorian hysteric to whom we now turn.

CHANGES IN MODERN HYSTERIA: DISAPPEARANCE OF
CONVERSION HYSTERIA

Abse (1959), Chodoff (1954), and others have observed that conversion hysteria has gradually disappeared from the clinical scene. McKegney (1967) has disputed this claim, contending that conversion hysteria simply presents itself currently in medical, rather than psychiatric, settings. His study, however, suffers from a definition of "conversion reaction" so loose as to include virtually any medically unfounded physical condition. The issue of the waning of conversion hysteria becomes clouded and complicated by Rangell's (1959) contention that conversion reactions ocur independently of hysterical character traits. What seems beyond dispute is that the *classical* hysterical conversion reactions documented by Charcot, Janet, and Freud, the grand hysterical fits, paralyses, and massive anesthesias, have become less frequent and occur among people of different sociocultural background than during Victorian times (Abse, 1959; Chodoff, 1954; author's own observations). The Victorian hysterics were mostly middle-class urban women, whereas, in contrast, in my own clinical experience lower-class and rural settings seem to be the last bastions of classical conversion reactions in women who present truly hysterical personalities.

Chodoff (1954) presented the following historical factors as responsible for the waning of the disorder in Western society: (1) people are no longer as simple and unsophisticated as earlier; (2) Europeans were closer to witchcraft; (3) class distinctions made for overawed and compliant patients; (4) prudery and sexual inhibition made repression of sexual impulses all the more necessary; (5) there was a belief in the inevitability of science (medicine) while now there is doubt and uneasiness about man's future and the wonders of science.

There is some truth in most of these hypotheses; however, none is a well-argued sociohistorical position. The first point implies a simple, linear, incremental view of history. According to such a view, people have become more complex and sophisticated over time. A social-science approach would consider the changing ethos of the culture and changes in socialization practices in its effort to understand *differences* in the personalities of people in a culture over time. Most facile explanations for the disappearance of conversion hysteria pivot on an assumption that people are too sophisticated to express their emotional problems somatically. In other words, people are too smart and worldly to become conversion hysterics.

Turning to Chodoff's second point, while Victorian Europeans were, of course, historically closer neighbors to the time of widespread belief in witchcraft, the late nineteenth-century middle-class European cannot be said to be the emotional pawn of witchcraft as Chodoff's statement implies. Rather, the late nineteenth century witnessed a widespread secularization of Western culture. The impact of such beliefs on this class would not appear to be any greater than the magical beliefs that constitute much of contemporary Western religion.

While Chodoff is probably correct that class boundaries were sharper during the Victorian era than they are today—and surely this factor must be taken into account in discussing lower-class hysterics treated by middle- and upper-class physicians—most of the hysterics who came to Freud's and Breuer's attention were of nearly the same social class as their doctors.

Prudishness and awe of science during the Victorian era, Chodoff's final two points, were both aspects of a culture which produced conversion hysteria; once more, however, Chodoff simply implies a connection rather than delineating a theory of the *process* by which this culture promoted this particular form of psychopathology.

Application of the historical perspective presented here suggests some answers to these questions: Did the disappearance of conversion hysteria mark the end of hysteria or did the form of hysteria change? Assuming, as will be argued, that hysteria is very much with us, why does it now often assume nonsymptomatic forms? What in the Victorian culture promoted conversion hysteria, and what in contemporary culture fosters the current forms of hysteria? The answers to these questions will form the foundation for the historical perspective on hysteria.

THE VICTORIAN HYSTERIC

Addressing the last question first, an exploration of the ethos of Victorian culture, particularly the position and image of women, is necessary. Out of this exploration it will become clear how the conversion reaction came to be the Victorian era's hysterical alternative.

Images of the Victorian Woman

The Victorian image of woman embodies several telling paradoxes. On the surface she was considered passive, naïve, and a bit dumb, but at the same time the culture expected her to be strong and in command. This paradox is apparent in the female characters in the fiction of Howells, a Victorian writer of rather prosaic, but almost photographic, tales of American domestic life during the Victorian era. In one short story, "Editha" (Howells, 1906), the protagonist is determined that her boy-friend go to war. Never telling him outright to go, she manipulates him unmercifully until he decides to do so, the whole time trying to appear the fragile, passive, completely harmless woman. Upon the boy-friend's death in battle, Editha pays a visit to his mother, who castigates her for having subtly coerced her son to go to war. The son is pictured fundamentally as a completely helpless pawn of these two women, a pawn who is under as much of an illusion about his own strength as Editha is about her innocence and passivity. In a story by Freeman (1891), similarly, a quiet, submissive pioneer woman shows herself in the end to be far more powerful and reasonable than her husband.

This paradox is most striking in the themes of the domestic novels of the nineteenth century, works written by and for women. On the surface these novels looked morally edifying and consequently were often approved, where earlier novels rarely had been by the church for its female parishioners and by men for their wives and daughters. As Papashvily (1956) points out, these novels were a "manual of arms" for women, a "quietly ruthless" attack on men and their institutions, an unconscious expression of women's grievances and the revenge they were unable either to experience or to express overtly.

These novels depicted women as helpless victims of exploitative and lecherous husbands, lovers, fathers, or brothers, while remaining themselves innocent, passionless, and in all ways virtuous. The heroine of the American domestic novel had to be tricked, drugged, or in some way ensnared by a scheming man, never stooping to extra- or premarital folly voluntarily. The fallen woman was absent from the domestic novel; men were portrayed as irresponsible or evil, and were either maimed or killed off by their female creators. These novels, and Papashvily's analysis of them, teach what is basic to the psychology of the Victorian woman: through a facade of weakness, righteousness, and passivity, aggressive and competitive feelings are indirectly and covertly aired — most often without the conscious recognition of the woman herself.

A related aspect of Victorian expectations of woman is illustrated in the stories: it fell to the Victorian woman to carry on the morality of a bygone era. The nineteenth century opened, according to Higham (1969), with a sense of boundlessness. The magic of industrial power promised to dissolve the limits of time and space of the preindustrial world. But as the nineteenth century progressed, it became apparent just how much the world had sacrificed for change. One response was to try to revive what seemed in retrospect to be the order and security of the preindustrial world. It somehow fell to woman to be the purveyor of the morality of this bygone social order. Thus, Editha does not overtly force her beau to war, for that would be inconsistent with the valor expected of men in that old, aristocratic world — rather, she tries to inculcate the morality in him, trying to get him to want to do the heroic thing, while she, the passive child-woman, watches adoringly. Consistent with this, M.

Murphy (1965) found, in his research on child-rearing practices during the Victorian era, that the mother was almost exclusively responsible for the religious and moral education of children during their first seven years.

The Victorian woman was expected to be herself a personification of this bygone morality—to be innocent, sexless, and aristocratic. As Fiedler (1960) pointed out, woman came to personify the essence of purity and the embodiment of virtue during the Victorian period, in contrast to the earlier Puritan image of woman as the epitome of evil and mystery. While in pre-Victorian times woman was portrayed as the seductress who would lead men down the pathway to sin, during the nineteenth century the man became the seducer and the woman the picture of helplessness, goodness, moral righteousness, and innocence. Fiedler traced the disappearance and transmutation of sexuality in the American domestic novel. The "sentimental love religion," as Fiedler termed it, pervaded popular novels written by and for women. Such novels were "tearful extravaganzas in which the female is portrayed as pure sentiment, the male as naked phallus . . ." The theme of the young girl, be she a Revolutionary colonial girl, Confederate lass, or farmer's daughter, defending her honor by escaping seduction repeated itself endlessly in these popular novels. Of course, with every defense of her sanctified virginity, the innocent maiden proved to be capable of great strength in her defeat and symbolic castration of her seducer. During the last third of the nineteenth centry, seduction scenes, even those involving the virtuous resistance by the woman of a man's advances, could no longer take place in the female novel, owing to what Fiedler described as the "almost intolerable gentility" of the female audience. Papashvily too described the portrayal of men in these female novels as bankrupt, ill, dying, or in a myriad of other ways irresponsible and castrated. She also noted a contrasting depiction of women as excelling in self-sacrifice, moral fortitude, Christian goodness, and secular innocence (Papashvily, 1956; Harland, 1910).

While the Victorian woman was raised to feel that she represented all that was pure and noble, a belief in the great vulnerability of women to uncontrollable passion which could sweep them from innocence lurked in the background. Thus while women were seen as innocent victims of lecherous men, and their virginity as the foundation of the social order, they were also seen as veritable sexual powderkegs. Girls were kept away from soft beds to prevent excessive sexual excitement (Sinclair, 1965). Cold baths and exercise befitting a woman were also promoted as ways of siphoning off these impulses before they reached a critical mass and exploded in hetero-sexual or autoerotic activity. P. Miller's (1965) intellectual history of America spelled out the many conflicts in the nineteenth-century American mind that eventuated in, among other things, the paradox in the image of Victorian woman—pure, weak, and moral, or passionate, angry, and managerial.

The growing split between home and marketplace around the mid-nineteenth century also had a profound impact on the image and way of life of the Victorian woman. Before the Industrial Revolution, when the locus of production of many goods was still the home, women were given recognition and endorsement for duties vital to the physical survival of the family. During this period women shared the privileges as well as the work. With the Industrial Revolution the home became a place of leisure and a greater range and quantity of goods came to be produced outside the home. In addition, surplus wealth no longer took the form of landed property that required feminine skills to develop and manage. Thus many of the activities that had defined women's lives were becoming usurped by industrial production and the public marketplace. Finally, the idle woman came to be a symbol of financial success—a trophy of her husband's affluence. Considering how extensive and arduous were the duties of women, particularly in America, during the preindustrial period, all this must have felt like an early, obligatory retire-ment for women. In harmony with the overt innocence and passivity of the heroines of the domestic novels, the culture now relegated women to a sphere of institutionalized passivity and uselessness (Papashvily, 1956). And, again in tune with the righteous examples set by these fictional heroines of the home, women were expected through indirection to be moral leaders of the culture (Bridges, 1965).

Images of Women in the Victorian American South

The conflicts in Victorian expectations of women were nowhere more stark and severe than in the American South. The trends present throughout the Victorian world appeared in sharper relief in the sociology of the American South, and consequently the Victorian form of hysterical personality has probably remained more prevalent there than anywhere else. The American South typified the cultural and social climate in which Victorian hysteria flourishes. The Victorian Southern woman, like the Victorian woman everywhere, was expected to embody an illusion of an earlier time—in the case of the Southern woman a romantic fiction of an aristocratic South. The Southern illusion about woman was more hollow than the European because what Cash (1941) has called the "cult of Southern womanhood" was not in the service of resurrecting something that had been, but a pretense at something that never was. Cash cogently argued that the South, in contrast to Europe, was never aristocratic, and the Southern woman therefore lived out an illusion of what had never been anything more than a pretense of high culture and aristocracy. The South did not succumb as did Europe and the American North to the pressures of scientific progress and urbanization, and thus resisted the "end of American innocence" (May, 1959) in the early twentieth century. The cult of Southern womanhood, the worship of women as bastions of purity, passionlessness, and morality, thus held on, and the post-bellum South looked to women to sustain illusions about itself that it knew were no longer viable—indeed, myths it probably fundamentally knew had never been true.

Scott (1970) contrasted the image of the Southern women in the nineteenth century as submissive, innocent, and childish with the heavy responsibility they actually carried, the greatest of which involved managing slaves. She pointed out a paradox which is central to the Victorian image of woman: women's self-denial and suffering in silence were said to be endearing to men. Perhaps less endearing, but considered as innately feminine, were women's piety and desire to limit man's natural vice and immorality. But at the same time, and herein lies the contradiction, she was thought always to need male protection and expected never to challenge her husband's judgment. A wife was expected to be amiable, sweet, prudent, and devoted, and differences between husband and wife were labeled a "calamity" in an essay by a college president in 1835. Evangelical religion echoed the ideal of a submissive, self-sacrificing woman intended to manage her husband's duties inconspicuously, to be silent in church, and never to voice discontent openly (Scott, 1970).

Similar to the contradictions in the Victorian image of woman was a paradox in the Southern ethos between the hedonism of the preplantation backwoodsman (Rourke, 1931; Cash, 1941) and the puritanical prohibition of pleasure. These two could exist side by side in the Southern mind—according to Cash, because it was essentially naïve and unrealistic. It was not, however, naïveté that permitted this paradox to continue unquestioned, but the prevalence of an ego in the Victorian Southerner that used repression, dissociation, denial, and the identification with mythical identities prescribed by the culture. As we shall see, the Victorian woman's attempts to avoid recognition of such stark conflicts in the culture's expectations and images of her were directly responsible for the prevalence of conversion as the Victorian hysterical alternative. The prominence and endurance of these trends in Southern culture have made it particularly fertile ground for both conversion hysteria and the hysterical personality which lives out the illusion of the naïve, chaste, hyperfeminine woman.

Identity Strains in the Victorian Woman

The Victorian woman was confronted, then, with carving out an identity from these many cultural demands, expectations, and prohibitions. While cultures inevitably make conflicting, often contradictory, demands on their members, the strains on the Victorian woman seem to have been particularly acute. She was told that she was to be the weak innocent of preindustrial times, while at the same time expected to be strong and active in her stringent enforcement and complete embodiment of that very preindustrial morality. Strength had to be covered by a façade of weakness, passion by gentility, and dominance over men by an exaggerated, even caricatured, femininity. When Chodoff claimed that the Victorian hysterics were less complex and sophisticated, he was caught up by the myth of the naïveté of Victorian woman. These illusions, needless to say, were not just for public display but deeply ingrained in each Victorian woman's most private sense of herself. How the ego of the Victorian woman sought to maintain inner harmony amid these illusions and myths is one key to why such women were so prone to develop the Victorian brand of hysteria, the classical hysterical reactions.

The Victorian Hysterical Alternatives

The Victorian woman sought to avoid realization of the stark, anxiety-arousing contradictions in the society's expectations of her, contradictions that tapped the universal, intrapsychic conflict between activity and passivity, masculinity and femininity, by a psychological maneuver recognized by Janet (1892-1894) as splitting of consciousness and by Breuer and Freud (1893-1895) as repression. An ego developed in the Victorian woman designed to keep the contradictory aspects of the culture's expectations of her separate from one another. There was great cultural pressure on the woman to maintain the conscious image of herself as a fragile, passive child, while in a second consciousness, split off from the first, as Janet conceived it, the sense of herself as strong and aggressive had to remain sequestered. While all people in all cultures must dismiss certain tabooed thoughts and feelings from awareness (indeed, Freud [1930] considered this dismissal an inevitable byproduct of civilization), the point is that the incongruities in the Victorian image of woman were so flagrant as to necessitate ego operations designed to disavow completely large areas of thought and feelings. Complete and wholesale dissociative trends became essential, then, for the maintenance of a woman's sense of integrity and unity. The Victorian woman could thus feel as if she were fragile and meek, while in her behavior, the meaning of which her ego was able to shield from awareness, she betrayed her passion for power, erotic pleasure, and moral control. Massive repression and dissociation became the most viable modes for resolving these cultural and intra-psychic dilemmas. These kinds of defensive maneuvers are prerequisite for severe dissociative states, hysterical fits, amnesias, and conversion reactions, the kinds of hysterical disorders common during the Victorian era. The fit or conversion symptom expressed thoughts and feelings that had to be totally banished from consciousness. The Victorian endorsement of naïveté and ignorance in women (Scott, 1970), of course, facilitated defenses of "not knowing," repression, denial, and dissociative clouding of the cognitive sphere.

Other aspects of the culture and its image of women combined with the above to make somatic expression of inner conflict the Victorian era's hysterical alternative. Rossi (1966) observed that the more vital a particular social role is to the maintenance and survival of the society, the greater the likelihood is that those required to assume that role will repress the negative end of their ambivalence toward it. In the Victorian culture, in some areas such as the American South more than others, the role of women was vital, for on her identity seemed to rest the last chance for the controlling class to return to a preindustrial, almost feudal, paradise. For a woman to become aware of a sexual impulse or doubts about her social role was to threaten the most treasured illusions of a society which desperately clung to them for survival. The great majority of Victorian women could not consciously consider the doubts and grievances concerning her position as a woman, as later became possible with the blossoming of the feminist movement during the first decade of the twentieth century. Victorian culture had put women in an emotional strait jacket, permitting them virtually no channels for overt expression of impulses, be they aggressive or erotic (Scott, 1970; Papashvily, 1956). Women were warned of the special dangers of illness attendant on over-exertion. Kept indoors, laced into tight bone corsets, the Victorian woman probably came to feel, very literally, fettered by her culture. From her fantasy life to the use of her muscles, she confronted cultural prohibitions and constraints. She was at once the embodiment of a bygone morality and in her stylish leisure an adornment to her home and proof of her husband's financial self-sufficiency (Sinclair, 1965; Papashvily, 1956). Again paradoxically, with reference to this last point, she had to maintain the illusion that she was a woman of leisure, though in reality she had many responsibilities and much to do, for she did not have the corps of servants that assisted her aristocratic mother or grandmother.

Somatization in the Victorian Hysteric

To love or to hate overtly and unromantically were close to impossible for the Victorian woman. To be weak and sick, however, were considered basic to feminine nature. To fall ill became one of the few ways within the limits of Victorian convention in which the Victorian woman could express inner passions and conflicts. (Of course, outside the limits of convention the psychotic or schizoid personality, as in every culture, expressed his own idiosyncratic, overtly deviant response to conflict.) Due probably both to the advances in the scientific study of disease and to the growing secularization of the culture during the later part of the nine-teenth century, concern with vulnerability to disease replaced earlier fears of divine vengeance. Howells's Editha, for example, remarks at the moment of great emotional crisis in the story that she took to her bed as was expected of a woman at such a moment. Papashvily (1956) noted that ill health remained a central theme in the domestic novel even after health standards began to improve around the middle of the nineteenth century. Fiedler (1960) observed that in the novel the sickbed came to replace the bed of sexual passion—that woman came to epitomize purity and frailness. Sinclair, too, observed that women were considered pure, though weak, during the Victorian era. Thomas Higginson

(1891), a moderate feminist, in spite of himself, expressed his culture's belief that women were extremely vulnerable to physical illness. Though he was trying to convince his audience that women had abilities on a par with men's and therefore deserved equal opportunities, he was continually amending his suggestions for equal treatment with the proviso that women be protected from overactivity in view of their vulnerability to disease. Howells termed middle-class American society during the Victorian era "a hospital for invalid females." Falling ill, therefore, was fostered by Victorian society as a channel for women to express—and in true hysterical fashion simultaneously disown—impulses and conflicts. Thus the dissociative, stringently repressive ego which developed in response to the social ecology of Victorian society combined with the prevalent Victorian belief in female proneness to disease to make conversion reaction the Victorian form of hysteria. The ego of the Victorian hysteric, characteristically in tune with the ethos of her time, chose a completely credible mode of expressing and disowning internal feelings—the psychological imitation of disease.

The social and religious constraints on the life plans of young Victorian women were often the source of conflicts that led them to resort to their culture's hysterical alternative. As Sinclair (1965) has shown, young Victorian women were put under great pressure to nurse obediently sick relatives, often wasting their youths in the process. Seidenberg and Papathomopoulos (1962), as noted before, discovered that all of Freud's classical hysterics nursed their fathers for substantial periods of time. They noted that the nursing required the suppression of the many emotions generated by caring for a very ill relative: resentment, guilt over the resentment, sadness, and fear. The conversion symptom expresses these many feelings symbolically, to enlist the caring and affection of others, often to terminate the nursing—and at the same time these strivings are passively attributed to the mysterious force of disease. In typical hysterical fashion, the hysteric is the innocent victim of forces not within her power to control. As the Apache shaman enlisted his culture's myths of passivity in relation to fickle, spiritual forces, to disown his own impulses, so the Victorian hysteric marshaled a myth current in her culture, the power of disease, to avoid acknowledgment of sexual and hostile wishes and feelings that ran counter to the dominant illusions about the nature of women.

"These are not my hatreds, loves, or ambivalences, but owing to the disease that has overtaken me"; such was the dynamic of the Victorian attempt at hysterical resolution. It was a solution which in characteristic hysterical fashion remained solidly within the limits of propriety and conventionality, and at the same time aroused enough concern, concern merited by one who was ill, to enlist the attention of people from whom to receive and toward whom to express, in disguised forms, the loves and hatreds unacceptable in a Victorian woman. Illness, the bane of Victorian women, became the language in which tabooed thoughts, feelings, and wishes could be disowned and, through the body, symbolically expressed. Unraveling these symbols and tracing their historical roots was, of course, Freud's first major accomplishment.[1]

Psychiatry Misled by Victorian Hysterics' Somatization

The conversion reactions of Victorian women were modern psychiatry's first confrontations with hysteria, a historical accident that had some unfortunate consequences for later thinking about the disorder. Because hysteria expressed itself as mock disease during this period, the disorder came to be considered, implicitly or explicitly, as a disease with physical symptoms diagnosed by its strictly physical manifestations. Imitating disease as hysteria did during this time, it naturally appeared as complexes of symptoms, differing from genuine disease only by the absence of primary physical lesions.

---

[1] This argument does not suggest that conversion hysteria did not exist before the Victorian era. It surely did. The point rather is that psychosomatic symptoms occurred frequently in middle-class Victorian society, probably more frequently than before the Industrial Revolution (but this is my own speculation), and that this somatic form of hysteria can be seen to fit well with some features of Victorian culture and its definition of women.

Because at the dawn of modern psychiatry hysteria mimicked disease and was consequently conceived of basically in terms of disease, psychiatry subsequently continued to try to view it as a disorder of *symptoms*, a symptom neurosis. It was not until the early 1930's that Wittels (1931) and Reich (1933) delineated the "hysterical character," but even it was described only as a character type conducive to the development of hysterical symptoms. Symptoms, not character, remained the focus of the definition of hysteria. When, in the late nineteenth and early twentieth centuries, hysteria gained the reputation as the great imitator of physical illness, expressing itself through somatic channels, hysteria *was* conversion and thus the two terms came to be virtually interchangeable. Unfortunately, as hysteria came to assume new forms with changes in the culture, as is its very essence, the theory of hysteria, lagging behind, persisted in the attempt to understand it as symptom and disease. As discrete conversion symptoms showed themselves with less frequency in clinical practice, some contended that hysteria was disappearing, others abandoned symptomatic definition, and tried to define it strictly dynamically (Fenichel, 1945), and still others, skirting the real issue of the change in the disorder, began describing the hysterical personality, listing its traits with the same superficiality as had been appropriate earlier to the simple description of symptoms (Lazare and Klerman, 1968; Chodoff and Lyons, 1958).

HYSTERIA'S ERA-SPECIFIC FORMS

What has happened over the past 100 years is that, characteristically, hysteria has changed with the times. In the late nineteenth century, consistent with the culture's myths of female passivity, it took the form of disease and gained a reputation in the psychiatric literature as the great imitator of physical illness (Abse, 1966). With the reorientation of Western culture that began in the 1890's (Higham, 1965), the range of social options of women broadened remarkably, and with it new modes for expressing conflict became possible for them. Falling ill became but one of many channels for women to express conflict hysterically. Finally, owing to the current cultural ambiance, to fall ill is markedly out of keeping with the myths and fantasies of both men and women, and consequently is no longer a common hysterical alternative. To be the helpless victim of one's society, the stars, one's unconscious, or mental disease are now our culturally sponsored myths of passivity and thus form the basis of current hysterical alternatives.

Thus when Rangell (1959) found that conversion reactions do not coincide in any regular way with hysterical character traits, he was making a discovery and at the same time observing a real historical *change* in the nature of hysteria. At one time conversion was hysteria, but by the 1950's, when Rangell wrote his paper, hysteria had come to assume new forms, no longer imitating physical disease. Hysteria is a symptom neurosis only when it expresses itself through mimicry of a disease with discrete symptoms, as was the case in the Victorian period and, by inference from Veith's (1965) history of the hysteric, was also the case in the Egyptian and Graeco-Roman periods. Hysteria has no specific cross-cultural manifestations, for it lives within the conventions of its host culture. Thus it is absurd to try to define hysteria by a catalogue of overt behavior, character traits, or symptom complexes, except for their parochial clinical utility.

Paradoxically, in my own clinical experience, patients from urban areas who now manifest classical conversion symptoms display borderline or psychotic personalities. This stands to reason: the Victorian woman's use of disease as her hysterical alternative reflected the high degree to which she was in tune with the ethos of her culture and its conventional limits for women — in short, it reflected her effective reality testing, sensitivity to the possibilities of her world, and generally well-oriented ego, which stand as enduring hallmarks of the hysteric. By contrast, to be the victim of hysterical fits, severe dissociations, and other classical hysterical symptoms in urban mid-twentieth century America is to be fundamentally out of touch with the culturally sponsored modes of disowning inner conflict, reflecting what is probably a schizoid, narcissistic — in short, borderline — ego structure. For an urban middle-class patient to display a classical conversion reaction, then, paradoxically suggests that she is certainly not a hysteric and is possibly far more disturbed. Moreover, the normal urban woman is not compelled by the culture for her psychic survival to resort to defensive strategies that tend to produce classical hysterical reactions when they miscarry. Thus the modern urban woman who develops a classical conversion reaction, beyond being out of tune with the more current channels of expression, develops an anachronistic set of defenses either out of a primitive, poorly differentiated ego structure, or out of inordinate trauma and conflict in her own personal history.

In my own experience, the last sources of true conversion hysteria in modern, Western culture are rural areas. Ziegler (1967) made this same observation. Angyal (1965) reported that even by the early twentieth century, "grand hysteria" had virtually disappeared from European urban areas, being found only in small secluded communities. Probably owing to the more traditional nature of the family and society in such areas, conversion hysteria has remained a viable hysterical alternative. The family has there remained in many respects unchanged from the urban Victorian family: the family is very close, the child's obedience and respect for authority is emphasized, the limits of acceptability are much narrower than in urban areas, and the chastity of single young women is still very important.

The Victorian hysterical mode, conversion, in many ways epitomized Victorian culture. Higham (1965) vividly described the *Weltanschauung* of the middle-class American during the Victorian era: "They had learned to live in cities, to sit in rooms cluttered with bric-a-brac, to limit the size of their families, to accept the authority of professional elites, to mask their aggression behind a thickening façade of gentility, and to comfort themselves with a faith in automatic, material progress." It was a period of docile compliance to ever more constriction, mechanization, and regulation of life. Combined with this, Americans had a personal sense of stagnating in this circumspect, studiously pursued gentility. In psychological terms, this was an "autoplastic" era, an era in which the self was continually being modified in large ways and tailored in small ones to conform to a quickly changing world. The pressures of industrialization and the society's flagrantly conflicting demands on the individual were dealt with, not by rebelling against or trying to change the world as it was coming to be, but by altering the self, creating ever new illusions about it and inhibiting it at every turn, all for the sake of gentility. Conversion hysteria is almost definitional of an autoplastic neurosis, for it strives to resolve conflict by changing and limiting the self. The self is amended so it will not wish to feel or think in ways condemned by the society. Moreover, the body becomes incapacitated, often making the sufferer an invalid, a most concrete and literal abbreviation of the self. As the modal Victorian mind was incapable of considering rebellion against or criticism of the social order, so hysteria, to remain consistent with the forms current in Victorian culture, could not assume alloplastic forms; that is, it could not express itself in neurotic attempts to change the environment. While clearly conversion served important interpersonal functions, the *subjective* experience of the conversion hysteric was that she was simply the victim of the disease, not intent on changing the environment, and it is this subjective sense that makes this form of hysteria autoplastic. In short, Victorian culture permitted painfully few *active* channels for the expression of normal feelings or neurotic conflicts, particularly for women, and consequently only attempts at resolution in which aspects of the self were inhibited, transformed, or denied were possible. Referring once more to Fiedler, as themes of seduction became sentimentalized, and then expurgated, from the American novel, to be replaced by a sentimental worship of the young, dying virgin, so illusions of weakness, illness, and invalidism, all autoplastic to the core, became the Victorian woman's only vehicles for hysterical, symbolic expression of the passions, resentments, memories, and fantasies condemned by her Victorian superego.

HYSTERIA IN TRANSITION: VICTORIAN TO MODERN HYSTERIA

Over the past 80 years the form of hysteria has evolved in accordance with changing cultural trends. May (1959) described the widespread changes in the social, international, and cultural attitudes of Americans during the early twentieth century. Focusing more on the American's subjective experience of his culture, Higham (1965) located the 1890's as a time of marked and important cultural transition. The reorientation of American culture that Higham described sheds great light on the nature of the transformation of hysteria during the twentieth century. In reaction to the constraints of decorum of the Victorian culture, an "activist mood" swept America in the 1890's. The circumspect, studious, effete identity was replaced by one of virility, power, and mastery. In response to the dullness and restrictions of an increasingly industrialized society, people turned to sports, an interest in untamed nature, and livelier music — in short, a lust for "spaciousness," health, and action.

This transition permitted the emergence of possible new identities for women. Her salient traits came to be, according to Higham, "boldness and radiant vigor." Macfadden, in 1901, wrote that physical exercise would enable a woman to develop muscular strength almost equal to a man's, a far cry from Higginson's warnings about the dangers of exertion for women only 10 years before, and from the myths about feminine sexual functioning rampant during the Victorian period (Sinclair, 1965). Women became far more aggressive in their desires for recognition in the political, legal, and social spheres, and the feminist movement picked up steam (Sinclair, 1965; May, 1959).

Thus, during the last decade of the nineteenth century, as Western culture seemed to depend less on illusions about women to maintain its identity, and as the culture as a whole turned toward action, women became much freer to experience consciously wishes to be competent and independent, to try to act on these wishes, and to try to change the society when prejudices thwarted these wishes. The whole culture now tended more to try to resolve conflict, be it on the personal or international level, by changing the world, where previously the characteristic response had been to try to amend, inhibit, and alter the self. The culture now promoted alloplastic solutions, those in which the world is changed to suit the self, instead of autoplastic ones in which the self is revised in accordance with the demands of the culture. As Higham observed in more historical terms, the military escapades throughout the Western world during the early twentieth century were an outgrowth of this transition to activity and alloplasticity. The technological remaking of life in the twentieth century is another social expression of the culture's alloplasticity. The form taken by hysteria came to express these trends.

With the expanded range of interpersonal action now open to women (and men as well), hysterical solutions were not limited to the autoplastic alternative of falling ill. The hysteric was now able to act out her conflicts in the interpersonal and political arena. Hysteria ceased to express itself exclusively as a mimicry of disease, and mapped itself out as a more general pattern of personal action — in short, it became character style. Just as Rangell's later contention that conversion symptoms exist independently of hysterical character traits is partly a historical observation, so Reich's and Wittels's descriptions of the hysterical character in the early 30's expressed *changes* in the appearance of hysteria.

Where the Victorian hysteric expressed feelings and thoughts unacceptable in consciousness by symbolization of body parts, the modern hysteric, making use of her new social options, has come to use the avenues of object choice and vicarious identification to express unconscious strivings and maintain the ubiquitous hysterial illusion of passivity.

Mrs. P., a 27-year-old divorcée, illustrates the modern hysteric's use of object choice to attempt to settle inner conflict. In an effort to disown tabooed sexual feelings toward an overseductive father, to act out unconscious fantasies of being raped by him and simultaneously taking his penis from him and making him weak and dependent on her, she repeatedly chose men who represented her father. When these men, as they were chosen to do, forced themselves on Mrs. P. sexually and brutally, she felt herself to be their unwilling victim. What she was "forced" to do, she felt, was not within her control, for she had been overpowered by men whom she just happened to fall in with—she did not wish to be raped and beaten, these were simply situations she was coerced into. From another point of view, she chose these men in order to disown both her rage at her father's weakness and her desire to build him up and make him strong. The men she chose presented a façade of strength, though without exception they showed themselves to be infantile, dependent, and incompetent. She disowned responsibility for her painful and incestuous feelings toward her father by repeating her relationship with him through attachments to men who symbolized him. From yet another point of view, it emerged that these men embodied the patient's regressive longing to be weak, which she vicariously enjoyed, but once more could experience as external to herself. Her "foggy," impressionistic cognitive style, as described by Shapiro (1965), permitted her to avoid recognition of her active choice in becoming involved with these men.

Thus what the Victorian hysteric expressed and disowned through the symbolic use of the body and its innervation, Mrs. P., as a modern hysteric, is able to express through transient involvements, part of a life style today considered risqué, but by no means insane for a divorcée—behavior which would have branded a middle-class Victorian woman as hopelessly deviant, and perhaps insane. *Mrs. P.'s neurosis mapped itself out in her pattern of relationships and life choices*, not in discrete, somatic symptoms. Her hysterical neurosis was embodied in her history and her agony over it, not in physical complaints. H. Deutsch's (1930) description of the "hysterical fate neurosis" is essentially a description of this modern version of hysteria. While some hysterics around the turn of the century undoubtedly continued to rely on autoplastic modes, action-dominated, characterological forms of hysteria were becoming viable hysterical solutions as alloplastic modes came to be increasingly the prerogative of women and the hallmark of the culture.

MODERN HYSTERIA: THE SEXY CHILD-WOMAN

The new social prerogatives afforded women, combined with remnants of Victorian myths of women as weak, innocent, and intellectually inferior, gave rise to a popular stereotype of woman current during the first half of the twentieth century—the "dumb blonde." This kind of woman was portrayed as unwittingly seductive, psychologically if not physiologically virginal, physically sexy, childish, and naïve. Parts played by Marilyn Monroe in her films epitomized this twentieth-century myth of woman. Fiedler noted that a retreat to childishness in women has been another means of avoiding sexuality in the American novel. Scott (1970) comments on the centrality of naïveté and ignorance in the image of the Southern woman. It is this American myth of feminine passivity that many twentieth-century hysterics have adopted and live out. The catalogue of hysterical character traits Easser and Lesser (1965) culled from the literature on the hysterical character—labile emotionality, suggestibility, excitability, active engagement with the world, presentation of the self as a flighty child-woman, and dislike of the mundane and unexciting—essentially describes this stereotype. Such a self-concept permits the hysteric to experience herself as too dumb or naïve to know what people want of her and consequently allows her to avoid acknowledging to herself what she wants of them. This in turn permits her to express her feelings alloplastically. For example, by involving herself with people who are doing "exciting things" she can vicariously participate in the excitement, but in the end disavow personal responsibility for her feelings, thoughts, or acts by remembering the situation as one which she was either helplessly forced into by others owing to her passivity or fell into out of ignorance or naïveté. Depending on the nature of the individual's unique conflicts, this character style can be used to seek people and situations which promise vicarious masochistic, incestuous, sexual, or aggressive experiences.

IMPACT OF POPULAR PSYCHOLOGY ON HYSTERIA

The psychological revolution in Western culture that has taken place during this century helped to determine the new form of hysteria. Heidbreder (1933) documented the indisputable truth that the twentieth century has witnessed an unprecedented expansion, diversification, and popularization of psychological theory. The promulgation of European psychoanalysis, American behaviorism, Lewinian cognitive-motivational theory, among many approaches, all informed the individual that within him resided a psyche, the scientific study of which was revealing forces and laws not within his control. Psychoanalysis presented him with his unconscious, behaviorism with his vulnerability to conditioning by the environment, and Gestalt psychology with the laws of his perceptual and cognitive functioning. People's concern with the psyche, with its power, fragility, and with their ignorance of its laws, was reflected in the proliferation of child-rearing manuals, culminating in the sanctification of Spock's book on child care. The sense of fragility of a child's psyche and the mystery and danger of the parents were both aspects of a growing feeling that inner life was no longer strictly one's own, but behaved according to wishes and laws known only to scientists.

Just as physical disease came to be concretely explained over the course of the nineteenth century by ever more elaborate medical laws of germs and disease, so during the twentieth century has the world of feelings, thoughts, and motivations come to be experienced less as a sphere governed by conscious will and more as an autonomous agency with a will of its own. Enforcing such a sense of passivity was, to be sure, in complete contradiction to the intent of psychoanalytic theory and technique, for Freud wished through analysis of personal needs and feelings to make one the master of one's history and therefore responsible for one's future. Paradoxically, the popularization of psychological theories gave the individual the sense of being the slave and victim of his psychology.

This trend gave the hysteric a new option. Just as she had

been prey to a wandering uterus in ancient Egypt and Greece, to the power of the Devil in medieval times, and to physical disease during the Victorian era, now she could experience herself as passive in relation to *psychological* forces outside her control. For example, rather than resorting to illness and invalidism to disown, and at the same time express, say, her resentment, the hysteric could now express and disavow resentment by claiming to herself and others that "the feelings just came over me, I don't know what happened, all of a sudden I felt angry." In short, she was now the victim of her psyche, as in other times she had been at the mercy of spirits or disease. Shapiro (1965) considers this very sense of being passively overwhelmed by feelings to be central to hysterical subjective experience.

In addition to locating the source of feelings in an independently functioning psyche or unconscious, the psychological revolution has brought with it another vehicle for hysteria: the imitation of mental disease. It is becoming increasingly common for hysterics to deal in what is becoming an accepted, among some even a fashionable, way of presenting themselves—as if they were depressed or psychotic. Clinically, I have seen patients who on first contact proclaim themselves to be "crazy," "compulsive," or "manic-depressive," and behave in many ways as if they were. Such patients often turn out to be neurotic, and the meaning of the behavior they present often emerges as imitation of mental disease, either a mental disease suffered by a member of their primary family or simply one current in the culture. It is a profound irony of our culture that to be "neurotic" or "a little crazy" is not to be considered insane— indeed, such people are often regarded as "interesting." Just as aping physical disease served as a hysterical alternative for Victorian women, imitating mental disease or acting crazy is a modern hysterical option.

RECENT FORMS OF HYSTERIA

With the rapid transitions of our culture in recent years, ever new alloplastic possibilities are opening up for the hysteric. Though the dumb blonde hysteric of the first half of this century resorted to alloplastic solutions, she strove to sustain a self-image as more or less incompetent and naïve, swept along by others to carry out her own unconscious wishes. The more recent hysteric seems to be resorting to more whole-hearted externalization of her inner experience, a trend that is consistent with the individual's increasing sense of oppression from without—oppression no longer at the hands of inner prohibitions, but at the hands of social and political powers. The hysteric is consequently coming to locate the source of her problems in political and social oppression. In claiming that her society will not allow her to be fulfilled, free, or recognized as competent, rather than acknowledging the conflicts within herself that prevent satisfaction, the hysteric is making use of a mode current in contemporary culture—externalization.

This is not to say that the re-evaluation of the culture and the openness with which it is criticized are without merit, but simply to point out that turning to criticism of the ills of the society is becoming a culturally fostered response to personal discontent, anxiety, and conflict. The germ theory of the Victorian period and the psychologies of the first half of the twentieth century were valid and important scientific contributions in themselves. They nevertheless generated popular myths, myths which were finally translated into neurotic solutions by people having difficulty in managing their lives. Similarly, although much social protest is valid and necessary, the point here is that owing to its current salience the very process of protest has been recruited for the hysterical resolution of conflicts. The hysteric's loves, hates, and inhibitions are now attributed to an uncaring, corrupt society. When things now go wrong, the first impulse is to look outward, to the society, for the source. Just as Victorian culture encouraged the use of dissociation—indeed, made its use a necessity for Victorian women to preserve their sanity—externalization, that is, relocating the source of conflict in the maladies of the world, is sponsored by current cultural attitudes. For example, a myth that emerges from many radical ideologies is that hate is not innate in man, but the outgrowth of political oppression and particular economic regimes. "I do not hate, but have been made to hate by my society," then becomes a hysterical solution. A related astrological externalization runs: "I do not hate, love, act, or bear responsibility for any of these, for I am at the mercy of my stars." Hysteria is not disappearing but, owing to its most basic nature, is continually transforming itself.

DIFFERENT FORMS OF HYSTERIA AND SELF-STRUCTURE

Schafer's (1968) model of self-structure helps articulate differences among the various versions of hysteria. In his discussion of internalization, Schafer argued for the usefulness of conceiving of several boundaries within the subjective sense of self: the self-as-agent (the "I"), the self-as-object (the "me"), and the self-as-place (the physical boundaries). To oversimplify his complex model, self-as-place refers to the person's sense of his bodily boundaries, self-as-agent refers to the internal part of himself experienced as capable of active approach to the world, and self-as-object refers to the part of himself that he feels to be passively acted on. In the neurotic, which whom we are dealing here, the self-as-agent and self-as-object, viewed topologically, are spheres included within the self-as-place.

According to this structural model, all hysteria can be viewed as an attempt to remove affects, motives, and impulses from within the sphere of self-as-agent. *Where* these psychic contents are relocated in hysteria differs among persons and among cultures. When hysteria expressed itself in the form of being a victim of witchcraft, the contents were moved experientially outside of *all* the self-boundaries, including the self-as-place boundary. The impulses were assigned to the Devil or a witch, and therefore felt to originate completely outside the body boundaries.

In the conversion hysteric, psychic contents are subjectively moved from within the self-as-agent outward, but remain within the self-as-place boundary, in the form of disease, and act on the self-as-object. The early twentieth-century hysteric continued to experience her thoughts, wishes, and feelings as outside the self-as-agent and inside the self-as-place spheres, for when such a hysteric talked of being overwhelmed by her feelings she was acknowledging that they came from within her, but felt that they lay outside of her control (outside the boundary of self-as-agent). The most modern versions of hysteria, in which conflicts are flagrantly externalized onto social or political targets, on a structural level repeat aspects of self-structure characteristic of the medieval victim of witchcraft: the current hysteric, who experiences the source of her conflict to be the ills of society, is, like the witchcraft victims, locating the source of her inner experience outside the boundary of self-as-place. In short, the *way* in which the hysteric experiences the self as passive in relation to inner intentions varies with the myths of passivity and defensive styles promoted by the culture.

Turning to the nature of the intrapsychic conflicts that have led all these Western hysterics to choose the hysteria of their times, we find a variety of phallic-Oedipal conflicts. Experiencing the self as passive by the processes mentioned can be in the service of avoiding responsibility for libidinal or aggressive strivings, as well as for such partial instincts as voyeurism or exhibitionism. The passivity can be designed to bring about actual brutality, physical or verbal, in a personality with a masochistic bent, or the unconscious desires may pivot on the fantasied fulfillment of an incestuous urge such as being loved sexually by the father. In some hysterics the myth of passivity and helplessness is designed to bolster a complementary illusion of the reliability, helpfulness, strength, or omnipotence of a parent. The myth of passivity may also serve to detect and punish the self under the impact of unconscious guilt for any of these wishes. That through the ages so many theories of hysteria have considered it a disorder of the genitals and so many medical treatments of it have involved treatment of the genitals (Veith, 1965) strongly suggests that conflicts around expression of sexual, probably incestuously sexual, urges has long been a common dynamic behind hysteria. Her disease, not she, asked that her genitals be examined and treated, and she remains, in addition, protected from realizing her unconscious desire to be raped by the doctor-father by the acceptability, indeed sanctity, of medical treatment.

HYSTERIA AND THE NUCLEAR FAMILY

The transgression of taboos, in thought or symbolically in acts, has without a doubt been at the root of much neurosis throughout history. Hysteria particularly seems to be the child of taboo, for the essence of hysteria is to disown thoughts and feelings incompatible with the internalized prohibitions of the culture. The Victorian period stands as an era in which incestuous ties within the family were probably very strong, and simultaneously the taboos against feelings of all sorts were very prominent. Sirjamaki (1953) considered the late nineteenth century the era of the most rapid growth of the nuclear family, bringing with it an intensification of the emotional attachments within the family. The late nineteenth century, according to Ariès (1962), marked something of a culmination of the growing child centeredness of the family and of the growing belief that strict family discipline was vital for the child's proper socialization. Victorian parents took far more seriously than earlier parents their responsibility to communicate to the child the taboos of the culture. D. Miller (1958), writing on the changes in American child-rearing styles, noted that from 1860 to 1914 there was a continuation of direct prohibition against autoerotic activity, coupled with a far greater appreciation of the child as a distinct individual, and less allegiance to the dictum to "break the child's will" that was characteristic of child-rearing attitudes before 1860. Thus the Victorian era was one in which the child was brought into the family, given somewhat more freedom and recognition, but at the same time parents were taking even more seriously than before their duty to enforce social regulations in child rearing. The consolidation of the nuclear family, the greater child centeredness of the family, the greater freedom accorded to children, combined with older prohibitions, made Victorians ripe for conflicts over incestuous feelings — in short, ripe for Oedipal conflicts.

As M. Murphy (1965) pointed out, child rearing during the

first six or seven years was solely the mother's responsibility during the Victorian era. The Victorian child was in close, and in fantasy exclusive, contact with the mother, and distant from the father (see Erikson's [1950] description of the German family of Hitler's childhood). This led naturally to intense Oedipal conflicts in both the men and the women raised in the culture. For the boy, the mother, the primary love object, was his, and the father distant, dangerous, and idealized; for the girl the primary love object, the father, remained an idealized, superior figure whom she wished to be loved by, to emulate, and to obey. His distance promoted fantasy about him, fantasy often condemned by the internalized mores of the culture and universal taboos (superego). The distance and the consequent fantasies of his omnipotence surely added fuel to Oedipal fires. Thus the Victorian woman who became hysterical seems often to have done so in an effort to flee incestuous feelings generated by the nuclearization of the family, the distance of the father, greater acknowledgment of children, all side by side with the continuation of sexual prohibitions.

CHILD-REARING CHANGES AND
MOVEMENT TOWARD ALLOPLASTICITY

Changes in child-rearing practices also shed some light on the transition to alloplastic forms of hysteria that has taken place in the last 60 years. In contrast to current trends, child rearing during the Victorian period was marked by an emphasis on breaking the child's independence in an effort to make him conform to the will of the parent. This was essentially training for autoplasticity—training the child to alter or abandon his own inclinations if they were at odds with the environment. Following the First World War, child rearing came to encourage independence in the child. Weaning remained early (ninth or tenth month), too much cuddling was considered bad for the child, and early, firm training for adulthood was at the heart of all rules of the day. With the beginning of the twentieth century, these practices were no longer carried out only in the name of custom, but also in the awesome name of science. Exemplifying the extremes to which this training for adulthood was taken, Watson, a respected psychologist of his day, advised against kissing children, and recommended shaking hands with them instead (D. Miller, 1958). This child-rearing regime, in contrast to the Victorian, served to promote alloplastic solutions. Before the 1940's there was, according to Miller, a clear-cut distinction between what the child wants and what he needs; the former could be ignored, whereas the latter required fulfillment. With the 1940's "wants" and "needs" became equated, and the child was permitted to fulfill his desires for pure pleasure, pleasure in and for itself. Other earlier tenets of child rearing were also revised. The child could be toilet trained *too* early; those in the child's environment were to foster what is "natural" in the child; and the child's desires were to be considered more seriously and increasingly catered to. In contrast to the more authoritarian attitude of Victorian culture, when the child asserted his will, the parent now rushed, in the name of psychological health and the nurturance of the child's "natural" assets, to gratify it. The parent was encouraged to let the child set his own time for weaning and toilet training, and in general to let him pace himself. The parent was, of course, simultaneously told to "set limits." Allowing the child to choose, while at the same time setting "reasonable" limits for him, is the dilemma of the modern middle-class parent. This pattern of child rearing may lead the child to expect the world readily to conform to his wishes. The child turns first to the world outside to fulfill needs, reduce inner tension, and resolve conflicts. In short, the adult who was raised under such a regime would understandably strive to alleviate conflict by trying to force the world to conform to his wishes, and rail against it when it does not. It follows that when conflict arises it may easily be felt to be the fault of an uncaring, selfish world — that is, the conflict is externalized.

When the contemporary parent is neurotogenic, he may either push the child into action or, out of indifference, allow the child to do whatever he wishes, both consistent with the drift of child-rearing practices. In contrast, the neurotogenic parent of the Victorian period, again in harmony with his culture, excessively prohibited the child's thought, action, and impulses. Thus when things went awry between the Victorian parent and child, inhibitions and repression were most often the result, whereas when contemporary child-rearing practices miscarry, alloplastic neurotic solutions are encouraged along with autoplastic ones. These changes in the philosophy and attitudes concerning child rearing surely contribute to some degree to the growth of alloplastic forms of hysteria, and the most recent appearance of externalization as a prominent hysterical mechanism.

HYSTERIA CONTRASTED WITH OTHER SYNDROMES

Though the hysterical personality does, as we have seen, vary enormously across cultures and over time, certain structural aspects remain the same and facilitate the adoption of the culture's hysterical alternative. As implied in Freud's comments on the feminine superego, in Siegman's paper (1954) on the use of pseudo emotionality as a defense in hysteria, and even in Eysenck's (1957) experimental approach to hysteria, the hysterical superego is relatively mild, unenduring, and tied to the pressures of the immediate situation or cultural climate. The obsessional's superego endures beyond the immediate interpersonal or cultural milieu, leading him to seem rigid and out of step with the morality of his world, to be living by harsh, idiosyncratic, often anachronistic, internal standards. Loyalty to his own standards, to his own prohibitions, and to his own will are the abiding drives of the obsessional. In contrast, the hysteric's superego is far more negotiable, its demands mirroring what is current and fashionable, and its aim far more interpersonal. Where the obsessional's superego is in the service of a stubborn, self-sufficient loyalty to his will, the hysteric's superego emphasizes what will bring acceptance, praise, and love from others (Wolowitz, 1971). The obsessional is willing, indeed usually motivated, to sacrifice the support and love of those around him to what *he* knows is "right," whereas for the hysteric what is right is largely defined by what will bring the support of important objects.[2] It is this quality of the hysteric's superego which permits him to be the "spokesman" for his culture and to live out so wholeheartedly the prevalent cultural stereotypes of what is attractive, innocent, and noticed.

The obsessional differs in several other major ways from the hysteric as defined here. Though the obsessional, like the hysteric, does not become labeled insane, he fails to use cultural forms with the fluency of the hysteric. Concerned more with such inner battles as controlling thoughts and aggressive, anal-sadistic feelings by keeping his own personal order within and without, his ego strives less to be noticed and more to be average enough to be anonymous and acceptable, if not stodgy.[3] He accommodates to the culture, but fails to use the currency of the culture with the creativity, ingenuity, and flair of the hysteric.

In addition to a negotiable superego, the permeability of the hysteric's ego boundaries facilitates his weaving a cultural stereotype into the fabric of his identity. Federn (1940) described the ease with which the hysteric can enlarge his ego boundaries to include another, searching ultimately for a reunion with the nurturing and protecting parent. In contrast, the obsessional's boundaries are firm, insulating him from the ebb and flow of his culture; what he knows he adheres to rigidly, but he cannot form the transient, empathic ties with another person or with a cultural ambiance that are the hysteric's specialty. For this reason the obsessional is often socially awkward, the more so the more novel the situation, in sharp contrast to the hysteric's ease, and excitement, at finding a new stage offering new parts to learn.

---

[2] Ultimately, of course, the obsessional is attempting to gain the acceptance of some introject; the hysteric, however, owing to his tendency toward wholesale displacement of infantile feelings onto current objects, tends to look more for approval from those in his *current* life.

[3] It should be added that in situations in which he feels under pressure (real or imagined) from others, the obsessional may come to cling so stubbornly to his positions that he may be significantly out of step with others—at times to the point of taking absurd, absolutist positions in an attempt to protect his intellectual turf and to resist what he imagines to be (and unconsciously wishes to be) attempts to force him into submission.

There is a developmental difference between the obsessional and hysterical personality. In the obsessional there has been a fixation at the anal phase, followed by a regression to the anal phase usually occurring during latency. In the obsessional, therefore, conflicts are found to a significant extent at both the anal and Oedipal levels. While the hysterical personality without significant pregenital fixations or regressions therefore struggles mainly with unacceptable sexual feelings toward love objects and secondarily with hostile feelings toward competitive objects, the obsessional, with a significant anal fixation, is struggling much more with a conflict over his strong anal-sadistic strivings, magical ego attitudes toward his aggressive thoughts or wishes, and a rigid, aggressivized superego.

Probably the most important difference, which is embedded in what has been said already, is that the hysteric tries to sustain within himself a sense of passivity, whereas the obsessional tries to sustain a sense of control, responsibility, and power (Salzman, 1968). Magical thinking, undoing, and rituals are the obsessional's rituals to create an illusion opposite to that sought by the hysteric, the illusion of control. The hysteric strives to flee responsibility for his inner experience by living out a cultural myth that provides an external target to replace the sense of internal will or motive, whereas the obsessional struggles to experience all external events as pawns of his thought and will.

The last difference also distinguishes the hysteric from the paranoid character. They both externalize in the broad sense, but the stance toward the target of the externalization is vastly different. Feeling himself to be in a life and death struggle to remain superior to those who would subdue him, the paranoid is totally unaware of any passive longings, of any desire to be controlled or subdued. In contrast, there is usually some sense of pleasure in passivity for the hysteric, though there may be particular areas in which he is conflicted over passivity, such as fear of the penis and phallic intrusion, in feeling moved by powerful forces beyond conscious control (beyond the self-as-agent boundary).

Another feature of the hysterical ego that emerges from

this cross-cultural analysis is its basic strength and resiliency. The shaman or the conversion hysteric may manifest rather flagrant alterations of consciousness, transiently bizarre behavior, and at times may appear psychotic. It is probably partly for this reason that Apache shamans were considered schizophrenic before their projective-test responses were carefully examined (Boyer, 1962). However, these episodes in the hysteric prove time and again to be transient regressions, during which he seems to be having rather immediate access to primitive impulses and regressed states of consciousness, but from which he can easily bounce back. Indeed, the shaman seems to *release himself* to such transient regressions as part of his religious duties, but remains in these states for only short periods of time. He can dip back into regressive modes and like an elastic band snap back to secondary-process thought and behavior, often artfully using the regressive episode for neurotic or social ends.

Another difference between hysterical and psychotic manifestations of similar behavior concerns the precipitating factors. The psychotic is often expressing a flood of impulse or ideation which his ego lacks energy or structure to modulate or modify. The psychotic behavior can often be seen to have its roots in a highly disordered, idiosyncratic process of thought—the overt expression of a chain of internal strategies based on psychotic reconstructions of reality and psychotic forms of logic in assessing that reality. In contrast, the hysterical episode is usually more directly triggered by an immediate, conflict-laden, libidinal impulse *toward an object* in the context of good reality testing, consensual logic, and such well-developed ego defenses as repression. Once more it becomes clear how vital it is to consider *how* the ego orchestrates behavior that appears bizarre or psychotic. The ego lets the self feel overwhelmed, lets its sense of intention and willfulness be washed away through paroxysms, conversions, affect storms, depending on the prevailing myths of passivity. In contrast to the psychotic, in whom the same behavior may be a last-ditch effort to maintain a sense of self and objects and to quiet primitive panic, this behavior is but one of a variety of strategies at the disposal of the hysterical ego.

This brings us to one of the most crucial diagnostic issues involving the approach to hysteria presented here—the nature of externalization in hysteria. It may be asked if we are not describing something which might better be termed externalization or projection. The clarification of this misunderstanding goes to the very heart of the difference between the hysteric and the psychotic. The psychotic, particularly the paranoid schizophrenic, experiences a great deal of his inner impulses, thoughts, and feelings as coming from outside himself. He is certainly resorting to externalization or projection; however, psychotic externalization is qualitatively completely different from hysterical externalization. First, the psychotic is disowning much larger portions of his inner experience than the hysteric typically does. Second, the function of the externalization is totally different. The hysteric resorts to the current myths of passivity, the fashionable, acceptable targets for his externalization, in order to avoid acknowledging a particular range of feelings toward a limited group of objects. The psychotic is bent on avoiding acknowledgment of a wide range of feelings, if not all his feelings, often toward virtually any object, because his ego simply cannot maintain its integrity under the pressure of any internally recognized urges or prohibitions. While the aim of psychotic externalization is to preserve the integrity of a shaky ego, in the hysteric externalization is more selective, oriented toward particular kinds of objects and certain kinds of feelings, and far less vital to his psychic survival. Moreover, the hysteric is so much more in contact with the consensual realities of his environment that he can choose a target for his externalization that is endorsed by the culture, whereas the psychotic's rift with reality leads him to cleave to idiosyncratic targets in his pervasive externalizations.

THE HYSTERIC'S VALUE FOR THE CULTURE

Thus far the hysteric's use of his sensitivity to cultural trends in the formation of his character and symptomatic style has been stressed. If one views culture as an organic process that is continually adjusting itself in response to internal and external pressures, continually seeking homeostasis, then it may well be asked if the culture needs the hysteric. It would seem that the hysteric may indeed be vital to the culture. In living out the myths treasured by his reference group, the hysteric becomes a living advocate of the moral and stylistic positions of the culture, a "yes man" for the social axioms of his milieu. In each historical example cited, and most particularly in the European and American Victorian versions, hysterics, in the very fabric of their personalities and life plans, were continually reapplying myths carefully guarded by the culture to protect itself from the shock and depression that result from rapid social and economic change. The hysteric may contribute to cultural stability. In remaining, for psychological reasons, within the limits of convention they are a natural conservative force.

This is not to say that the hysteric simply embodies and lives out the *status quo*, for he may be something of a pacesetter, a cultural prophet oblivious to his prophecy. Though the hysteric remains within the bounds of convention, his sensitivity to the ambience of his culture makes him sensitive to emerging cultural trends just before they enter the mainstream of the social ethos. In art, sports, and popular intellectual pursuits, and even more in such visual, exhibitionistic areas as fashion, interior decorating, and cocktail-party conversation, the hysteric frequently allies himself with what is coming into vogue. Again functioning to stabilize the culture, the hysteric promotes modest, minor change that rarely challenges anything basic to the society. The changes they respond to and try to be early participants in are more often of style than of ideology, though recently in American culture the former has at times tried to pass as the latter. The hysteric, in his excitement and participation in changes of style, can help a society foster the illusion of change, promoting a sense of self-satisfaction that things are moving ahead, without really disrupting and reconstructing anything important. These changes which the hysteric is inclined to usher in need not necessarily be completely trivial. However, even if the changes have substance the hysteric will strive to embody them only if their divergence from what has come before is slight. The hysteric enjoys change, but only as he enjoys sexuality—to flirt with it, but to remain safe from it and essentially passively without responsibility for it.[4]

The hysteric will willingly be in the vanguard of change; however, the change must meet certain requirements—it must be safe, it must somehow provide a myth of passivity, and it must depart in only minor or stylistic ways from what is conventional, accepted, and appreciated by the culture. The hysteric advertises change without really participating in any fundamental social change, and the society, for better or worse, evolves that much more slowly.

CONCLUSION

Hysteria has eluded definition partly because a transcultural perspective has been neglected. Hysteria expresses itself through conventions and stereotypes so woven into the fabric of its culture that it becomes definable only when studied in several cultures.

Hysteria cannot be defined by a particular symptom picture, personality pattern, or behavior pattern, for the "content" of the hysterical solution differs radically with the nature of the culture and atmosphere of the period. Nor can hysteria be defined solely on the basis of unconscious conflicts. Hysteria is a personality constellation.

People presenting this type of personality have phallic-

[4] In my opinion, hysterics were in the late 1960's a disaster for radical movements. In the U.S. in the 1960's political activity was truly fashionable, and the political arena became very attractive to the hysterical personality. Submission to strong, charismatic political leaders and wholesale externalization of guilt onto the society, "the system," insured a reliable myth of passivity. People who 10 years before would have been found in fraternities or sororities protecting their chastity were now in political movements protecting their goodness, innocence, and righteousness. Movements that considered themselves radical drew many such people, and at rallies radical leaders could get them fired up about revolutionary issues. The leaders came to believe their followers were truly radical and would join in wholesale disruptions of society. When the leaders then tried to spur their followers to revolutionary acts, to their surprise they lost large portions of their following. It is my hunch that among those who fell away were many hysterical personalities. The call to arms of the radical leaders was for them too severe a change, departing too precipitously from what was conventional, involving the threat of *active* participation and with it the danger of true responsibility.

Oedipal conflicts, ego defenses, and an ego style that can be recognized across cultures and eras. This ego organization, which includes a sensitivity to the consensually accepted style of the culture, a capacity to know the limits of social acceptability and to regress within them, and an essential ego intactness and resiliency, mediates among the forces of id, superego, and external world by characterological patterns that draw on culturally sponsored myths. The type of resolution such people seek, one syntonic with their sense of self, is that the self be a passive object or victim of forces outside its control and not in any important respect active, doing, and responsible. In fact, however, in the various expressions of this personality constellation the unconscious, active, phallic strivings are clear in the hysteric's behavior and in its impact on the people and culture around him.

Though the psychotic, like the hysteric, may strive to disown responsibility for his wishes and use the forms of his culture in doing so, in marked contrast to the hysteric his mode of resolution is blatantly idiosyncratic, out of tune with what is recognized as within the bounds of convention, and therefore labeled insane. Central to the definition of hysteria is its conventionality, reflecting the strength of an ego that permits it to conform with accuracy and sensitivity to the demands of the environment. Though the obsessional, like the hysteric, does not become labeled insane, he differs from the hysteric in two fundamental ways: the ego maneuvers he displays—undoing, reaction formation, compartmentalization, among others—differ from hysterical mechanisms, are more readily definable and identifiable in behavior, and tend to show more cross-cultural similarity than hysterical modes; and he attempts to sustain within himself not a sense of passivity as does the hysteric, but a heightened sense of control, responsibility, and power (Salzman, 1968).

Within a culture, hysteria can be defined for immediate clinical purposes by the form it outwardly manifests (behavior pattern, symptoms, etc.) in conjunction with the dynamics that tend to generate this picture; but from a theoretical standpoint, in the development of more scientific study of psychopathology, hysteria has to be defined as a metapsychological concept whose study must include historical and cross-cultural perspectives. It can be generally defined only by the nature of the drives, the nature of the ego, the process by which the ego uses cultural forms, the position of the hysteric in the culture, and the over-all aim of the hysterical mechanism.

In the next and final chapter, the historical and cross-cultural perspectives on hysteria will be integrated with the provisional definition presented at the conclusion of Chapter 2. With this as a foundation a comprehensive definition of the hysterical personality and neurosis will be presented, and then illustrated with two cases.

5

COMPREHENSIVE DEFINITION
AND CASE ILLUSTRATION

In this final chapter I will attempt to synthesize a definition and description of hysteria by drawing on common elements in the previous accounts of the syndrome and the
aspects that endure across cultures and eras. This description
is meant to be an ideal type, a point of reference for clinical
diagnosis. It is not to be taken as a rigid set of criteria into
which to force actual patients and their emotional difficulties.

For this diagnostic description to be of real use, it must be
recognized that diagnosis is a complex process that demands
the assessment of many areas of functioning. People are
simply too complicated to be categorized according to a
simple, superficial check list of traits. To diagnose a patient
as hysterical on the basis of flirtatiousness, coquettishness,
and the presence of nonorganic somatic complaints is to
make just such a meaningless, misleading assessment. For
diagnosis to be an effective clinical guide, unconscious
conflicts, ego structure, specific defenses, character style, and
the extent of intrapsychic and interpersonal conflict must be
systematically examined and re-examined throughout contact with the patient. Such data should then be assessed using
common psychological configurations as reference points.

Though the description of hysteria presented here is drawn
from the work of many authors discussed earlier, it is
impossible to specify the contributions of specific authors;
consequently, specific citations will not be given.

DEFINITION OF TERMS: HYSTERICAL PERSONALITY, HYSTERIA, HYSTERICAL CHARACTER

Hysterical personality is defined as a personality configuration and does not imply the presence of psychopathology. It is simply a personality type with characteristic ego style, defenses, cognitive structure, superego structure, and interpersonal modes. It also denotes the attainment of a particular level of psychosexual and psychosocial development.

Hysterical neurosis or hysteria refers to conflicts and symptoms of neurotic turmoil within the hysterical personality. Symptoms may range from conversion symptoms to maladaptive, unconsciously directed patterns of life choices. Whether circumscribed or more global, the symptom must be essentially ego dystonic: that is, it must be recognized as maladaptive and there must be a resultant wish for it to be alleviated or altered. Conversion hysteria refers to a form of hysteria in which physical symptoms are a direct outgrowth of neurotic conflict within a hysterical personality. Conversion symptoms, however, can exist in many types of personalities. Anxiety hysteria (phobia) refers to another form of hysteria in which the neurotic conflict within a hysterical personality takes the form of a fearful attitude toward a specific stimulus. Once again, it should be remembered that phobias exist in many types of personalities.

Hysterical character refers to a hysterical personality in which the expression of unconscious conflict has become indistinguishable from basic attitudes and coping modes, and is ego syntonic: that is, such traits, attitudes, and action patterns are not considered by the conscious ego to be the source of serious difficulty or in need of change.

DRIVE DEVELOPMENT AND POINT OF MAJOR FIXATION

The hysterical personality has traversed the pregenital stages of libidinal and aggressive development generally successfully. There are no extensive pregenital arrests in libidinal, aggressive, or narcissistic development or massive regressions to pregenital periods during later infantile development. Though there may be some libidinal fixation at pregenital stages and transient regression to oral and anal fixations, neurotic conflict, when it occurs, results primarily from fixation at the phallic-Oedipal level and regressive and defensive attempts to flee from such conflicts. The unconscious wishes that produce neurotic conflict involve classical, triangular, Oedipal rivalries. The conflicts revolve around forbidden or frightening wishes toward incestuous objects (infantile perception and experience of parents). Although the specific nature of the intrapsychic conflict varies widely in individual cases of hysteria, the unconscious wishes in the male hysteric involve to a significant extent sexual longing for the mother and fear of retaliation and castration from the father for such fantasies. In the male hysteric there is also commonly a negative Oedipal conflict, involving an unconscious wish to replace mother vis-à-vis father. The competitive, rivalrous, and murderous wishes toward the father are also conflictual because the father is an object of love in his own right. In female hysterics, the unconscious wish involves a phallic-Oedipal fantasy of being penetrated phallicly by the father, obtaining a penis-child from him, and finally replacing the mother. Connected with such wishes are the fear of losing the mother's positive regard, fear of retaliation from her, and finally, fear of the destructive power imputed to the phallus. In both the male and female situation there is, in addition, an unconscious fear that the opposite-sexed parent will be displaced, that the imagined sexual act will be frightening, and that damage either to the self or to the object will result. In contrast to the phallic-narcissistic personality or other patients with phallic, immediately pre-Oedipal fixations, the hysteric is primarily concerned with the exclusive libidinal possession of the incestuous object.

EXTENT OF CONFLICT IN HYSTERIA

When the hysterical personality manifests neurotic, ego-dystonic conflict and thus becomes a case of true "hysteria," the impact of the conflict is limited to particular areas of life activity. By definition, many areas of functioning should remain intact. The major conflicts might show themselves in work situations, while the capacity for recreation is little affected. Or work relationships might be virtually free of neurotic conflicts, while heterosexual relationships are conflictual. The expressions of neurotic conflict are often painful and disruptive, but essential capacities for caring for oneself in a generally independent fashion endure. In short, the hysterical personality is sufficiently intact so that neurotic conflict does not massively disrupt its functioning. Libidinal development has progressed to the phallic-Oedipal period and ego development too has been substantial and solid.

HYSTERICAL EGO

The ego of the hysterical personality has undergone substantial development during early life. Though certain ego capacities are inhibited and others are hypertrophied, the ego structure is not seriously distorted. In its healthiest form, it could be considered one of several normal or "well-adapting" ego configurations; when not taxed by neurotic conflict, this sort of ego can function consistently and smoothly in many areas. (The capacities of the ego reflect, along with the extent of libidinal development, over-all psychological development.)

It should be remembered that though the ego is being described separately from drive development, in actuality their development and operation within the adult hysterical personality are intimately related. The case presented at the conclusion of this chapter will more clearly illustrate the interactions of id, ego, and superego in the hysterical personality.

For purposes of discussion the hysterical ego will be divided into cognitive style, ego style, ego structure, affective experience, prime defenses, nature of relationships, experience of objects, superego structure, and relationships with social reality.

COGNITIVE STYLE

Fundamentally, the hysterical personality is capable of solid secondary-process thinking. There is, however, during crises and in affect-laden situations, a tendency to turn away from the basically logical, cause-and-effect mode of thinking. In these contexts, the hysterical personality is prone to think in vague, impressionistic ways, tending toward global, intuitive (not necessarily accurate) approaches to the problems of the moment. At these times events are remembered through the veil of affects experienced during them and are therefore often distorted. At moments of crisis or in such affectively loaded situations as sexual encounters, the hysterical personality feels a dislike for ordinary, logical approaches to problem solving, experiencing them as dull and commonplace.

Even when cognition is clear in the hysterical personality, it is seldom rich in verbal ideation or freewheeling fantasy. Cognitive style dovetails with the predominance of repression as a defense to produce diminished, stereotyped verbal thinking. Though the hysteric is often remarkably sensitive to style and fashion, the truly creative use of fantasy necessary for artistic pursuits is seldom present. If true creativity is present in such personalities, it is usually in nonverbal realms, such as the visual arts or music.

EGO STYLE

The hysterical personality is characterized by a use of passivity to disguise, inhibit, and disown personal resources and accomplishments. Identity is often formed around implicit myths of one's own passivity in relation to pressures and powers outside of his control. The self-images the hysteric draws on change with the culture. This characteristic of the hysteric has contributed to the definitional confusion surrounding the syndrome, for the hysterical personality, like a mirror, reflects the current cultural forms and changes with them, often in substantial ways. Active, assertive strivings are disguised from others and the self through use of a currently accepted social role or stereotype. Others are usually surprised at the capacities actually possessed by the hysterical personality, for his own myths about himself suggest helplessness and childishness.

In affectively neutral situations, external reality is generally accurately, though conventionally, perceived. In conflictual situations, however, reality is distorted by unconscious wishes. What is inconsistent with the unconscious fantasy of a wished-for libidinal object, for example, may simply not be recognized or acknowledged.

While unconscious fantasy is to some extent continually distorting people and events, there is a dearth of free conscious fantasy and ideation. The hysterical personality has difficulty anticipating future interpersonal situations because he is unable to use fantasy, daydream, or playful thinking for anticipating the future or for substitute gratification.

The hysterical personality is oriented toward maintaining the approval of parental-Oedipal objects. He is particularly sensitive to what will be pleasing, flattering, and gratifying to others. The wish for approval and to be pleasing leads the hysteric to be very ready to alter and amend the self. But though the hysteric quickly picks up the atmosphere or ambience of a situation and seems to alter himself in accord with it, in actuality he often exerts very substantial control over the situation. The hysteric and those in the environment often do not recognize the power he is subtly wielding.

EGO STRUCTURE

There is a basic strength to the hysterical personality's ego. It is differentiated and generally functions smoothly. Though neurotic behavior and symptoms may be guided by unconscious wishes transformed by the primary process, conscious thought is predominantly of a secondary-process sort.

The hysterical personality has basically well-established synthetic and integrative ego capacities; a capacity for delay and planning is also firmly rooted. These capacities, like others, are often unavailable in anxiety states or affect storms. Nevertheless, the hysterical personality is, when it is absolutely necessary, capable of recruiting enough ego control, even in the midst of crisis, to permit basic independent life functioning.

Though the hysteric often appears to be flamboyant and whimsical, such positions are guided by ego activity and do not reflect a loss of ego control of impulses. The hysterical personality may seem to be without inner capacity to control, channel, and direct impulses. In fact, the ego capacities are remarkably well established. Here again, the hysterical personality maintains a self-image that is out of keeping with his actual ego resources.

AFFECTIVE EXPERIENCE

The hysterical personality avoids the direct public expression of urges and impulses. Affects are internally engineered by the unconscious ego to be those acceptable in a given situation, to test the interpersonal climate, to ascertain how others will respond. Those affects that are called for socially are dramatized or expressed in an exaggerated fashion. For example, if there has been a death or a tragedy, the hysterical personality tends to be aware of in himself, and to express, only sadness, the culture's morally "right" reaction. Though the hysteric seems to be spontaneous and expressive, affects and affective expression are often invoked defensively, commonly substituting for other affects or for more direct, basic, but impolite versions of themselves.

In the hysterical personality, affects may cloud or color experience and interfere transiently with accurate perception of objects. But, like fantasy, these affects are not rich, plentiful, or easily accessible to consciousness. The hysterical personality is readily responsive to what is pleasing or displeasing to others, and can invoke a set of stereotyped affective experiences in response to needs to maintain attachment to parental Oedipal substitutes, but lacks depth and richness of subjective feelings. Emotions are not *necessarily* phony or "put on," but simply emerge in consciousness in a narrow, shallow form. It is the unconscious ego, not conscious will, that produces affects designed to draw approval and love.

PRIME DEFENSES

The hysterical personality is inclined toward defenses of "not knowing," "not seeing," and "not recognizing": repression, blocking, dissociation (and more subtle mild dissociative trends), and hysterical denial. Hysterical denial involves only some aspects of a situation and is not as massive as denial that originates earlier in development.

Another dominant hysterical defense is displacement. As the hysterical personality is commonly struggling to establish a fantasy tie to an incestuous object while avoiding the intrafamilial taboos and imagined retaliations, displacement is an understandable defense. An object is sought that has the qualities of or is in some way associated with the original tabooed object, and infantile longings are then played out more safely with this object.

Though these defenses predominate, the hysterical personality, by virtue of his advanced psychosexual development, has potential access to defenses of earlier psychosexual stages more or less successfully traversed. At moments of severe stress, he may regress to an oral dependence, and, to a lesser extent, to a stubborn, anal, willful stance. Moreover, virtually all hysterical personalities have inherited and integrated necessary reaction formations from the anal stage. It has been noted that such reaction formations are an important factor in making the "true hysteric" analyzable (Zetzel, 1968).

To avoid loss of love, the hysterical personality employs a defense variously described as living vicariously, having a pseudo self, idealizing and clinging to objects, and enlarging ego (self-) boundaries to include a libidinal object. These are the many sides of the hysterical tendency toward identificatory experience. The hysterical personality tends to mold himself around his partner, to live through him, to change on the surface, to be pleasing, decorative, or attractive to him. There is a fear that direct experience, experience which is not checked against the object's reaction, will entail the risk of losing the object's love, being replaced as the "special" or "best" person in the eyes of the object, or being physically hurt by objects.

NATURE OF RELATIONSHIPS

The hysterical personality has problems with relationships, but is generally capable of forming and maintaining them. The extent of his difficulties is directly related to the amount of intimacy or sexual responsiveness demanded by the partner. The hysterical personality does not have difficulty beginning relationships — indeed, may have unusual facility in doing so. Nor are his relationships always brief and chaotic; many are long-standing.

When the hysterical personality suffers from neurotic conflict (hysteria), his difficulties are often in the area of object choices and the enduring harmony of the relationship. The hysterical patient expects relationships to conform to unconscious, infantile, fairy-tale images of love and romance and grows depressed and angry when the object fails to measure up to his fantasies. There is often a phase during which the hysteric, through hysterical denial, dissociation, and narrowed, wish-fulfilling cognition, manages not to see aspects of the object that do not correspond to the fantasy. With time, the object's reality becomes undeniable, and its lack of congruence with the infantile images causes disappointment and often subsequent conflict within the relationship (this is in contrast to people with less capacity for accurate experience of objects, who may never see aspects of objects that deviate from their fixed fantasies about them [Brodey, 1965]).

The hysterical personality lives through objects, often resulting in the object's feeling that he is living for two people, which he commonly grows to resent. The hysteric tends to identify himself transiently with the goals and values of those he is involved with. At times, via an attachment to an object, his superego is modified and compromised by the object's moral and ethical attitudes.

PERCEPTION OF OTHERS

Object representations are basically stable, relatively differentiated, and multifaceted. Object images are not fluid or diminished, as are those of borderline personalities. Again, in contrast to the borderline personality, objects are ambivalently regarded, not split into highly idealized or utterly demeaned images. While objects are idealized as part of the hysterical personality's attempts to sustain the illusion that an infantile object has at last been found, there is *fundamentally* a rich spectrum of object representations which, in appropriate intrapsychic circumstances, are accessible to the ego. Though the hysterical personality may misperceive objects as judgmental or all-protecting, he is capable of relatively realistic perception of them and maintains a basic sense of trust in many of them.

SUPEREGO STRUCTURE

While the hysterical personality's superego has a basic integrity, it is neither rigid nor uncompromising. It can in many ways be amended and altered in accord with what is pleasing to significant objects or in accord with an infantile fantasy of parental values. The hysterical personality can sustain an illusion that responsibility and accountability have been turned over to a significant object.

The hysterical personality can externalize superego pressure in a particular way: by appealing to convention, precedent, and the example of others, he characteristically rationalizes morally questionable behavior with "They all do it, so why not me?" Whereas the obsessive might cling subbornly to a highly specific, personally defined set of commandments, the hysteric often strives to find an excuse to unburden himself of such internal superego pressure. To do this, he often attaches himself to someone who will enforce moral restraints. The hysterical personality will try to skirt his parent-moralizers' mandates, but at the same time will say, "He (she) is good for me." The superego is neither defective nor primitive. Rather, an effort is made to locate it outside the self by coercing an object to purvey and enforce the superego's commandments, which are then, with pouting and teasing assent, conformed to. Keeping the superego at a distance is characteristic of the hysterical ego.

RELATIONSHIP TO SOCIAL REALITY

The hysterical personality has often been difficult to identify because a most basic mechanism of this character style involves its own transformation. The hysterical personality is sensitive to what is currently in vogue in fashions, style, and interpersonal patterns, and to what is soon to be "in" in these spheres. He responds to social and cultural atmospheres and draws on popular social myths to build images and myths of himself. In order to establish the ego's preferred stance of pseudo passivity in relation to a powerful, protecting object, the hysterical personality draws on popular ideas which place the self at the mercy of uncontrollable forces. At different times these ideas have been religious forces, the power of one's own uncontrollable id, the immutable power of political forces, and the power of the stars. As the hysterical personality's identity is to a large extent composed of popular stereotypes, it shifts with cultural and social changes, and may appear on the surface to be totally different in another culture or subculture. Consequently, the hysterical personality cannot possibly be defined on the basis of obvious, surface aspects of behavior or symptoms. Rather, his very conventionality must be considered a basic defining feature. Though it probably makes little sense to approach the diagnosis of any type of personality configuration or psychopathology on the basis of surface behavior, it is particularly misleading to do so with the hysterical personality.

THE HYSTERICAL PERSONALITY'S SELF-FULFILLING
EXPECTATIONS OF OTHERS

The hysterical personality's need to engineer relationships which are congruent with infantile paradigms (both wished-for relationships and, via the repetition compulsion, feared or distasteful relationships) often leads him to a narrow assortment of *actual* relationships with other people. Consciously and unconsciously, he chooses people who promise either to fulfill an infantile wish or to repeat traumatic infantile relationships (in the hope that they will turn out better this time) and then endeavors to see and respond to those aspects of the other that confirm the infantile wish or memory. His capacity subtly to coerce the object (often chosen for his coercibility) to repeat the wish or memory leaves the hysterical personality unaware of other relationship possibilities and further confirms a neurotic conception of others. The hysterical personality thus experiences only neurotically distorted relationships, and his neurotic preconceptions become even more solidified. He will come to feel, for example, that "all men are unreliable" or that "all women seem annoyed with me," etc. His proclivity to externalize, to place responsibility and blame on the object, and to see the self as helpless in the face of such inexorable realities is reaffirmed.

The hysterical personality chooses certain types of objects and unconsciously quite forcibly encourages certain responses from them—more so than does the obsessive personality, who tends toward inhibition and cognitive control and less toward actual control and manipulation of those in his environment. If the obsessive is to maintain a fixed, stereotyped, neurotically preconceived image of others, he must defensively rationalize or deny what he is exposed to in others, whereas the hysterical personality may subtly coerce reality to behave as he wishes it to. Consequently, in the psychotherapy of hysterical personality, it is crucial to help him understand the regular, expectable impact he is having on interpersonal situations.

HYSTERICAL DISTORTION: WISHES AND FEARS

The hysterical personality's distortions have been illustrated predominantly by noting the wish-fulfilling, "rose-colored-glasses" aspects of his cognitive style. Distortions may also involve an expectation that objects will behave in unreliable, cold, or hostile ways. The hysterical personality will commonly see certain objects as repeating what were experienced (often via projection or externalization) as the negative characteristics of infantile objects. These negative expectations, like the wish-fulfilling, fairy-talelike ones, are usually patterned on unconscious memories of specific objects, or memories of wishes or fears in relation to them. As these expectations are the product of a relatively late period of fixation, including a basically intact ego structure, they tend to be infantile, but should be distinguished from the primitive, malevolent, and omnipotent expectations of objects which the borderline personality consciously maintains. When these distortions are pointed out to the hysterical personality, he can reflect on them. The borderline, by contrast, maintains his more primitive, less differentiated, much more inhuman expectations of objects as conscious convictions.

THE DEFENSIVE FANTASY OF INNOCENCE

The seemingly "oral" aspects of the hysterical personality are often, it seems to me, not an expression of libidinal fixation or regression, but rather a defensive *fantasy*, one designed to bolster denials of sexually exciting events and repression of sexual feelings. While proclaiming a wish for a "close, warm, open and understanding relationship with a soft, sensitive man," the hysterical personality can avoid recognizing the sexually exciting and gratifying features of the relationship. Consistent with the hysterical personality's capacity to resonate with the accepted and stylish social currents, he will describe the relationship in terms so automatically accepted as conforming to wholesome contemporary values that the defensive aspect of the image is often difficult to discern. Currently the hysterical personality is seeking relationships characterized by total "frankness, honesty, and openness." This standard is so contemporary that the diagnostician or therapist may overlook its function, particularly the erotic wishes it serves to exclude. Neither the cultural currency nor the oral quality of the content of the hysterical personality's fantasies of objects should obscure their defensive function. If these fantasies are assessed as having a true oral base, and interpretations are geared toward the presumed underlying oral conflicts, the defensive structure of the hysteric will often be bolstered, for the fantasy of himself as a little child with conflicts about feeding and being cared for is ego syntonic. This fantasy of passive, childlike innocence also serves to avoid the aggressive and self-destructive potential of relationships with others. This trusting, "innocent" expectation of objects is often part of an unconscious attempt to draw punishment from or act aggressively with the admired object. Standards and personal judgment are suspended and turned over to the object, who is then magically considered responsible for whatever happens. This permits the hysterical personality tabooed experiences but often it also has built-in punishment for these pleasures.

THE MYTH OF PASSIVITY DISTINGUISHED FROM
PRIMITIVE FORMS OF EXTERNALIZATION

Basic to the definition of the hysterical personality presented here is his maintenance of an ego-syntonic illusion of helplessness and passivity in relation to forces outside his control. This process needs to be more fully explored and differentiated from other forms of externalization and projection which are not characteristically hysterical. On such a distinction rests such crucial diagnostic differences as that between the hysterical defensive use of an illusion of passivity, paranoid projection, and borderline externalization.

The myth of passivity is characterized by several basic features. (1) The person has a sense of external pressures that "force" him to act in a certain fashion or to feel certain affects. (The power may be located in another person, in social or family pressure, or in part of himself over which he feels no control, e.g., "My feelings are making me do things I don't wish to.") (2) The process by which this external influence acts on the self is left vague—that is, the steps by which it occurs are often not thought about or questioned. (3) However, if the person is forced to spell out the process, he will rationalize it and not view it consciously as a magical influence on the self. (4) He may "blame" the external world for an action that worked out badly, but there is a general feeling of comfort and acceptance of the imagined pressure and of his helplessness vis-à-vis the object. The anger at the object will be for giving bad advice, poor guidance, or ineffective coercion, not for the coercive or patronizing behavior itself. (5) The stance toward the object is unconsciously experienced as some version of loving protection and/or sexual penetration by the object. (6) The motives of the object are left quite comfortably vague, global, and diffuse.

These features reflect basic aspects of the hysterical ego and libidinal constellations. The hysteric's tendency to see objects as protecting parents is obvious. There is, as well, the hysteric's tendency to see phallic-genital wishes as located in the object, not in the "innocent" self. The fantasy of participating in a vicarious, identificatory way in the power of the object is also apparent. The hysterical personality's "foggy" consciousness and the mild dissociative current in his cognition shows itself in the absence of clear and careful questioning of the process by which the self is influenced. This is not magical thinking, for there is very little conscious cognition; rather, there is a diffusion of attention, a retreat from logic, and an alteration of consciousness. There is little self-consciousness or shame about this vague, illogical mode of thought; rather, it is experienced as innocent, feminine (in women), castrated (in men), and its harmless, childish quality is felt to be alluring to the infantile objects (the parents).

Paranoid projection differs from this in many fundamental respects. The projected forces are usually aggressive, malevolent, and murderous. They are feared and avoided by the self. There is a heightened attention to the environment (in contrast to hysterical vagueness, dissociative tendencies, and foggy cognition). There is an increase in highly complex, pseudological thinking about the external forces in an attempt to seek refuge from them or control over them. When pressed, the paranoid person often cannot, as can the hysteric, view these forces realistically; his attempts to explain the external forces reflect defects in reality testing and in thinking. Finally, the imagined forces themselves are projections of relatively more primitive, pregenital impulses (impulses to eat, to kill sadistically, or to humiliate), whereas for the hysterical personality the imagined external forces are of a phallic-Oedipal nature, including relatively less ambivalently split, more modulated, and more fused libidinal and aggressive impulses.

The externalization in borderlines is also very different from the hysterical myth of passivity. The borderline externalizes larger aspects of the self, often leading to a sense of self-fragmentation and fluidity. He tends even more flagrantly than the paranoid to project highly infantile and/or primitively sadistic wishes onto others and to fear that these wishes will be turned toward, and annihilate, the self. Most important, the externalizations of the borderline are often but a part of mutual introjection and projection that comprises an experience of objects as incompletely separated from the self, as if they could still magically and omnipotently soothe the self or destroy it, as if they were inside the self. By suspending judgment and by attempting to deny his experience of boundaries between himself and love objects, the hysterical personality can maintain the *illusion* that the object can give power to the self, leading, for example, to a sense that the object is the source of disowned sexual and aggressive wishes. There remains, however, an enduring distinction between self and object images.

These primitive forms of externalization must also be distinguished from hysterical phobic patterns. In the hysteric phobic avoidance of the feared stimulus is sufficient to relieve anxiety, whereas in the paranoid or borderline the object of these primitive projections must be controlled, manipulated, subdued, etc. This often leads to a strong, deeply ambivalent tie to the object in which the person tries time and again to quell his own projected wishes or change his own "bad" self. This latter pattern involves, in essence, a projective identification, whereas the former is characterized more simply by projection of wishes followed by avoidance. To state the point slightly differently, in the hysterical phobic it is wishes (phallic, Oedipal loves and hates) that are projected (and usually also displaced), whereas in the more primitive personality self-fragments along with wishes and impulses are located in the object.

THOUGHT, ACTION, SUPEREGO, AND EGO PROCESSES: STRUCTURAL CONSIDERATIONS IN HYSTERICAL SYMPTOM FORMATION

As has been described, the hysterical personality can engineer situations to bring pleasure (and punishment) without recognizing his own role in bringing about the situations in which he then "finds" himself. The nature of the hysterical ego and superego facilitates major life actions and choices whose roots are completely obscured from the patient's consciousness. Let us briefly explore these structural dimensions and their interaction.

The ego of the hysterical personality shows extensive repression of impulses, superego contents, anxiety and other affects, along with a cognitive style that tends to turn away from rational thought about relationships as an activitiy considered cold, rote, and uninteresting. Rational thinking about relationships is sometimes experienced by the hysterical personality as too masculine and therefore even more unacceptable. This leads to a dearth of consciously avowed, verbally organized standards. At the same time, the hysterical ego shows a tendency to express conflicts in *nonverbal, nonthinking channels*. The major channels are the motor and somatic systems. Via action, dissociated or unconscious strivings are expressed. Many symptoms of the hysterical neurotic manifest this trend: conversion hysterics have no conscious memory of the core conflicts or traumas, little conscious anxiety about their symptoms, and a somatic symptom (conversion or hysterical attack). In some more modern versions, the hysterical personality expresses unconscious fantasies using larger, more extended action patterns. Impulses and superego prohibitions are not conscious and patterns of action (conversion symptom or stereotyped relationship pattern) express the unconscious fantasy and the punishment for it. Guilt as an affect is not intensely felt; instead, the actions themselves serve a self-punishing function. The hysterical ego, then, by its inclination to action, disdain for thought and planning, and tendency to repress superego contents, plays out conflicts in *action*, such as object choice, relationship pattern, phobic avoidance, or somatic symptoms, depending partly on the social context. The hysterical personality's world of conscious and preconscious thought, ideas, and reflections tends to be shallow, whereas his world of unconscious fantasy is rich, and regularly expressed through action channels. His dearth of conscious ideation allows him to disown responsibility for the forbidden wishes that are being regularly lived out in relationships. Moreover, this restricted ideation, at the behest of the punitive side of the superego, often serves to engineer situations that substantially endanger the self or entail needless suffering and discontent.

The repression of the superego contents and the continuing intrapsychic need to inflict punishment on the self often lead the hysterical personality to view self-defeating and self-destructive behavior as a "mistake," "accident," or error, unintended on any level, with no implication for the self.

This review reflects the hysterical personality's tendency to view himself and others in terms of his current and overt action, and to overlook the possible unsavory or objectionable motives in the self or others that might lie behind. This buttresses his need to defeat himself, for he learns little about his personal motives and conflicts from his difficulties. Feelings of guilt or conscious struggle are often not painful enough to motivate change or serious inspection of behavior. Feelings of guilt or a sense of danger are superego-triggered affects that can be most adaptive and self-protecting. When these feelings are bypassed, as is often the case in the hysterical personality, self-destructive behavior may take their place. This pattern was most probably being observed in the "*belle indifférence*" of the nineteenth-century conversion hysteric.

The essence of the hysterical personality is a tendency to express (especially in neurotic contexts) unconscious fantasies and conflicts in action or inhibition of action (usually involving objects), rather than in thought. Paralysis, phobic avoidance, a tendency to show and exhibit, to accept and trust the overt and obvious in others, hysterical body language, and concern with the appearance of the body, all reflect a heightened cathexis of the sphere of the ego that perceives, cognizes, and responds to active, overt, interpersonal, and mundane areas of experience. Blurred perception, foggy cognition, a disdain for synthesizing thought about relationships, pseudo stupidity, reflect the complementary hysterical tendency to avoid recognizing internal fantasies, wishes, and instinctual urges. This all might be termed repression, and indeed to a significant degree it involves repression, but more than that it is a composite of several dimensions: it is a repressive ego style, a reflection of a self-image built around a myth of a beautiful, stupid woman-child and a consciousness that is narrow, shallow, and bound up more with action channels than with opportunities for guiding and self-regulating thought and feeling.

These dimensions can be more clearly focused by comparing the obsessional's use of thought with the hysterical personality's use of action.

HYSTERICAL ACTION VERSUS
OBSESSIONAL COGNITIVE "TRIAL" ACTION

A central difference between the obsessional and hysterical personalities lies in their access to and use of thought and action. The hysterical ego makes more ready use of action, whereas the obsessional ego automatically resorts to thought and rumination. The hysterical personality experiments with new situations and new people through active commerce with them. A prime hysterical mode involves rushing, sometimes dramatically, into new situations and sizing up the new people by their responses to his actions. The hysterical personality seems at these times to be "pushy" or "demanding," and others often feel coerced, cajoled, or teased. The hysterical personality judges others by their reaction to himself. This does not necessarily imply that hysterical personalities are self-centered, narcissistic, or crave attention; rather, these behaviors reflect an *ego mode* oriented toward getting to know the object. This trend makes general sense of behavior commonly observed in hysterical personalities. They tend toward "acting out" conflicts and are often described as extraverted, flamboyant, or lively. The hysterical access to action and the complementing dearth of thought (particularly in emotionally charged situations) lead him to play out an intrapsychic conflict in a wholesale way in his choice of sexual partner, stance toward the partner, or behavior in social situations.

The trend being described is part and parcel of the hysterical personality's tendency to manifest transference longings clearly and intensely. The tendency toward action, toward reliving and recreating infantile conflicts in current relationships, leads the hysterical personality in psychotherapy toward experientially immediate longings for the psychotherapist—that is, transference longings. This tendency may at times pose special problems, for when this "acting in" (transference) is not interpreted effectively by the therapist, the hysterical personality is more likely to act out these conflicts with people outside the psychotherapy.

By contrast, the ego mode of the obsessional personality tends more toward thought, control, and inhibition of action. The obsessional experiments less with action and relies more on thought in the face of life tasks. He considers and reconsiders, delays and rehearses, doubts and weighs. When he considers a plan, he strives to take into account all possible outcomes. If any eventuality is omitted, the obsessional fears he will be surprised by it and be left helpless, foolish, or humiliated. The obsessional experiences action, even relatively minor acts, as committing, defining, and unchangeable. He often remembers his acts in detail, and ruminates later about his performance and others' reactions to it. In contrast, the hysterical personality views his actions more "experimentally" and much less seriously; like much that he experiences, they can be quickly forgotten, by being suppressed, repressed, and dissociated. In psychotherapy, the obsessional presents a much more muted, diffuse experience of conscious and preconscious transference wishes or derivatives of these wishes. He meets the experience of such wishes with rationalization and compartmentalization.

The two personality types are also distinguished by the nature of their self-observation. The hysterical personality has the capacity for self-observation, but does not automatically use it. Often, indeed, he depends on an object (at times a therapist) to encourage him to question his actions, consider their consequences, and evaluate their aims. He lives in his experiencing ego and tends to resist systematic observation of his behavior, particularly around exciting and conflictual heterosexual situations. The obsessional, in contrast, is prone to survey and monitor his behavior continually in order to handle his fears (and fend off his wishes) that he will make a mess, be seen as childish, or be out of control. In some obsessionals, this reflection on the self becomes so pervasive that little is experienced as spontaneous or enjoyable, and everything is instead experienced as production or accomplishment. The obsessional's self-observation is in the service of the superego, whereas the hysteric's self-observation, halting and resistant though it is, is more in the service of the ego.

PSYCHODIAGNOSTIC TESTING

Psychological testing remains a useful approach to the diagnosis of hysterical personality and neurosis. The contributions by Rapaport, Gill, and Schafer (1968) and Schafer (1948, 1954) continue to be the best and most systematic, projective-test indices of hysterical personality. (See Chapter 2, pp. 74-83, for a complete review of this material.)

At this point a few additional diagnostic-test dimensions and indices necessary for the diagnosis of hysterical personality will be mentioned. The hysterical personality is distinguished from more primitive, borderline (particularly infantile) personalities on the basis of the status of passivity, the integration and differentiation of object representations, the nature of impulse control, the nature of dominant drive energies (oral, anal or phallic-Oedipal), and related ego states. Projective tests, including the more recently devised Early Memories Test (Mayman, 1968), permit these areas to be effectively tapped. The Early Memories Test (in which the patient is asked to give a set of memories from his early life) provides memories that are viewed not as history, but as expessing the nature of internalized relationship paradigms, including dominant and subsidiary affect states, action modes, and ego orientations. The memories are interpreted by the diagnostician with an eye to the variety-narrowness, richness-specificity, warmth-coldness, subtlety-bluntness of the images of self and other, the sense of contact with the objects in the memories, the psychosexual and psychosocial modality of the interaction, among other dimensions. This test is essential for distinguishing higher-level neurotic personalities, such as the hysterical, from more primitive personalities. The former present an image of objects that have certain features: (a) there is an essential affective contact with the object, (b) images of the object reflect somewhat modulated, ambivalent strivings toward it, (c) there is some variety to the objects remembered, (d) to some extent objects are seen in terms of their own needs, not merely in terms of how they can fulfill the needs of the self.

The early memories of borderline personalities are very different in these respects: (a) the ties with objects are either very tenuous or highly conflictual, (b) a sense of the imminent loss of the object, or of its malevolence, is ever-present, (c) a pessimistic ominousness surrounds the object and the events, (d) objects are viewed in rigid, stereotyped fashion, only to the extent that they meet or frustrate the needs of the self, *or* split into "all good" or "all bad" images, (e) the interactions in the memories are generally character-zied by a primitive, brutal quality or a magical, unreal sense of ecstasy, or both.

A diagnosis of hysterical personality rests on establishing that the self- and object representations are relatively enduring and differentiated. (They may, of course, be defensively narrowed and restricted, but the test as a whole should reflect the presence of more integrated and whole images of objects.) This is not sufficient for the diagnosis, but it is a *necessary* condition, and one that can be investigated in the Early Memories Test.

In addition to this basic distinction between the hysterical personality and more disturbed personalities, the former regularly shows certain other patterns on the Early Memories Test (and analogous patterns on the TAT). (a) The memories are stereotyped, often resembling corny, maudlin movies, but the remembered objects retain an essential realness and from time to time a real depth. (b) The memories have an overnice, nonconflictual quality. Too much works out too well, there is little ambiguity or uncertainty, and people are viewed in excessively altruistic terms. (c) The self is seen as helped, guided, taught, and praised by a strong, helpful parent. As the patient tells them, these memories bring a sense of comfort and security, at times even excitement. Independent, autonomous activity usually appears as well, but these memories are less pleasantly related, often formally more disjointed, and end less happily. (d) There are often triangular Oedipal themes that the patient, in relating the memory, is totally unaware of. (e) In hysterical personalities where repression is rigid, the memories may be sparse and few, and reported with blocking and hesitation; in many hysterical personalities this repressive pressure shows itself in lack of insight into the implications of the memory and in pollyanna-ish, if not sparse, memories.

THE HYSTERICAL EGO AND PHALLIC-OEDIPAL CONFLICTS

Though in portions of this monograph hysterical ego processes have been discussed independently of unconscious conflicts, these ego processes are inseparable from the conflicts diagnostic of hysterical personality. The hysterical personality presents fixations at the phallic-Oedipal stage. These fixations date to a period of development when verbal and secondary-process thinking are firmly established, and consequently wishes toward the infantile objects at this stage are organized into relatively coherent, verbally encoded thoughts. In comparison to earlier points in development, at the phallic-Oedipal stage object images are relatively differentiated, enduring, and consistent. The wishes toward objects are laid down in memories which include an image of an object and the self, both with many specific qualities. This internal object image is patterned on the unique traits of an infantile object, in contrast to the rudimentary and interchangeable internal object images which result from much more primitive, cognitively and intellectually simpler experience of objects characteristic of earlier points in development. There is also, by the phallic-Oedipal period, a greater capacity for complex fantasy and ideation than was present earlier. Thus there is sufficient psychic structure and cognitive "equipment" to imagine some rather complex, perverse, and incestuous relationships with relatively stably perceived infantile objects, to fantasize the consequences of such wishes, and to remember them both.

In order to ward off wishes occurring in this stably encoded, highly differentiated form, new defenses and defensive styles must develop. These defenses must function to avoid such mental contents, to cast them in their entirety out of awareness. Repression is the prime defense, for it relegates a whole complex of thoughts to the unconscious. Alterations of consciousness (hysterical vagueness, inattention to details, and dissociation) also serve to avoid thoughts in the preconscious and to render vague and unclear thoughts in the conscious. The search for the "happy idea" (Sullivan, 1956) is another defense which has as its goal the replacement of an unwelcome sexual or aggressive thought by a global, affectively positive, idea. Maintenance of a myth of passivity serves to avoid the recognition that any wishes are the responsibility of the self. The differentiation of object representations, and the capacity to pretend or imagine oneself in the role of another, also make transient identification another way of escaping one's wishes and fears.

In sum, the phallic-Oedipal libidinal fixation, characterized by enduring, complex wishes toward well-discriminated and differentiated self- and object images, is met with an equally differentiated cognitive-defensive style which is capable of excluding complex, verbally represented wishes from consciousness. Indeed, and most important, it is the same differentiated ego that produces the wishes in this form as strives to fend them off. Though, of course, ego processes developed during the anal period, such as reaction formation, magical thinking, and doing and undoing, play some role in the ego operation of the hysterical personality, the primacy of strictly secondary-process thinking makes such defensive techniques increasingly inadequate to the demands of the phallic-Oedipal period.

HYSTERICAL PERSONALITY AND THE OEDIPUS COMPLEX

The predominance of Oedipal conflicts and the attendant ego and superego processes and tendencies remain basic to the definition of the hysterical personality. The structure of the Oedipal period of development and its relationship to the hysterical personality and hysterical neurosis has been left until last because it involves the most detailed study, not because it is in any way less important than the other features.

It would be to invite the same confusions and limitations of definition if the presence or absence of Oedipal fantasies was used as the *sole* defining feature of the hysterical personality. Oedipal conflicts are considered a necessary but not sufficient condition for the diagnosis of hysterical personality and hysterical neurosis. Moreover, these conflicts must be considered not simply in terms of the content of the fantasies, but in terms of ego development, object relations, and drive development characteristic of the Oedipal phase, for the hysterical personality reflects the phase-specific functioning in all these areas.

The Oedipus complex really refers to a whole set of intrapsychic urges and prohibitions, both libidinal and aggressive, both narcissistic and object directed. It refers to a developmental phase as well as to a constellation of conflicts and structures in the adult. This "complex" of fantasies, urges, and fears has a different theoretical status from the unfolding of the instinctual drives (oral, anal, and phallic) in the id or the development of the ego. It is neither a structure nor a function, neither a single unconscious fantasy nor a defense. It is a *complex*, and one which involves such intricate

relationships of fantasies, drives, prohibitions, and identifications that it can best be described by a poetic image drawn
from Sophocles' drama, *Oedipus Rex*.

The Oedipus complex refers to a constellation of many fantasies as they interact and conflict, and as they are resolved or
unresolved during development. It involves drive development, object relations, fantasies, behavioral modalities, and
ego accomplishments. It may seem at first easy to define, but
this appearance is deceiving. Attempts to define it give one the
feeling of trying to survey something from many vantage
points without capturing its essence directly. Let us content
ourselves, then, with these various partial views.

The easiest aspects of the Oedipus complex to define are the
basic sexual and aggressive fantasies toward the parents which
arise during development and emerge later in the psychoanalysis of adults. In the boy, phallic instinctual drives are
turned toward the mother, and the father is experienced as a
rival who is interfering with and potentially retaliative for the
exclusive sexual relationship the boy seeks with the mother.
The father is a competitor for the mother and there are death
wishes toward him, yet these are mingled with the boy's loving
feelings for the father. The boy's realization that there are castrated people, women and girls, leads him to fear retaliation
for his fantasies of doing something sexual with his penis to his
mother. He fears castration from the father (and, to a much
lesser extent, from the mother in normal development) and
the loss of the love of both parents. Beyond retaliation from
the father, the little boy's death wishes conflict with his wish to
maintain the father, for he is an important libidinal object in
his own right.

Under the pressure of castration anxiety and anxiety about
loss of love, the boy suspends his sexual interest in the mother,
represses the phallic-sexual fantasies toward her, identifies
with the father, and internalizes the restrictions and limitations of his relationships with parents (and others), forming
the first cohesive and reliable superego content.[1] The *external*

---

[1] Consistent with Hartmann and Loewenstein's (1962) view, the superego is
seen to coalesce as the Oedipus complex is resolved or partially resolved. (Earlier

circumstances that forced the child to set aside the phallic-sexual feelings toward the mother are, in normal development, replaced by internal standards, controls, prohibitions—many modeled on the parents themselves.

Owing to the child's essential bisexuality there is also within the boy a network of negative Oedipal fantasies: the fantasy of playing the mother's part with the father and experiencing the mother as the competitor. Whether the negative or positive Oedipal complex predominates will strongly influence later personality development and later potential psychopathology. Freud illustrated the positive Oedipus complex most clearly in the case of an infantile anxiety hysteria (phobia), "Little Hans," whose fear of horses involved the displacement of his fear of his father's retaliation for his phallic-sexual wishes. The libidinal strivings toward the father were secondarily present, and served to render more conflictual his death wishes toward his father. Freud illustrated the negative Oedipus complex in his case of the Wolf Man, whose *primary* psychic conflict involved his wish to be penetrated by the father.[2]

The negative Oedipal wishes lead to conflict arising from virtually the same source as the positive Oedipal wishes: to play the feminine part in a relationship with the father necessitates being a woman and losing the penis. It also means risking the mother's retaliatory withdrawal of her love. Thus in both cases a narcissistic cathexis of a body part, the penis, comes into conflict with the cathexis of a parental object. To insure the safety of the penis and the maintenance of parental love, and upon the realization that Oedipal wishes cannot possibly be fulfilled, the object cathexes are replaced by identifications and libidinal trends become desexualized, sublimated, partially inhibited, and transformed into affection. This paves the way for the latency period, which is characterized by the development of channels for sublimated energies.

In very skeletal form, this is the nature of the Oedipal stage

superegolike functions are viewed as genetic determinants of the superego.) This constitutes the ego-superego-ego-ideal system that is essential for psychic integrity.

[2] This patient, of course, can now be seen probably not to have been neurotic, but the case is still a good illustration of negative Oedipal fantasies.

for the boy. The nature of the Oedipal stage and of resulting Oedipal conflicts in girls is much more complex and, until recently, has been less well understood. As hysterical personality seems to occur somewhat more often in women, it is of utmost importance that the female Oedipal phase be examined in detail.

FEMALE OEDIPAL-PHASE DEVELOPMENT

Though Freud originally viewed the development of the girl's Oedipus complex as a mirror image of the boy's development, it became apparent that the female pattern was both more complex and more obscure. The girl must, during development, change her primary sexual object from the mother to the father and the leading erogenous zone from the clitoris to the vagina. The girl was seen as entering the phallic period, much like the boy, with the mother as the object of her phallic strivings. This was considered in early psychoanalysis to be either a pre-Oedipal phase or part of the Oedipal phase proper (Freud, 1931; Lampl-de Groot, 1927). Following Nagera (1975), it will be considered here as part of the Oedipal phase, for the strivings are phallic, the genitals are the leading erogenous zone, and the dominant sexual fantasies involve a triangle consisting of a love object, the self, and a rival object.

The question of possession of or lack of a penis and other sexual insignia is a concern for the girl as well as for the boy during the Oedipal phase. When the girl discovers that there are people with penises, she assumes all people have, will have, or have had a penis, and develops fantasies that she will grow one, has one hidden, or had one that was lost. As it becomes clear to her that she does not have one or has lost it, she turns in anger from the mother, who is blamed for not giving her the penis (or for taking it away), toward the father to give her the penis and/or a baby as a substitute. There ensues rivalry and competition with the mother for an exclusive relationship with the father.

A clarifying study of female sexuality and the Oedipus complex has recently been made by Nagera (1975). He points

up the confusions in the literature concerning the female
Oedipus complex and female sexuality and, drawing on
both psychoanalytic observation of children and the psychoanalysis of adults, delineates more clearly than others
previously the vicissitudes of female Oedipal conflicts. The
theoretical perspectives afforded by this work have important
implications for the psychoanalytic understanding of the
Oedipal conflicts in the hysterical personality.

Nagera conceptualizes two substages within the female
Oedipal phase. During the first stage, called the phallic-
Oedipal stage, the little girl's sexuality is predominantly
phallic, masculine, and she tends to seek the mother as the
primary object and to view the father as a rival. During the
second stage in normal development, there is a shift on many
levels (to be discussed below) resulting in a passive, feminine
orientation, with the father as the primary sexual object.

Thus far, this is a clarifying systematization of the
dominant psychoanalytic thinking. Nagera's real contribution is to discriminate several constellations in each of these
two stages, pointing up the importance of considering the
interaction of the unfolding infantile sexuality and the choice
of primary libidinal object. In the first stage, the normal
dominant constellation involves intense cathexis of the
clitoris, active masculine sexuality (a wish to penetrate)
directed toward the mother, and an attitude of rivalry with
the father. This is termed *positive complex first stage*. As
part of the girl's bisexuality, there is a secondary,
less-cathected constellation which draws on the feminine
component of the girl's sexuality. In this constellation the
father is the primary object and the sexuality is passive-
feminine. In normal development, this is a secondary,
less-cathected constellation and is called the *negative
complex first stage*. In addition, still within the first stage of
the female Oedipus complex, there is an abnormal
constellation, called the *inverted complex first stage*, in
which there is a strong cathexis of the father as love object
from a masculine position, with the mother as the rival. Thus
the negative complex refers to a normal, secondary cathexis
of the father with a feminine element of the girl's bisexual

potential, while the first stage inverted complex, which also takes the father as the primary object, does so on the basis of the *masculine* side of the girl's bisexual potential. Moreover, the cathexis of the inverted complex, when it exists, is much stronger than the more normal, mild negative complex. This stands to reason, for the active phallic strivings (based on clitoridal erogeneity) are phase dominant, which makes the active-masculine cathexis of either parental object intense and the female sexual stance toward either subsidiary. According to Nagera, the first stage of the Oedipal phase, in contrast to the pregenital phases (oral and anal), has certain characteristic ego, behavioral, and object-relational aspects. There are advances in ego development, a greater interest in the father, less primitively ambivalent, sadomasochistic, controlling-controlled aspects in the relationship with the mother, and an interest in a highly charged, triangular relationship emerges. Ego interests in the phallic phase, first stage, are turned toward the phase-dominant zone, the genitals, and increasingly away from anal processes and the ego interests attendant on them. Sexual "researches" become a prime ego interest and theories concerning the absence of the penis or its later appearance develop. These "researches" may be interfered with by the presence of especially strong penis envy (or pregenital fixations).

The second stage of the female Oedipal phase in normal development is characterized by shifts in several areas. The father replaces the mother as the primary sexual object (mother becomes rival), clitoridal erogeneity is abandoned or suppressed, there is a shift from a masculine to a feminine position on the level of sexual and ego development, some ego acceptance of the absence of the penis emerges, and acceptance of substitutes for it (babies). There are changes in the ideas of intercourse, and the beginnings of a feminine identification. The feminine bisexual components are now predominant, the father is the object of most intense cathexis, and fantasies of sexual contact and play patterns become altered by identification. This pattern is termed *positive second stage* (Oedipal) *complex*. The normal, less cathected pole of the child's sexuality is the *negative second*

stage (Oedipal) *complex* in which the mother is the object
and is approached from a masculine position. As with the
previous stage, Nagera stresses that in normal development
there must be shifts in *both* the dominant sexual position and
the choice of the sexual object. Through suppression of the
masculine fantasies associated with clitoridal masturbation,
including repression or renunciation of active-masculine ego
modes, and the ego acceptance of the absence of the penis
and its comfort with substitutes for it, the shift into the
second stage of the female Oedipal stage is accomplished.
Going beyond previous authors, Nagera sees the shift in
choice of object as only part of the essential shift in the
Oedipal phase. There must be shifts on several dimensions,
especially object choice and sexual orientation. When one of
these two shifts either fails to occur or takes place in a distorted fashion, one of the vicissitudes of the second stage may
come to predominate (the negative or inverted second stage
complex) and have specific neurotic consequences.

Nagera emphasizes that the nature of the dominant
Oedipal (second stage) or phallic-Oedipal (first stage) constellation must be defined if the patient's neurotic conflicts
are to be fully understood. In this *inverted, second stage* constellation the dominant sexual position is a feminine, passive
one with ego beliefs and interests consistent with the feminine
interests of the stage. The aberration in this constellation lies
in the object of these strivings being the mother (the mother
which the ego at this stage knows does not possess a phallus).
The objects, which Freud had early realized are more loosely
attached to the drive than its source or aim, are altered in
this constellation. This alteration commonly occurs if the
girl's sexual overtures to the father are rejected, if fear of
murderous, competitive feelings toward the mother becomes
too intense, or if the father's seductiveness is frightening to
the girl. In these cases the feminine position is maintained,
but a defensive shift of object takes place, from the father to
the mother. If the shift to an inverted position is complete
the outcome may be a homosexual object choice (with the
self playing a feminine role) in adulthood. When the shift is
less complete and transient, it constitutes one of several con-

stellations seen in the hysterical personality, to be discussed below.

There are, then, three positions, "normal," "negative," and "inverted," for each of the two stages. Each position, in addition to including the masculine or feminine mode of impulse discharge, also comprehends the economic, qualitative factors, such as which object and which sexual position receives the dominant cathexis, and which the secondary cathexis. A diagram constructed by Nagera (Figure 1) clearly presents the six positions that constitute the two phases of the female Oedipus complex.

The diagram indicates by capitalization and the number of pluses and minuses the object in each constellation which receives strong or weak cathexis, be it of a positive or negative sort. The size of the sexual symbols reflects the dominant sexual position of the drives (masculine or feminine).

This more differentiated approach helps us to isolate more precisely the nature of fixations or regressions in female psychopathology. Fixation can occur at one of the positions of the first or second stage. A regression to one or several previous stages, or from stage two to one, may occur during development. Moreover, partial fixation at the first stage may interfere with a complete movement to the second stage, resulting in a mixed clinical picture in which aspects of stages one and two appear together. The nature of these fixations and regressions of course depends on rate of ego development, object relations, and other areas. This clarification of development permits a more systematic assessment of several dimensions of personality seen in both children and adults: the dominant sexual position (including dominant erotogenic zone and dominant ego modes), the choice of objects, and the relative intensity of the cathexis of various objects. It permits a more accurate clinical assessment of women who in fantasy or reality choose women as primary sexual objects. If there has been a true fixation or regression to stage one, then the clinical picture is characterized by the predominance of active-masculine approaches to the mother, by ego attitudes of a similar nature, and by

	FIRST STAGE PHALLIC-OEDIPAL		SECOND STAGE OEDIPAL	
	Positive	*Inverted*	*Positive*	*Inverted*
	MOTHER + + + FATHER – – – (a)	FATHER + + + MOTHER – – – (e)	FATHER + + + MOTHER – – – (b)	MOTHER + + + FATHER – – – (f)
	Negative father + mother – (c)		*Negative* mother + father – (d)	

Figure 1

Nagera's Diagram of the Female Oedipus Complex

ego beliefs such as the existence of the hidden maternal penis. If the woman shows, rather, an inclination to play a passive, feminine role with the female object, seems to have established some feminine identification with the mother, and shows ego beliefs and attitudes that bear the marks of the second stage, then a true regression has not occurred; rather, an inverted second-stage constellation has consolidated. These two types of patients will present some very different unconscious fantasies and conflicts, and interpretive efforts with them should take into account the differences in their psychosexual orientation.

For another example, the typology permits better discrimination among intrapsychic conflicts in female patients who choose men as the primary love object. The nature of the patient's fantasies, sexual conflicts, and ego attitudes will differ according to whether the object is approached from a predominantly masculine (first-stage) or feminine (second-stage) position, or from a combination of the two positions. Of course, in many cases several of these constellations appear as partial fixations or regressions. In some cases, the conflict between the wishes, fears, and attitudes of the two constellations may be the central psychopathological conflict presented by the patient.

Nagera also views the unfolding of these two stages on the levels of ego and id in the context of earlier fixations. A fixation at, say, the first stage of the Oedipal phase may be a result of anal fixations which led to a belief that intercourse with a man, from a feminine position, would be demeaning, endangering, killing or profoundly painful. A fixation at the positive first-stage constellation may then be a likely result.

OEDIPAL CONFLICTS IN FEMALE HYSTERICAL NEUROTICS

Core Oedipal conflicts in the female hysterical personality can be considered by reference to the recent theoretical contributions of Nagera described above. With this theory, it is possible to say more than that the hysterical woman presents an "Oedipal fixation" or "Oedipal conflict." The more precise description of the phallic-Oedipal conflicts offered by this theory permits better understanding of which fixations are universal to the hysterical personality, indeed partly definitional of it, and which others account for the variations among different hysterical personalities.

The hysterical personality presents, whether in conflictual or nonconflictual forms, a strong cathexis of the Oedipal father, a wish to replace the mother in her relationship with him, and a wish for a penis-baby from the father. Both the sexuality and the ego modes of the hysterical personality are of a predominantly passive-feminine sort. While this represents the predominant position on the level of ego, drive, and object relations in hysterical women, other sexual modes (such as unconscious masculine strivings) and other objects (the mother as opposed to the father) and other images of the self (as a man rather than as a woman) may also be present and in conflict with the dominant position.

This dominant Oedipal constellation just described is the positive second stage of the female Oedipal phase in Nagera's framework (cell b, Figure 1). This constellation, involving a shift to a feminine position, temporary suppression of active-masculine aspects of clitoridal sexuality, a shift to the father as the primary object of sexual impulses, some ego knowledge of the absence of a penis in women, and the emergence of identifications with the mother, is the point of major fixation in the hysterical personality and hysterical neurotic. In some hysterical personalities there is no substantial fixation at or regression during development to the first stage of the Oedipal phase or pregenital phases (oral or anal phase). In these personalities object choices and potential neurotic conflicts revolve around the continued cathexis of the infantile Oedipal object. There is in such personalities an inability to shift cathexis from the father primarily and the mother (via the negative complex) secondarily to the nonincestuous object. In his object choices the person looks repeatedly for a parent, predominantly a father, not a husband or lover. If this pattern has spilled over into other areas, employers, friends, and even passing acquaintances are unconsciously expected to conform to the unconscious infantile images of the father or mother. The search for the

Oedipal object may express itself in a pattern of repeated disappointment in men and sexual difficulties with them, or in less conflictual form as a wish-fulfilling assumption that the object really is like the infantile Oedipal object. This kind of wish-fulfilling assumption about the object, however, may lead to an ignoring of aspects of the object which the person ought realistically and self-protectively to be wary of. The need to see the object in these terms, along with the hysterical equation of naïveté and femininity, is a basic ingredient in the psychology of hysterical gullibility. This type of fixation has implications for ego beliefs, for there is a fixation on rather dichotomous and rigid ego beliefs about what is characteristically masculine and feminine, ideas that are formed at the height of the Oedipal "researches" concerning the differences between the sexes. This contributes to the hyperfeminine behavior presented by the hysterical female and the hypermasculine behavior she expects from her partner.

This fixation may be due to vulnerabilities introduced by a particularly conflictual oral- or anal-stage development, by the inherent intensity of the Oedipal conflict, or by environmental conditions that interfere with the integration of these sexual strivings. An excessively gratifying or frustrating relationship with the father, a coldness experienced in him to sexual and affectionate overtures, an internal or external interference with the processes of identification with the mother, or actual loss by death or divorce of the father or mother, are all potent factors in promoting this sort of fixation.

This, then, is the common denominator of the Oedipal constellation in the female hysterical personality. In many (perhaps most) female hysterical personalities and neurotics there are one or more partial fixations at or regressions to the first stage of the female Oedipal phase and, to a substantially smaller degree, to the anal or oral phases. These partial fixations or regressions help to explain the variations in conflicts among patients whose character structures are hysterical (by the definition described here) and whose conflicts are, generally speaking, "Oedipal."

The basic variations are the following: (1) fixation exclusively at positive Oedipal (second stage), with little or no fixation or regression to phallic-Oedipal (stage one) (cell b, Figure 1), (2) dominant fixation at positive Oedipal position (stage two), with a secondary partial fixation at or regression during development to positive phallic-Oedipal (stage one) position (cell b, primary fixation, and cell a, secondary fixation), (3) dominant fixation at positive Oedipal position (stage two), with a secondary partial fixation at or regression during development to inverted phallic-Oedipal position (stage one) (primary fixation in cell b, secondary in cell e), (4) dominant fixation at positive Oedipal position (stage two) alongside of which exists a secondary fixation to the inverted Oedipal position (stage two) (this is not a true regression as is a shift from stage two to stage one) (primary fixation at cell b, and secondary at cell f).

Each of these variations has specific characterological and symptomatic consequences in adult hysterical women. Examples of these will be sketched.

1. Fixation at positive Oedipal stage (stage two).

The conflicts here devolve from the unconscious search for the Oedipal father, the wish for a baby from him, murderous, rivalrous feelings toward the Oedipal mother, all in the context of unconscious Oedipal-phase "theories" of sexual intercourse, childbirth, etc. There is often narcissistic injury at the father's preference for the mother. Some neurotic consequences of this pattern: (a) a compulsive need to get or be pregnant; (b) hysterical somatic difficulties that express the unconscious, infantile theories of intercourse or childbirth (for example, *globus hystericus* as an expression of a fellatio fantasy involving an infantile theory of conception through the mouth); (c) fear of the size or destructiveness of the penis, fear that it will rip or hurt (often exacerbated by witnessing parental intercourse or by anal conflicts), leading to sexual inhibitions, phobias, or frigidity, or, in some cases, choice of objects unconsciously experienced as castrated (e.g., impotent men); (d) unconscious attempts to find idealized father substitutes with an unconscious expectation that they will give the magic penis-baby, an expectation that is either buttressed by hysterical denials, foggy cognition, etc., or is repeatedly disappointed. These men are experienced as larger than life, to duplicate the infantile awe of the size of the father's penis, his accomplishments, and his power; (e) a tendency to become involved with much older men; (f) a tendency to "find oneself" in triangular relationships, in competition with older women (e.g., continually becoming involved with married men and being very interested in being compared by the man with his wife); (g) a pattern of intense, bitter competition with particular women (derivatives of death wishes toward the mother) leading to difficulties in relationships with women, and also guilt over or fear of retaliation from these women for these wishes. This leads the person at times to a chronic expectation that other women will be condemning or suspicious of her; (h) many relationships are unconsciously experienced as incestuous and, if the guilt over Oedipal wishes is strong, sexual excitement with the object must be repressed and the whole relationship may have to be subverted and include much suffering. Objects may be chosen, out of flight from the unconscious incestuous meaning of romantic ties, to be as different as possible from the father, while they often turn out to resemble him in many ways.

2. Fixation primarily at positive Oedipal (stage two), with secondary partial fixation at, or regression to, positive phallic-Oedipal (stage one) position (cells b and a, Figure 1).

Here the neurotic problems in (1) above are potentially present. In addition, there are potential conflicts and characterological compromises between the dominant psychosexual position of a feminine, passive stance toward the father as the primary object and a secondary phallic-masculine position with the mother of the first Oedipal phase as the object. This type of secondary fixation has a wide variety of potential neurotic consequences, involving both the unconscious sexual theories about the primary libidinal object (father or mother) and the nature of the internal drives and ego stance toward the object (phallic-masculine or feminine). Furthermore, this constellation presents a clinical picture in which ego orientations of the phallic-Oedipal and Oedipal periods are found side by side. Thus, for example, the patient may at times clearly be operating on a strong unconscious assumption that she has a hidden penis and that all people are endowed with the same genitals (consistent with the phallic-Oedipal stage) and at other times or in other interpersonal contexts evince a greater acceptance of the lack of a penis and a greater acceptance of her femininity (consistent with the second stage of the Oedipal phase). Similarly, with some objects or in certain circumstances a feminine attitude in sexual relations is acceptable, while in others a masculine position is sought and the feminine position scorned. A prime conflict for this type of personality involves deep ambivalence toward men, for the man, equated unconsciously with the infantile father, is alternately considered a rival of the phallic-Oedipal stage (first stage) or the love object of the Oedipal stage (second stage).

A few illustrations of some potential neurotic outcomes of this: (a) potential neurotic outcomes discussed under (1) above; (b) intense ambivalence about being a woman, often involving resentment toward "feminine women" and the self; (c) exaggerated overt feminine behavior and appearance disguising unconscious masculine trends (e.g., under the guise of ingenuousness and hyperfemininity, the woman is actually very competitive with men); (d) choice of men involved with other women, with a special interest in being known by the women (the fantasy life of such patients often betrays the unconscious phallic-Oedipal strivings toward the mother); (e) a tendency to behave in a very feminine fashion with men and more assertively and/or protectively with women; (f) choice of an object which is experienced in different aspects as both masculine and feminine (e.g., a man who outside of the home has an air of bravado, but privately is dependent on women to look after him in a most infantile way); love objects must have traits that are associated by the person with the infantile images of both parents; (g) intense conflicts about activity and passivity, particularly in the sexual sphere, leading to a tendency to be, for example, seductive with men and then aggressive, controlling, and rejecting of them.

This pattern commonly presents itself as a partial fixation

in hysterical women. The intense conflicts about sexual identity, the hyperfeminine behavior masking strong masculine strivings, and the existence side by side of beliefs in the hidden phallus and a magical fantasy of receiving it from the father are often observed as central to hysterical conflicts. The hysterical personality also shows this dual fixation in many areas by presenting an ego "style" characteristic of the positive Oedipal position while at the same time presenting unconscious rivalrous feelings with men, particularly for the attention of other women. This contributes significantly to the hysterical pseudo passivity and the defenses described in this paper as "myths of passivity."

3. Dominant fixation at positive Oedipal position (stage two), with a secondary partial fixation at, or regression during development to, inverted phallic-Oedipal position (stage one) (primary fixation in cell b, secondary in cell e).

Here, in addition to the conflicts described in (1), there is a secondary set of conflicts revolving around a masculine-phallic stance toward the father. The primary object in these two constellations is the father; however, the stance toward him is an alternation between or combination of masculine and feminine trends. As in (2) above, the ego beliefs in a hidden female penis and awareness of lack of this penis may exist side by side. Also similar to (2), there are often special contexts in which feminine strivings predominate and others in which masculine strivings predominate. The major difference between this combination of fixations and the dual fixations of (2) is that on both the phallic-Oedipal (stage one) and Oedipal (stage two) levels the *father* is the primary object. The internal images of the nature of the relationship with the father as expressed in later relationships shows wishes to love him at certain times or in certain contexts both as another man (or boy) and as a woman (or girl).

Some neurotic consequences of this : (a) the consequences described in (1) above; (b) beyond expecting men to be like the father, there are attempts to establish a relationship with men in which the self is viewed both as the man's little girl and his little boy; (c) an especially intense competitiveness with other women, competing with them with the internal image of the self as a superior man and as a competing woman; this often leads to difficulties in identifying with women and thus particularly strong fixations at both the first and second stages of the Oedipal phase; (d) an especially strong death wish toward the mother, leading to substantial unconscious guilt and to actual difficulties relating to women; (e) an enjoyment in relating to men as "one of the guys"; women who maintain an essentially feminine position with their husbands and children in the home situation but relate to other men in a "tomboyish" fashion present a less conflictual resolution of this dual fixation; (f) a conflict, as in (2), about being active or passive in relation to men; (g) a feeling of being in meaningful contact only when with men, a need to relate only to men, a feeling of boredom, discontent, or contempt for women.

4. Dominant fixation at the positive Oedipal position (stage two) alongside of which exists a secondary fixation at the inverted Oedipal position (stage two) (not true regression, but two constellations at the same stage). (Cells b and f, Figure 1).

In this constellation stage one has been superseded relatively completely by stage two. The feminine position has been established more firmly than in (2) and (3) above. The only difference from constellation (1) above is that here there is a secondary fixation at the inverted Oedipal position in which the mother is the love object and father the rival. The woman here has given up the first stage of phallic-Oedipal belief in the universal existence of the penis, has suppressed the masculine component of clitoridal sexuality, and has turned to a major degree to the father from a feminine position. The secondary fixation in the inverted position involves a shift from father to mother. Fear of the mother's retaliation for Oedipal wishes toward the father, fear of the phallus, the actual loss of the father (or mother), are several possible causes of this secondary fixation.

Some neurotic consequences of this : (a) the consequences outlined in (1); (b) a turning toward women as safer, less threatening, than men; (c) a submissive, at times apologetic, attitude toward women, especially following competitive wishes toward them; (d) absence of masculine strivings and penis envy as central neurotic conflicts; feminine position is somewhat more acceptable than in other constellations.

A special word needs to be added concerning this constellation, for it is my impression that it is often misread as indicating an oral fixation. The woman's attachment to the mother from a feminine position is often viewed as a passive dependence whose roots are considered to lie in the oral phase of psychosexual development. While this phase may in some respects resemble such oral dependency, the dynamics, the level of ego development, etc., are entirely different. It may be that some limited oral conflicts have facilitated the development of the inverted Oedipal position (stage two), but the fixation is essentially an Oedipal one.

Pregenital components may be seen in any of these paradigms. Developmental conflicts during the oral or anal phases in some cases tend to promote fixation at these Oedipal stages. For example, unresolved anal conflicts may lead the child at the Oedipal phase, second stage, to view intercourse as a sadistic, aggressive, and humiliating event. This may lead to a greater fear of the feminine position and a fear of the penis, leading then to a fixation at a positive position of the Oedipal phase (stage two) or regression to the "safety" of the positive phallic-Oedipal stage one (phallic position vis-à-vis mother). The presence of unconscious fellatio fantasies commonly seen in hysterical conflicts is another example of the role of pregenital components in the unconscious fantasy and wishes of the hysterical personality. Fellatio fantasies, which are often associated with Oedipal-phase beliefs in oral conception, may have some strictly oral components. While these components are present, the diagnostician must appreciate the vast qualitative differences between this minimal oral fixation and the more pervasive oral arrests or regressions seen in borderline or severely depressive personalities. The hysterical personality does not show the pervasive regression of libido and deformation of the ego seen in obsessional neurosis or in the more severe character psychopathologies. Pregenital conflicts are always present in neurotics, but the major libidinal fixation in hysterical personalities is at the positive Oedipal (second stage) position.[3]

It should be noted that though the positive Oedipal position is the most "normal" Oedipal constellation developmentally, a fixation at and regression to this stage often has severe neurotic consequences for the adult. Though a feminine position has been adopted and the father has been taken as the object, identification with the mother may be rudimentary, and shifts from intrafamilial love objects to nonincestuous ones are incomplete. Full sexual responsiveness is often hampered as well.

Why, it might be asked, cannot the hysterical personality be fixated at the positive or inverted *stage one* position? The answer is simply that such a fixation tends to yield a personality style and set of neurotic conflicts inconsistent with the hysterical personality. A woman with a fixation at stage one (positive or inverted position) has an overtly and deliberately masculine approach, including at times a conscious wish to be a man. Such a woman is not inclined to resort to the defensive strategy involving an illusion of passivity in relation to internal states and external events which is an essential hysterical ego mode. The overt masculine identification seen in such women leads them to be overtly aggressive, intrusive, critical, and very self-sufficient, all inconsistent with characteristic hysterical ego modes and preferred modes of self-presentation. Moreover, in the case of the positive first stage fixation, the woman may well choose a woman as the primary love object, while the hysterical woman chooses men (albeit ambivalently) as primary love objects.

THE PHALLIC ATTACHMENT TO THE MOTHER
IN FEMALE HYSTERICAL PERSONALITY

A long-standing debate about the genesis of hysteria in women concerns the nature of the libidinal fixation. Some

---

[3] The nature of the anal regressive material in the psychotherapy of a male hysterical personality is illustrated below.

consider the basic point of fixation to be oral, others consider it to be phallic-Oedipal, without significant drive regression. The latter was Freud's position, and he considered it one essential difference between hysteria and obsessive-compulsive neurosis. Clinically, one can see what those who claim an oral genesis for the disorder are responding to. The hysterical personality expresses the wish for warm, close, nonsexual, "dependent" relationships with men and women. They seek "tenderness" in relationships and are often disappointed when relationships do not include it. This is often read as an expression of oral wishes; these wishes are, however, open to an entirely different interpretation. Though the wishes are for a dependent, tender tie, the lack of the intense, desperate craving which characterizes truly oral-libidinal fixation suggests that these wishes reflect a *fantasy* of such a tie, which refers to a different point of psychosexual development.

Could it be that in many cases the wishes for such a tie in hysterical women express a phallic wish toward the mother resulting from the first portion of the feminine Oedipal phase? The longing for the mother may not express a wish for the pregenital mother, but rather a wish for both active and passive *phallic* contact with the mother merged with defenses against these phallic wishes.

OEDIPAL CONFLICTS IN MALE HYSTERICAL NEUROTICS

In the male, the Oedipus complex is brought to an end in part out of fear of the father and his castrating potential. In women the Oedipus complex is ushered in by the recognition of her penislessness. While both hysterical men and women seek to displace the parent (either in the negative or positive Oedipal constellation), the neurotic conflicts in men are more concerned with protecting the body from imagined injury that would result from the retaliation from the parents (usually the father, sometimes the mother as well). The hysterical neurosis in men consequently revolves around neurotic compromises designed to symbolically hide, avoid, or repent phallic wishes in order to insure safety from and love of the father. Thus both male and female hysterical personalities are unconsciously seeking incestuous objects of the Oedipal phase, but the male hysterical neurotic's conflicts center more on the fear of castration and retaliation, and the female hysterical neurotic's conflicts emphasize more the attempt to transform and alter the self in order to please the object.

In the male hysterical personality, the unconscious fantasy is to engage in some infantile construction of phallic-sexual intercourse with the mother. Again, as in women, the nature of the infantile sexual theories during childhood determines the nature of the unconscious neurotic fantasy. Basic to the neurotic struggles of the male hysterical personality is his unconscious search for the Oedipal mother. As castration fear is so much more prominent in the hysterical difficulties of men, the conflicts are determined as much by fear of the father and the superego as by search for the Oedipal mother. Choice of objects, the nature of heterosexual relationships, and neurotic symptoms all express both the unconscious libidinal wishes for the mother and the inhibition of phallic-genital and competitive urges.

The possible consequences of this neurotic complex are many. The following will serve as illustrations:

1. Heterosexual objects are unconsciously equated with the mother. Often these objects must be experienced consciously as completely unlike, indeed diametrically opposed to, the mother.

2. The illusion may be maintained that the woman, not the self, initiated, and is therefore "responsible" for, sexual contact.

3. In sexual activity, the self acts in a way unconsciously considered "feminine."

4. Sexual inhibitions, including impotence, may be present.

5. Work inhibitions may exist as unconscious punishment for phallic-genital success with a sexual partner or for competitive strivings in relation to men unconsciously equated with the father.

When the fear of castration and retaliation is strong, the

hysterical neurosis may revolve around a pattern of relationships with men, particularly older men in positions of authority. This very common male hysterical pattern shows itself in a tendency to behave obsequiously with older men and men toward whom competitive and hostile feelings are directed. This neurotic pattern also shows itself in several self-defeating work patterns: (1) a tendency to work ambitiously and effectively but never quite actualizing one's full potential; (2) always remaining second in command in spite of the potential and wish to lead; (3) putting oneself with childlike trust in the hands of a powerful man (or group) with the *conscious* fantasy of being looked after and protected. This pattern often simultaneously involves unconscious self-punitive tendencies to be abused and taken advantage of by the man. This fawning, trusting, dependent relationship represents a reversal of competitive, murderous feelings, and also often functions to draw punishment and abuse from the object as a price for the murderous wishes. Another neurotic solution to this basic male hysterical conflict involves identifications with women, as if to say, "I'm no phallic danger, for I am already a woman, already castrated." These men may show effeminate traits, feminine interests, and relate to women as asexual platonic friends. At times they get involved in transient, overt homosexual relationships. Another common neurotic expression of this conflict involves public presentation of hypermasculine behavior, while intimate relationships are characterized by dependence and inhibition of sexual contact.

GENERAL FEATURES OF THE OEDIPUS COMPLEX

The Oedipal phase has some developmental features pertinent to our full understanding of the hysterical personality. It includes elaboration and development of many aspects of the personality. In the previous section drive development, sexual object choice, and dominant ego beliefs were discussed. Here the attempt will be to describe some less tangible but very important features of the Oedipal phase and to spell out some distinctions between this phase and those that precede it. The implications of these general developmental features for the hysterical personality will then be suggested.

During the Oedipal phase drives become more directed toward whole objects. In boys the aim is not phallic superiority vis-à-vis the father as an end in itself as it is in the immediately pre-Oedipal portion of the phallic stage. Rather, the aim is to protect, help, love, and receive a response from the mother. The aim is to direct sexual energies into a relationship and to receive a sexual response from the object. In both sexes, in contrast to the anal period during which the strivings are to control, dominate, and forcefully possess the object, to own the object as a thing, during the Oedipal period the object becomes valued for its novelty, spontaneity, and *its* act of loving control of the self. The aim becomes to have a relationship through which needs (now more modulated, less ambivalent, and less sadistic than earlier) can be satisfied.

The needs themselves change. Wishes to be appreciated and to appreciate replace the wish of the immediately preceding phallic-narcissistic stage to be admired, to impress, and to show off. The aim becomes less to impress an audience with oneself in order to confirm the size of the penis or the body and more to please and entertain the object. The aim of the Oedipal period, following the physical structure of the male and female genitals themselves, is to complement and complete the object. Viewed slightly differently, children during the phallic-narcissistic period commonly evince wishes to have the anatomical equipment of both sexes. Denial and fantasy formation help the phallic-narcissistic child to maintain a hermaphroditic illusion. When the limits of one's physiology become undeniable (as they do with the development of reality testing and more sophisticated cognition during the Oedipal period), the child of either sex seeks to establish this infantile omnipotent hermaphroditic state, but now via some sexual connection with the object. With the development of many aspects of the ego, with more differentiated self- and object images, and the general toning down of drives, the child is not buffeted between the desperate attempts at activity or passivity characteristic of the oral period or the stubborn and deeply ambivalent active or passive positions of the anal period. There is in normal development a coalescing of active and passive positions toward close objects. For normal development to proceed, the positive Oedipal position must predominate.

With the development of more complex cognitive capacities, the elaboration of internalized object images, development of memory, and more refined sense of time, the fantasies about relationships can be more elaborate, structured, and complex. The fantasies that develop during this period and undergo repression as it concludes are therefore often very specific and elaborate. When uncovered they look more like stories (fairy tales at times) than simply ideational representations of drive or need states. Though these fantasies often draw on the magical thinking of earlier development, there is nevertheless some attempt to rationalize the fantasy according to basic reality constraints (similar to the way secondary revision provides some sense of order among the manifest images following the basic wish-fulfilling function of dream work). The need to have wishes square with reality reflects a development in the ego, particularly reality testing. The wish to be the exclusive lover of the parent becomes connected for the child with the reality that someone else is thereby excluded—that exclusiveness means only one person can occupy a role and another therefore cannot fill it. Fantasies, then, must be created which take account of a more demanding set of realities known by the ego than was the case earlier when reality could be magically altered by thought or ritual. Consequently conflicts that date to this nexus in development are characterized by highly structured, often complex fantasies concerning objects and relationships with them. To anticipate a point described below, this is the reason the hysterical personality commonly seeks a particularly stereotyped, romanticized relationship in which the object has certain qualities and the relationship must follow a prescribed course.

With the developments in cognitive capacities, drive and

affect modulation, and recognition of limitations in objects and self, there develops a more modulated ambivalence toward the parents. The rage and intense ecstasy toward objects characteristic of the separation-individuation period have been integrated and modified; images of objects as all-frustrating and all-gratifying have to some extent been synthesized, the omnipotence of the object is to some extent given up, and an acceptance of objects with both negative and positive features becomes possible. The earlier assumption of the omnipotence of the objects, that is, the experience by the infant toward the end of the primary narcissistic phase of an omnipotent self-other, is now replaced by fantasies that express the *wish* for such a situation, a wish that exists side by side with a more realistic understanding of the assets and limitations of the object. For example, in the hysterical personality the object's sexual aspects are often idealized, and fantasies of intercourse seem to hold the potential for an all-protecting bond with the object. This is, however, a much more circumscribed idealization, and it exists side by side with a more realistically attuned awareness.

The development of cognitive capacities and the capacity to empathize with objects permits relationships between other people and between the self and others to be pondered and contrasted. There is a capacity to objectify the relationships between self and other as well as other and other. Beyond wishing for love or nurturance from an object or for things from it, at the Oedipal stage there develop wishes to have the *relationship* shared by two other people. This involves in a new and very profound way an awareness of triadic relationships among people and paves the way for the development of jealousy. With the movement from the envy of the oral period through the bitter aggressive wishes to have the possessions of an object of the anal period to the true jealousy that arises from conceptualizing triadic ties, the foundation is laid for the concern with triangular relationships involving mother, father, and self which is the core of the Oedipus complex. In other words, the Oedipal stage involves wishes to give love to and to receive it from a particular object in a particular way. There is a synthesis of narcissistic and object-related strivings, with the aim a love relationship that follows a certain pattern. The aim is not just the pleasure of the self, but the pleasure of the other that is vicariously enjoyed by the self. There is delight in both the self's capacity to entertain and bring pleasure to the object and empathic, vicarious enjoyment of the object's pleasure. This sense of contact is one of the essential cornerstones for enduring ties with objects. There is enjoyment of the object's pleasure, a sense of pleasure when helping the love object, and a general protectiveness toward it.

ORAL, ANAL, AND PHALLIC-NARCISSISTIC STAGES
DISTINGUISHED FROM THE OEDIPAL PHASE

The developmental tasks of the earliest phases of development, including the stage of autoeroticism, primary narcissism, and separation-individuation, differ from those of the Oedipal phase in the most fundamental ways. The tasks of the former stages involve constitution of a body ego, a sense of basic integrity and consistency of the self, the initial regulation of drives, and the gradual dissolution of the assumption of an infantile, objectless, all-gratifying paradise, leading to the formation of a boundary between self and object. These most basic processes, described by Spitz, Mahler, and Anna Freud, among many others, form the essential foundation for the later development of internalized object representations, the modulation of affect, and the formation of psychic structures. The implications of this stage for the integration of libidinal, aggressive, and narcissistic energies have been extensively discussed by Hartmann (1939), Kernberg (1967), and Kohut (1971), among others. When these processes go awry, psychosis or borderline personality (Kernberg, 1967) results. Primitive projection, splitting of object representations, and unharnessed aggressive energy emerge in these personalities. Objects are viewed largely as need-gratifying or frustrating, and a desperate clinging alternates with bitter, degrading negativism toward them. These expressions of disruption at the earliest developmental stages are not clinically present in the hysterical personality as defined here. The hysterical personality has traversed these stages relatively unscathed. Though there may be some minor oral and anal fixations on the libidinal level, the major fixations are Oedipal, and the ego is essentially without major defects.

The differences between the phallic-narcissistic and anal stages are not as obvious, and fixations at these stages are in practice harder to identify. Ultimately, however, a clear understanding of some general features of these stages and of the essential clinical features of patients in whom the different phases have been especially conflictual will foster a more precise definition of what is unique about the intrapsychic conflicts found in the hysterical personality.

In one important respect the Oedipal phase is more similar to the oral phase than to the anal: they are both predominantly object seeking. In important respects the anal stage involves objects as sources of control, power, and restraint; it is characterized by the establishing of control over body contents and actions. Seeking autonomy, the establishing of boundaries of social control and ownership of possessions makes this stage in important respects a more self-directed one than either the oral or the Oedipal phase. The anal stage is oriented toward leaving one's own personal stamp on people or things by making them conform to one's wishes even if this means that the object must set aside its own needs.

The phallic-narcissistic phase, in important ways drawing on urethroerotic libido, falls between the anal and Oedipal periods and in several respects represents a point of transition between the two. During the phallic-narcissistic stage there is increased erogeneity of the genitals, as opposed to the earlier pleasure in the sphincter and anus. Yet the use of the genitals during this phase is not unlike the use of the feces — they are valued for their size (and depreciated for their smallness), exhibited to others, and prized in themselves. (Excitement in the genitals is bound up with the instincts to look and to show, which are also important component instincts in anal eroticism.) Phallic-narcissistic-phase pride in the size of the genitals and the body as a whole is similar to the anal-phase pride in producing large and firm feces, a production of the self valued for size and exhibited to others. Another aim during this phase, again similar in many respects to the anal phase, is the use of the genitals to exert power for its own sake, to dominate something with it, to force the submission of others with it. The interest in control of body contents characteristic of the anal stage evolves into control over self-presentation in the phallic-narcissistic stage. There is then a shift from the feces to showing the body as a whole, but control of the body continues to be a central issue.

While objects are surely psychosexually important for the child during the anal stage, they take on a special importance in the phallic-narcissistic and Oedipal phases. In the phallic-narcissistic phase the child becomes concerned with more specific comparisons between himself and others. In the anal phase the child struggles to control objects or body contents; in the phallic-narcissistic phase he seeks less to control the other and more to perform better than the other, to impress the other, and ultimately to compete with the other in more defined areas. The mode during the phallic-narcissistic phase becomes, of course, intrusive and instrumental, and less possessive and controlling. The intense and often split ambivalences of the anal phase develop into better coordination of aggressive and libidinal impulses. These coordinated impulses fuel the child's wish to have his parents be proud of and loving toward him for his assertive, exhibitionistic behavior—in short, he feels himself to be both giving and receiving love from his parents by showing off actively and assertively with them. The anal phase is characterized by global and pervasive attempts to establish independence from the objects in the environment and to bring them under the control of the self. During the phallic-narcissistic phase the attempt to compete with and to outdo the object in more defined areas becomes primary, and the need to resist control by the object becomes secondary.

During this stage the child's comparisons of his own genital size, body size, and actual potential with those of objects becomes much more realistic. The immutable reality of the parents' greater competence and size becomes undeniable. The unhappy results of comparisons between the self and the parents are met with fantasies of the tables being turned. A child of about four said, "When we grow up again, you'll be the boy and I'll be the daddy." But in normal development these fantasies are recognized to be hopes, at best to be achieved in the future, and are gradually seen not to alter present realities. The child's realization that his competence and size are inferior to the parents' comes to play an important role in the dynamics of the Oedipus complex. The phallic-narcissistic phase involves imitation and some internalization of the parents' behavior. Children at this stage become, for example, very much interested in their clothing, in looking like their parents, etc. The alternation between imitation and competitiveness of the phallic-narcissistic phase replaces battles over control and stubborn independence of the anal phase. The anal-stage striving for independence is replaced by the phallic-narcissistic striving for instrumentality.

With elaboration of cognition, increased experience, and a better social sense, the phallic-narcissistic child seeks to compete with his parents in specific ways. The anal-stage wish to have power equal to that of the parents is replaced by the wish to have specific traits and abilities of the parents. This stage in many ways paves the way for both the Oedipus complex and later latency pursuits.

What, then, are the essentials of the shift from the phallic-Oedipal (or first stage of Oedipal phase) to the Oedipal phase (or second stage of Oedipal phase) in men and women? What are the characteristics that distinguish this stage from those that precede it?

From the point of view of object relations, the Oedipal phase involves the focusing of libidinal and aggressive energies toward objects perceived in a far more differentiated fashion than before. The object can be experienced in terms of its various roles, functions, and particularly as it changes in its relationships with various people.

Owing to the increased erogeneity of the genitals, and therefore interest in the genitals of others, a general interest in sex differences develops. The boy's awareness of the penisless mother, and the girl's recognition of the existence of penises, beyond leading to castration anxiety and penis envy also provoke curiosity about the differences between men and women and the sex role of the self in its relationships with each. A concern with the masculinity and femininity of certain behavior, and the capacity of objects, particularly the parents, to assume active and passive roles with each other, becomes central to the child.

In a profound sense the Oedipal struggle involves the child's confronting the limitations of his social and family reality, the essential and immutable inequality in the family relationships, in his biology, in his prerogatives. It is with the waning of magical thinking, a better sense of time, and the development of the concept of conservation of matter that the child becomes capable of recognizing the existence of these limits. It is obvious, therefore, that the Oedipus complex cannot emerge until the ego has developed the capacity to recognize these limits. The Oedipus complex can thus be seen both as an indication of substantial accomplishment in ego development and, in part, as a result of these accomplishments.

Through the development of a capacity to see objects behaving differently with others, the child comes to realize that his relationship with his mother and father is profoundly different from their relationship with each other. He comes to recognize that he may control each and be controlled by each, but this is merely possession, not the mutuality he sees in their relationship with each other. The aim then becomes to have a certain type of relationship with the parents, modeled in most respects on their relationship with each other. The wish to possess the primary object exclusively, a striving common to all developmental phases, now involves working toward the achievement of an interlocking of self and object based on an elaborated fantasy (and theory) of human interaction. This involves perception of and internal construction of the parental relationship. These conceptions of how people relate produce enduring ego beliefs and attributes, particular self- and object representations, and unconscious fantasies. The goal during this phase then becomes more than to have the attention of, or control over, the parents. It involves forming a particular relationship with the object, one which has the earmarks of the parents' relationship with each other. The need to empathize with the object then becomes central to this new kind of exclusive possession of the parent. Possession of a relationship with certain features, certain roles and sex role definitions, a certain mix of activity and passivity, is now the aim, not simply to control the object, to be autonomous of it, or to impress it with the size and power of the body or genitals. The essential limitation the child comes to face is that he may possess the parent, but will never have the kind of relationship with the parent he wishes. It is the specificity of these fantasies that fuels the identification of the child with the parents' behavior in their relationship with each other. These processes help form styles of interacting and are the precursors of the more consolidated identifications which emerge toward the end of the Oedipal period.

The advances in cognitive capacities that coincide with the phallic phase promote the development of structuralized fantasies. The child can now understand and remember fiction, for example. These capacities, in combination with more complex fantasy activity, spur an interest in fairy tales, make-believe, and "let's pretend" games. With the development of a sense of the limits of the reality in which he finds himself, the child seeks fictional options to extend the limits of his physicality and his relationships. Fairy tales, of course, capture common childhood wishes, become the focus of interest in many children, and may play an organizing role in their mental lives. These fairy tales then serve to organize further the child's sense of the triadic relationships in his family and to provide a more complex structure to his fantasies and wishes. These fantasies are far more structured, organized, and elaborated than the impulse-ridden, less object-related wishes and fantasies of the oral and anal periods.

With the search for an interlocking, complementary relationship with the primary object, the interdependence of the objects becomes salient. The child comes to understand (not necessarily, of course, able to conceptualize) that to establish a relationship such as the parents have with each other involves *conditions* and particularly renunciations. Needs must be delayed and channeled. Drives must be turned to pursuits that are in the interest of the relationship, not just the self. Most of all, pregenital impulses must be renounced as a condition for the emulation of the parental relationship. The putting aside of such impulses is decisive for the Oedipal conflicts to become focused and resolved without libidinal regression, and is the foundation for the spurt in the development of channels of sublimation characteristic of the latency period.

The Oedipal period is characterized, then, by a striving for a relationship with an object through which phallic excitement is gratified. The size of genitals, the extent of instrumental competence, are pressed into the service of attaining an exclusive relationship. The aim becomes more competition *for an object* and less, as in previous phases, competition to establish the superior power, autonomy, or control of the self. Part of what is sought is a kind of response from the object that the child observes the parents eliciting from each other. Envy is gradually replaced by a true triangular jealousy, which is a dominant affect of the Oedipal phase.

The child's awareness of the differences between his relationship with his parents and their relationship with each other, along with the concept that an exclusive monogamous tie is simply, by definition, impossible for three, then leads to the wish to exclude and extrude the rival parent (at different moments both parents are rivals for the child). This, then, becomes the basis for death wishes toward parents.

What needs to be emphasized, and this is of prime significance for an understanding of the hysterical personality, is that for the Oedipus complex to become a focused developmental conflict, substantial developmental achievements, particularly in the sphere of ego functioning, are required. If there have been faults in the development of the ego, the experience of this Oedipal deadlock, the impossibility of fulfilling the Oedipal wishes, becomes obscured by a retreat, for example, to the magical thinking of the anal stage or the denial of the oral period. When this sort of ego regression occurs during development, the Oedipal conflicts may be viewed only as triggering an ego regression, and the ensuing distortion of the ego and regression of the drives push the Oedipus complex into the background. When psychopathology results from this regression on the level of ego and drives, it is not a hysterical neurosis, but rather an obsessional or mixed neurosis.

There are, of course, many other cases in which developmental arrests of many sorts (ego, drives, separation-individuation, impulse modulation, etc.) have precluded the development in childhood of an Oedipal conflict; that is, in which the Oedipal phase has not been reached. These cases, of course, fall outside of the neurotic spectrum. An essential point concerning the hysterical personality and neurosis is that for an Oedipal conflict to be possible, substantial developmental achievements on the level of ego and object relations are necessary, and for the conflict to be settled without regression these accomplishments must be quite stable and enduring. When there is then a neurosis with predominantly or exclusively Oedipal conflicts at its roots, as is the case with hysterical neurosis, these previous developmental achievements should be present in the patient's personality. This section has stressed, then, the ego-developmental and object-relational accomplishments that are prerequisite for and basic to the Oedipus complex. Though an admittedly brief overview of psychosexual development, it has highlighted the ego and interpersonal facets of the Oedipal phase of development. These developmental advances on the level of ego and object relations must be clearly understood, for they are found in the ego structure of Oedipally fixated personalities, many of whom are hysterical personalities.

OEDIPAL CONFLICTS AND OEDIPAL-LEVEL ACHIEVEMENT:
THE CORE OF THE HYSTERICAL PERSONALITY

Most authors agree that hysteria has its roots in fixation at the phallic-Oedipal period. How does the structure of the hysterical personality and neurosis reflect the characteristics of this developmental phase? On the basis of the preceding, highly schematic outline of the phallic-Oedipal period, an attempt will be made in what follows to spell out the various continuities between the Oedipal phase and the hysterical personality and neurosis.

The hysterical personality is concerned with infantile relationships and, when a neurosis develops, it involves conflicts over attempts to achieve an unconscious fantasy of an infantile relationship. The hysterical personality pursues a relationship patterned on an infantile wish toward the parents, a now unconscious wish that has the structure and complexity characteristic of the Oedipal phase. The object and the relationship must conform to an often complex set of unconscious requirements, for the phase from which these fantasies date permits relatively complex understandings of human interaction. The developmental achievements during the pre-Oedipal period have given the hysterical personality a relatively differentiated view of objects and therefore not any object will meet his needs (as is commonly the case in borderline personalities operating at a strictly need-gratifying level); rather, an object must have certain *qualities*.

Beyond a search for an *object* with certain qualities, the hysterical personality is in pursuit of a *relationship* with certain qualities, patterned on unconscious, complex structured fantasies about, and unconsciously remembered infantile constructions of, the parents' relationship with each other. The hysterical personality finds himself in competitive relationships with others, often marked by attempts to impress and exhibit to the other. At its roots, however, the competition with objects is in the service of obtaining an exclusive relationship with an object. The experience of objects, consistent with the Oedipal phase, involves a wish for an interdependence with objects, an attempt to complement the object and to be complemented by it. The hysterical personality seeks to please the primary love object, to be the special person in the other's eyes, to give and receive love from the object. In contrast to the obsessional personality, the hysterical personality is often disappointed if he becomes *conscious* that he has coerced or forced the object to care or love, though often he is, without realizing it, behaving quite coercively and manipulatively. The aim is to have the object love the self freely—"just because he (she) loves me." Indeed, the hysterical personality often must avoid realizing his own active and coercive behavior, for this makes him feel that the object is not really loving. The hysterical personality is often so insecure about his capacity to be loved as an adult that he becomes fearful that he has forced affection from the object. Many hysterical neurotics present conflict over the failure of a relationship to achieve a perfect, harmonious complementarity.

In hysterical neuroses, the attempt to please the object is felt to demand that various facets of the self be altered or exaggerated. Isomorphic with the Oedipal phase from which his psychopathology arises, the hysterical neurotic often feels that the love object will be pleased *only if the self presents an exaggerated masculinity or femininity,* images based on infantile constructions of the parents' behavior with each other. The hysterical neurotic feels such an image is essential to maintain the love object, and may feel a sense of artificiality in his behavior with the object. His need to maintain an exclusive relationship with an object often results, under the auspices of the repetition compulsion, in a pattern of forming triangular relationships characterized by intense jealousy and attempts to form an exclusive relationship with one or both of the other members of the triangle. Most important, the hysterical neurotic maps his neurosis out in an arena which is of concern during the Oedipal phase, that of intimate relationship. Consistent with the developmental achievements the child has made at the dawn of the Oedipal phase, the hysterical neurotic often functions effectively in areas not directly involving intimate, usually heterosexual, relationships.

Consistent with, on the one hand, the cognitive advances of the Oedipal phase and the Oedipal-phase child's beginning understanding of the limits of his anatomy and interpersonal prerogatives, and on the other hand his complex fantasies of a phallic-genital relationship with a parent, the hysterical neurotic has an awareness of what is possible realistically, and simultaneously presents a pattern of actions based on infantile fantasies of objects. To oversimplify, he knows consciously that there is no Prince or Princess Charming, yet continually operates as if there is and as if he can, if he behaves properly, find such a person. The latter trend is largely unconscious, though buttressed by pseudo naïveté and a diffuse, unplanful approach to objects which is woven into many interpersonal patterns. These ego trends permit the unconscious material to map itself into action and relationship patterns, though the patient has no awareness of them. This is what has been characterized, from Freud's earliest writings, as the split in the ego in the hysterical personality. Unconsciously generated patterns of action remain largely unconnected with the ego's awareness of what is really possible. Actions involving search for intimate relationships are consciously experienced by the hysterical personality as motiveless and unconnected with conscious ideation. Patterns of interaction, no less than somatic symptoms, express unconscious wishes and affects but fail to register in the person's conscious experience. Only by reading the messages of his actions and connecting them with the derivatives of his unconscious thoughts can the hysterical personality come to repair this split. Such is one essential goal of psychotherapy or psychoanalysis with such patients.

Having had a reasonably normal development of the ego through the pregenital phases, the hysterical personality cannot resort to the distortions of thought seen in obsessional and more disturbed personalities. To avoid recognition of, for instance, the limitations of the object or the relationship with it, the hysterical personality must make sure he does not see the realities or think about them. But if he is made aware of the facts, he will find it hard to misunderstand them. The defenses must then be geared to avoiding seeing and knowing. These include dissociation, forgetting, repression, foggy cognition (making ideas vague—which is different from the warping of thought processes), ego strategies that steer clear of specifics, and "perception" narrowed by the unconscious fantasy itself.

Though the hysterical personality often tends to idealize or degrade the love object, to be enamored with him at one moment and enraged at another, there is an essential consolidation of the object's negative and positive, pleasing and annoying, aspects. The hysterical personality, like the child at the height of the Oedipus complex, knows that to murder the rival is also to lose the loving and loved aspects of that object. The hysterical personality and the Oedipal-stage child are aware, at least consciously, that if someone is gone, he is not here, that both are not simultaneously possible. The hysterical personality will often, through ego efforts not to look, attend, or think, avoid this reality. To operate on unconscious fantasy, for example to act as if the rival object can be murdered yet still be there to protect, involves ego efforts to avoid thinking. If the hysterical personality attends to reality, he has the intellectual functions that force him to see the inconsistency. It is the presence of these firm and enduring cognitive substrates that makes repression such a necessary defense for such patients, for repression completely precludes conscious thinking.

The hysterical neurotic tends to feel jealous, not primitively envious. In contrast to infantile or borderline personalities whose conflicts reflect pregenital developmental difficulties, and who consequently seek to have the qualities of objects as if they were food or things, the hysterical neurotic's search for a relationship leads to jealousy of those who seem to enjoy wished-for relationships. The hysterical neurotic reflects an understanding developed during the Oedipal period that a relationship cannot be wrested or grabbed from others, that such an oral or anal mode of taking it destroys it.

The hysterical neurotic is often depressed by the fear that he will never have the particular relationship he sees and wants. This leads to attempts to identify with both the rival object and the sought-after object so as to become part of the relationship. The hysterical personality is inclined to change his manner and to claim to have certain interests when he is in the presence of the valued object.

The hysterical personality's concern about loss of control

(particularly of strong, genuine affect) is reminiscent of anal concerns, and his tendency to try to impress others and be noticed as special by them is reminiscent of the phallic-narcissistic phase. However, in both cases the hysterical personality's aims are more object-directed. To be out of control during the anal phase involves a humiliating sense of loss of sphincter control, which in itself feels destructive, self-disorganizing, and dependent. During the Oedipal period loss of control is renounced more because it is usually felt to displease the object and to jeopardize the wished-for relationship with it. Indeed, if the object is felt to enjoy the self's loss of control, the hysterical personality, again isomorphic with Oedipal-phase conflicts, will let himself lose control, or at least seem to. The fear of humiliation, of being shamed, is subordinated to the wished-for intimate tie with the object.

The hysterical personality reflects the Oedipal-phase child's growing awareness of the nature of relationships. If the Oedipal phase is reached without major distortions or arrests of the ego and drives, an enduring and reliable internal world of mental representations should have begun to develop. These self- and object representations are more than images; they are an internal coordination of affects, action modalities, self-experiences, drive states, expectations, and memories. They are relationship paradigms — templates, as it were, for potential relationships. By the Oedipal period a variety of relationship paradigms should be encoded intra-psychically, giving the child the capacity to discriminate relationships not solely on the basis of the person he is with, but also on the basis of the characteristics of the interaction. All of this makes it possible for the Oedipal-phase child to be much more subtle in eliciting what he desires from objects. The child moves from the very obvious attempts to control and possess of the anal period to much more subtle, "manipulative" behavior with those in his environment.

In the hysterical personality, these developmental accomplishments show themselves in his sensitivity to the interpersonal, social, and cultural currents and modes of his world and in his capacity to coerce those around him to behave in certain ways toward him. The hysterical ego can unconsciously engineer situations and relationships among people that match unconscious infantile fantasies and wishes (as well as self-punitive arrangements), while consciously feeling that he is a victim of circumstance and the whims of others. The interpersonal "savvy" of the hysterical personality permits him unconsciously to set up situations in which he is the central, powerful, and most loved member. He does not experience himself, however, as having these "unsavory" active or aggressive motives, and retreats into an illusion of passivity, helplessness, and victimization. The point is that the effectiveness of the hysterical personality's unconscious engineering and alteration of his relationships reflects a sense of people congruent with Oedipal-phase development.

The Oedipal roots of the hysterical neurosis facilitate the expression of neurotic conflicts in the interpersonal sphere. In contrast to the very "private" obsessional thoughts and rituals, or the psychotic's autistic behavior, the hysterical neurotic, even if he develops a somatic symptom, is speaking with his symptoms to people in his world. His relationships, then, are often the arena in which his neurosis shows itself.

The pseudo stupidity or naïveté of the hysterical personality can also be better understood from the point of view of the wish for a complementary, interlocking relationship in the Oedipal phase of development. The different roles, strengths, and weaknesses of each parent become more apparent to the child by the Oedipal phase. The parents (and other objects) are often seen as helping each other, providing the other with what the other lacks. This experience of objects is, of course, part and parcel of emerging concepts about the penis and its presence in one parent and absence in the other. The motif of complementarity pervades the Oedipal period and helps subordinate the pregenital, particularly anal, drives. In the hysterical neurotic, infantile notions of the parents' maleness and femaleness complementing each other often become exaggerated, and he comes to feel that object ties, which are unconsciously infantile ones, are possible *only* if traits in the object are *not* matched by the same traits in the self, and conversely, that traits in the self are not found in the object. This dichotomy often shows itself in the hysterical neurotic's tendency to exaggerate some aspect of his sex-typical behavior and to expect the object to do the same. For example, to play out this infantile fantasy of idyllic complementarity, the hysterical neurotic often feels he must be as stupid, naïve, and confused as the object is bright, worldly, and organized. The competitive drives, particularly the phallic (masculine) narcissistic ones, are experienced as unacceptable. They are often unconsciously acted out in the relationship, leading the object to feel challenged and competed with. The hysterical neurotic's conscious fantasy does not include these competitive drives; indeed, they are felt to threaten the infantile fantasy of harmonious interlocking. In some hysterical neurotics, particularly in males, there may be an exaggeration of some stereotypically masculine traits, a repression of the passive feminine pole of his bisexuality and a living out, unconsciously, of his feminine strivings. These exaggerations of competitiveness or lack of it are often at the root of such hysterical behaviors as pseudo stupidity, hysterical naïveté, exaggerated masculine or feminine behavior, and the seductive, teasing exhibition of weakness and incompetence. The familiar image of the highly intelligent woman, or man, who throws up his hands in confusion when asked to change a light bulb or a tire and who then turns appreciatively to a more "competent" helper, captures this process. The hysterical neurotic feels that this sort of pseudo ignorance (or pseudo intelligence; see the case of male hysterical personality below) is a prerequisite for a tie with the infantile object. The pseudo strength or pseudo weakness is bound directly to unconscious early-childhood fantasies of power and weakness, the relative strength of the parents, and the power of the phallus. The incompetence of the self is equated with a passive, feminine welcoming of the competence of the object, which is often unconsciously equated with taking in the paternal phallus. By this path, the exhibition of incompetence and pseudo stupidity is eroticized.

Certain aspects of the Oedipal phase of development lead the hysterical personality to have more conflicts over tabooed libidinal wishes than over aggression per se, and to turn to repression and displacement as preferred defenses. The

Oedipal phase of development, more than other phases, rests on a growing recognition that sexual wishes are "right" when directed toward certain objects and "wrong" when directed toward other objects. The "morality" that is contributed by the anal stage is a morality of control of aggression, of black and white (dirty and clean) actions, and of stubbornly personal "standards." The Oedipal period involves the beginning of an awareness of rules, customs, and patterns based less on control of aggression and more on unquestioned (often puzzling) family, social, and religious commandments (such as the incest taboo) concerning the expression of sexual, loving impulses with the genitals. Certain objects have been defined as appropriate for sexual gratification ("When you grow up you will marry someone") and some not (incestuous objects). While hysterical conflicts of course involve the expression or inhibition of aggression, such as the conflicts surrounding fear of murderous wishes toward the Oedipal rival or retaliation from him for sexual wishes, the aggression is a means to or punishment for more central *libidinal wishes*. While in the anal stage sadistic wishes constitute a primary drive in itself (associated with wishes to smear) and consequently conflicts over any expression of aggression plague the obsessive-compulsive personality, in the hysterical personality aggression is more in the service of libidinal strivings and conflicts over it arise only when internal libidinal wishes transgress certain family and social prohibitions. Thus the hysterical personality has conflicts not about the expression of libidinal or aggressive impulses per se, but about the expression of these wishes toward the wrong, tabooed objects.

The reason for the hysterical personality's tendency to use displacement and repression follows partly from the above: if the wish is taboo because it is directed at an *inappropriate* object, then the *displacement* of the wish or the repression of the fantasy of that object makes the wish more acceptable. In the obsessive-compulsive, the impulse-connected aspects of the wish itself must be more thoroughly and continuously eradicated by reaction formation, undoing, projection, etc. In the hysterical personality there is greater acceptance of impulses if the object is an appropriate one or if the true object of the incestuous impulse can be kept from awareness. Repression and displacement are ideal for this purpose and are therefore dominant hysterical defenses. These defenses are less effective in completely warding off the aggressive impulses with which the hysterical personality, in comparison to the obsessional, has less conflict. In fending off the conscious recognition of the object of the libidinal wish, the secondary conflicts over aggression toward or from the rival are avoided.

The Oedipus complex promotes the development of a set of defensive images of self and objects as "innocuous" and asexual. These images are divided into those that are dirty-sexual-immoral and those that are clean-asexual (e.g., the whore-Madonna view of women). One important aspect of the Oedipal phase involves fantasies of mutual sexual excitement with the parents. Previously, the fantasies inclued the wish to stimulate control or approval from the pregenital mother. The Oedipal phase ushers in a conception of sexual excitement in the parents themselves and the possibility of providing such excitement for them and being mutually excited with them. The ego feels endangered by possible excitement toward the parent and also by the parent's excitement in response to the self. In an attempt to feel protected from the danger of these excitements, images of the parents as asexual, proper, and "cold" are constructed. These images ward off the possibility that the parents will be washed away in a mutually exciting and frightening fashion by insuring that they will be asexual protectors against excessive excitement. The images of parents as asexual often simultaneously express the unconcious fantasy that parents do not find sexual interest *in each other*, and would be more interested and excited by the self. The image of the parents' asexuality involves, then, both a wish to be sexual with them and a defense against the danger inherent in such acts. Hysterical people commonly see others as "sexual" or "asexual." This pattern shows itself in the hysteric's experience of objects as nice, asexual, and wholesome, or lecherous, sexual, and illicit. In some hysterics there is a need to place everyone immediately into one of these two categories. When an object who has been assigned to the former category makes sexual advances, the hysterical personality is often surprised and frightened, and feels betrayed and fooled. The image of the "sexual" object is usually made up of several components: it involves memories of infantile masturbatory excitement accompanied by fantasies about parents, infantile conceptions of adult sexual excitement and contact (that it is brutal, animalistic, or dirty, for example), and understanding and misunderstanding of primal-scene experience. This commonly results in the hysteric's experiencing sexual excitement in himself or others as distorting, animalistic, grotesque, improper, and ugly. Though there may be no conflict over anal-sadistic aggression, these images of sex as disgusting of course draw on residues from the anal period. The male hysterical patient discussed later in this chapter expressed this typical hysterical image of sexual contact through a screen memory of looking at pictures of bare-chested African women in an anthropology textbook, seeing them as disgusting, deformed, and "just not beautiful," not aesthetic. He preferred what he described as a cold, quiet, and motionless beauty in women, a preference which turned out to be a reaction against his infantile attitudes about sexual excitement itself.

The superego of the hysterical personality shows its distinctly Oedipal heritage and constitutes a prime diagnostic differentiator. The Oedipal-stage superego is composed of internalizations of parents' demands, ideals, prohibitions, and guidance that date from a relatively advanced point in development. The superego therefore shows virtually none of the primitive, severe, malevolent, cannibalistic qualities seen in persons whose superego internalizations date predominantly from the oral phase. In these borderline personalities the superego (or superego precursors) is composed of unintegrated primitive images of external and internal drive states, based mainly on oral-sadistic aggression and projected versions of it. The hysterical superego is much more rooted in a sense of rules, guidelines, and limits of the later, Oedipal, phase of development when the world is seen much more realistically and when the drives (particularly the aggressive drives) have been brought under better ego control and have themselves advanced to less sadistically and nakedly destructive forms.

Consistent with the Oedipal phase when the central areas of life concern and conflict involve genital excitement directed at significant objects, the superego that consolidates during this stage, and which is seen in the hysterical personality, is embedded in what might be called *relationship morals*. Rather than an anal-phase morality involving honor (in opposition to shame), sovereignty (in opposition to helplessness and control from the outside), and independence, the hysterical superego contents are much more relativistic, responding severely to wishes toward certain objects and much more mildly when these *same* wishes are directed toward other objects.

In a very basic sense the superego is oriented toward maintaining significant relationships, toward insuring nontaboo routes to pleasure with others. In some forms of hysterical psychopathology the need to maintain a relationship may lead to delinquency in the service of the relationship (and often in the service of self-punishment). Such persons have in some areas a "psychopathic" quality, for they seem to care less about the larger, impersonal needs of the community than about the preservation of their relationships. The hysterical superego tends to emphasize the personal, and to underemphasize the community, in some cases including its laws. This characteristic is *not* definitional of the disorder, however, and does not indicate that hysterics are more psychopathic, conscienceless, or uncontrolled than anyone else. It suggests only that when delinquency occurs, it tends to be a result of a wish to serve, help, or attract a love object.

The hysterical superego is rooted in interpersonal, human values, tending to be flexible and relativistic (changes with relationships). The obsessional superego is less flexible, less contingent on the interpersonal environment, and based more on impersonal principles that should apply in all situations. Each superego pattern has its assets and liabilities, contexts in which it is adaptive and constructive, and others in which it is not. The rigidity and impersonal quality of the obsessional superego may lead him to be strict and fair or rigid and inhuman. Similarly, the flexibility of the hysterical superego may lead him to be flexible and sensitive to individual situations and the needs of particular people, or so circumstantial as to hold firm to few enduring, situation-free standards. The hysterical superego often revolves around the mores of immediate significant interpersonal relationships, in contrast to the stubbornly independent mottoes and oaths of the obsessional. The hysterical superego differs from that of the obsessional, but in my opinion is neither "weaker" nor "stronger," neither more nor less moral.

Another characteristic of the hysterical superego reflects its Oedipal-phase heritage: its verbal contents can be warded off by the predominant ego defense of the Oedipal phase, repression. Thus verbal representations of superego prohibitions are repressed and unavailable to conscious ego processes. This contributes in large measure to the hysteric's tendency to self-defeating, impulsive action.

The superego of the hysterical personality reflects the hysterical ego and cognitive "style." The superego seems to rest less on explicit verbal mandates than does the superego of the word-conscious obsessional. The movement from the anal to the phallic-Oedipal phases involves a de-emphasis of words and thoughts and a heightened emphasis on less explicitly verbal patterns, emphasizing instead the harmonies of human interactions. Though this sense of interaction patterns may not be verbal or explicit, there is often complex cognition that permits this understanding. This is yet another factor that promotes superego and ego processes rooted in an "implicit" feeling for what is appropriate and fitting in a particular situation.

HYSTERIA: THE BASIC NEUROSIS

As the hysterical personality presents a relatively delimited conflict within a basically intact ego structure and uses repression and displacement as primary defenses, neurosis within the hysterical personality (hysteria) is in many ways, in psychoanalytic terms, the basic neurosis. Once conscious, now repressed libidinal and aggressive thoughts express themselves, in spite of the repressive block, in the form of derivatives. These derivatives are in some very direct way related to the unconscious thoughts or wishes that push toward awareness. They are compromises between prototypical unconscious longings, Oedipal longings, and a prototypical ego defense, repression. Hysteria is prototypical because repression is the prime mechanism by which conscious experience is relegated to the unconscious and the power of the unconscious content is basic to neurosis and everyday parapraxes. Indeed, it was through the discovery of the dynamic unconscious that psychoanalysis went beyond previous theories.

Hysteria is also prototypical because the repression of unacceptable wishes and fantasies occurs during a phase in which verbal and symbolic processes have reached a high level of development. Consequently the derivatives and conflicts emerge in verbal and symbolic forms most available to understanding by the adult ego.

DEPRESSION IN FEMALE HYSTERICS

Along with other symptoms and character problems, many female hysterical patients present depression and depressive affects, inferences from which have an important bearing on formulations about this personality type. It seems from both the literature and from clinical discussion that depression in hysterical patients (as well as in other types of patients) is taken to reflect difficulties arising during the first two years of life. Depression is considered to be specifically related to difficulties during the oral period, including object loss, deprivation, and insufficient or unreliable gratification from the mother. It is probable that those who believe hysteria involves either a major or partial fixation at the oral period are basing their conclusion at least in part on the presence of depression in hysterical patients.

While it is surely true that depression often has anaclitic roots, it seems increasingly likely that the nature of depression differs from person to person. Brenner (1977) has recently attempted a different approach to depression found in some women patients. He considers that depression in some women results from the infantile discovery of their lack of a penis—that is, is related to their "castration complex" (a term used by Freud which Brenner prefers to "penis envy"). The depression results from an ego perception that damage has already occurred and that the loss is irreparable. He believes that these depressive feelings play a role comparable to that of anxiety. Anxiety is an ego reaction to some real or imagined *future* danger, whereas depression is an ego reaction to something experienced as a past and immutable fact. Depression can be a conflict-signaling affect, like anxiety as described by Freud (1926). The little girl's awareness of her "castration," which is often accompanied by a fantasy of having been deprived of the penis or having lost it because of some transgression (usually masturbation), leads to depression. This depression, like anxiety, is a signal for defensive activity. In this situation it is not the outcome of a compromise between impulse and a defensive process—that is, a symptom—but a *primary* response of the ego to unpleasure, unpleasure concerning the immutable "fact" of having been castrated. This depressive affect, again like anxiety, is a *signal* or trigger for defensive activity and in some cases for the formation of a symptom. The depressive affect, then, is not a symptom in the psychoanalytic sense, that is, a final compromise among intrapsychic forces, but is rather an intrapsychic event that *triggers* defensive activity, conflict, and symptom formation. Depressive affects therefore can be pathogenic. In the little girl this depressive reaction may lead, for example, to an unconscious fantasy of secretly having a penis inside her, or of growing a penis, fantasies which in adulthood may be expressed in symptom, character, or object relations.

Brenner's contribution helps address the question of pregenital fixation and regression in hysteria. He is saying essentially that in some female patients depression may not have fundamentally anaclitic roots, but may result from their infantile perception of themselves as lacking a penis and the fantasies attendant to that perception, often including believing themselves to have been castrated. The depression is viewed essentially as resulting from phallic-phase, not oral-phase, conflicts. The depression found in female hysterics may therefore be connected with phallic conflicts, supporting Freud's contention that hysterical patients present phallic-Oedipal conflict without significant pregenital regression.

NARCISSISTIC CONCERNS IN HYSTERICAL PATIENTS

Certain types of narcissistic concerns in hysterical patients also seem to have been viewed as originating in very early development. Feelings of inadequacy, sensitivity to criticism, and feelings of inferiority to others are frequently found in the hysterical personality. Rather than viewing these experiences as arising from an unstable tie to the mother involving a poor fit between the infant's needs and the mother's capacity to gauge them and to help the infant manage them, it is important to keep in mind the role of narcissism during the Oedipal phase. While this phase is correctly viewed predominantly in terms of conflicts between libidinal instinctual drives and the fear of castration or loss of love, the Oedipal-phase child suffers significant narcissistic assaults because he really is smaller, less competent, and generally less powerful than the parents, and really is physically incapable of consummating a sexual relationship with the parents. The impossibility of such a relationship is a very significant assault on the child's phallic narcissism (Nathan Segel, personal communication, 1977). These phallic-Oedipal narcissistic assaults, like depressive affects and anxiety, can trigger conflict. They may lead to an unconscious fantasy of phallic grandiosity including, for example, a body-phallus equation. An adult hysteric may have an unconscious self-image of being a little child, and a defensive need then for continual assertion of phallic superiority. These narcissistic concerns in hysterical patients may well have entirely phallic-Oedipal, not pregenital, sources.

The case that follows is meant to be an illustration of a hysterical neurotic. The patient does not illustrate absolutely every characteristic described above, but does present most of the major facets. The reader will be struck with how ordinary and familiar is this case. The patient has no flagrant or bizarre symptoms, functions well in many areas, and is unusual in very few ways. Transculturally and transhistorically, this is the very essence of the hysteric: he tends to be, in terms of his own culture and era, generally successful at basic life activities, at times even excelling in his work, usually aware of and in general conforming to what is in vogue and what will soon be convention.

Description of Patient and Neurotic Problem

Miss F. was a 24-year-old single woman who worked as a public relations consultant for an advertising firm. She was of slightly above average height and full figure, well-dressed, poised, talkative, intelligent, and had a warm smile. She behaved more seductively than she consciously realized, at times drawing the attention of men without understanding how. Her dress, manner, and taste were very contemporary. Though occasionally her manner revealed a muffled brazenness, a wish to impress and shock, she nevertheless interacted with enough control and comfort with others to have a range of acquaintances and a few close female friends. She had always made friends with men easily, but her relationships with them always followed the same abortive pattern. It was primarily to understand and change this pattern that she sought intensive psychotherapy. At the beginning of each relationship with a man, she would generate idealized fantasies about him and grow anxious that she was failing to please or interest him. The idealization usually centered on ideas of his superior intelligence, self-assuredness, and clear-sightedness; she always overestimated these qualities and quickly became disappointed as the inevitable flaws became obvious. Her perceptual and cognitive style were such that she managed to avoid seeing these imperfections until the reality of the partner's humanness was no longer deniable. During the idealized period of these relationships the patient often felt she lacked the intelligence to maintain the man's interest, though in reality she was intelligent and articulate. Almost immediately upon meeting a man she would feel a compulsion to have sexual intercourse with him. She was consciously proud of her acceptability, indeed her prowess, as a sexual partner. Her concern was, at the outset of relationships, with her sexual performance, not with her pleasure in sexual encounters. Her perception of these men was basically wish-fulfilling; she saw them as highly intelligent and powerful and potentially expert in areas she identified as masculine: technical fields, math, geography, etc. When the usual difficulties in the relationship emerged, the patient would almost reflexively assume it was *her* fault. This seemed less motivated by a self-punitive masochistic attitude than by a need to protect her image of the man, to avoid seeing his contributions to difficulties; her basic motives seemed to be to blame herself and to exonerate him. It was also clear that these patterns were in part rooted in a feeling that men would be bored or disgusted if they really knew her.

Soon after beginning a relationship with a man, she would find herself increasingly curious either about previous women in the man's life or about other women with whom the man was in any way involved. She found herself probing the man for details, sometimes quite intimate ones, about other women, her curiosity centering on their beauty, sexual responsiveness, and intelligence. She would often have to inquire about such women in very indirect ways in order to buttress her own and the partner's denials that she was curious about them.

Though she defined these difficulties as, in some way, her fault, she could never specify what she had actually done to bring them about. In contrast to her capacity to identify the complex factors at work in her business relationships, she was remarkably global, vague, and illogical about the specific causes and effects of events in her close relationships with men. She often forgot large portions of recent conflictual interactions with men, again in striking contrast to her capacity to remember details of non-affect-laden work situations.

She generally tended to select phallic-narcissistic men who needed to "show off" with women. Several of them seemed to expend substantial internal effort on self-consciously engineering an "image" to impress women. Obviously, just below the surface in many of these men were phallic insecurities, fear of women, and in a few cases a profound neediness. One such man was a self-proclaimed Buddhist priest-psychotherapist who placed himself in a teacher relationship with the patient. He told her he had complete control of his mind, could transcend the boundaries of the ordinary workaday world, and left the patient thoroughly in awe of him. She felt that somehow, by contact with this man, by leaning on him, she would acquire the calmness and wisdom she imputed to him. In particular it was through intimate, sexual contact with him that she imagined she would come to share his wonders. She seemingly turned over to this man virtually all mutual decisions. She felt comfortable putting herself in his hands, and encouraged in herself and in him the myth that she was the passive, starry-eyed pupil of a wise man. In reality, through flattery and seductive coaxing, she maintained her share of control over the relationship. It was pleasurable and comfortable to maintain the illusion that the man was the source of power and responsibility. This seemed to free her from her guilt, her "ownership" of her feelings, and in addition made her feel she would be more desirable to him. Though she was capable of careful evaluation of people in many areas of her life, she avoided enlisting these capacities in assessing this man and others in his position. Though on some level she knew her view of him was unrealistic, she had such a strong wish to live out her unconscious fantasy of being a helpless little girl in the hands of a strong father that she defensively avoided applying her usual perceptiveness to him.

Another symptom the patient complained of was her "mindless" use of skin lotions for dry skin. The lotions were aggravating an allergic reaction, yet she seemed unable to stop using them. She reported, "I use them because I think I have dry skin, but I don't know what dry skin even feels like any more. I don't know if I ever even had it." Though this seemed to be a compulsive symptom, closer examination revealed its basically hysterical nature. She had no thoughts when she used the lotion, the habit had no driven, tortured quality as would a truly compulsive symptom. Rather, what was most striking was its mindless, automatic quality. The patient felt she was a victim of the habit, implying without realizing it that the habit was not hers, but came from without and overtook her. Though she knew these treatments were harmful, she was not particularly frightened about her habit and did not seem uncomfortable with her sense of passivity in relation to it.

Finally, the patient sought treatment to understand better what she felt was an excessive reaction to a woman under whom she worked at her job. Her supervisor, a man, had been somewhat critical of the patient's work and she regularly grew quite depressed about this. She compared herself to another woman in the same position as herself, who was, she felt, much better liked by the superior. She grew depressed after contact with either the supervisor or the other woman, and found it increasingly difficult to continue on her job.

Background

Miss F. was the oldest of four children, with a sister four years her junior and two brothers, eight and 10 years younger. Her father was a successful lawyer, her mother a mildly depressed housewife with numerous somatic complaints, many organic, some probably psychosomatic. The patient always viewed herself as the "pretty" sister and her younger sister as the less attractive, more intelligent one. The patient, however, did reasonably well in school, had a variety of friends, and performed well at a good university. By her report of her parents she seems to have accomplished her developmental tasks on schedule: bottle fed until 10 months, weened easily; toilet trained relatively easily by two years; walked at 14 months, talked in full sentences by 18 months;

no arrest or regression of gross and fine motor development. At the age of four, around the time of her sister's birth, she became somewhat more cautious, less exploratory, more irritable, and more prone to tantrums. At five this stage passed; she became more interested in dressing up, particularly for her father, and was described as a very feminine little girl.

The patient remembered little of this at the beginning of treatment, and indeed remembered little about her life before the age of 16. Most of the developmental information was reconstructed from memory fragments and information from the parents (gathered by the patient during treatment), who seemed to be adequate family historians.

Patient's View of Parents

The patient experienced her father as a very successful though eccentric man who was secretly very unhappy in his marriage. She was motivated to infer from a wide range of the father's behavior that he was unhappy with his wife. For example, she interpreted his spending time alone with his hobbies, reading, and his interest in playing tennis with other men as indications of strong dissatisfaction with his wife. At the beginning of treatment she viewed the father as having lost an intellectual curiosity about the world she was sure he had had when he was younger. This too seemed to her, in some unexplained way, to be a direct result of his unfulfilling marriage and in particular the fault of his wife. There was clearly still a great admiration for her father, though a note of disappointment in him as well.

The patient viewed her mother as a pitiful, ill woman who never enjoyed anything in life. Though this may have been a true picture of the mother's state at the time the patient entered treatment, it turned out to be an inaccurate assessment of the mother earlier in her life. Side by side with these views of her parents, the patient showed an affection for both of them.

Early in treatment it became clear that the patient needed to see her parents' marriage as worse than it was and to see her mother as much more ill and unhappy than she had actually been. The patient also needed to see her parents as much less supportive of each other than it turned out they actually were.

Review of Hysterical Elements

On the basis of this brief review we can see many hallmarks of the hysterical personality in the patient's presenting complaints, view of her parents, and overview of developmental history and life situation.

Conflicts Circumscribed. First, the conflicts with which the patient struggles are limited to particular sectors of her life, and are not severely incapacitating or overwhelming. Though her close heterosexual relationships are conflictual, other relationships are not; though one work relationship is conflictual, other aspects of her work performance are little affected.

Intact Ego Structure. Her ego structure is in general well established; she operates on a secondary-process level most of the time, is capable of delay of gratification, has basically good impulse control, is not subject to direct intrusions of primitive, unconscious material into consciousness. She shows no thought disorder, seems to have significant intellectual resources, and has intact self-boundaries.

Wish-Fulfilling Distortions of Relationships. She shows the characteristic hysterical tendency to experience important objects through the veil of unconscious, wish-fulfilling fantasy. Perceptual and cognitive acuity would be suspended in an effort to make the object appear congruent with an unconscious infantile fantasy of an idealized parent. In other areas, cognition proves to be clear, subtle, and smooth. The unconscious fantasy seems, even initially, to be a childhood fantasy of being a helpless, fragile little girl in the hands of a powerful, flawless phallic father who is exciting and in whose power the child feels she vicariously participates. Conscious images of the mother, as well as the repeated curiosity about "other women," reflect the patient's competitive strivings toward the mother. The patient's unconscious wish is clearly Oedipal; she turns toward the father for a powerful, protecting relationship through which she imagines she will obtain his strength, a baby, or a penis. The mother is seen as damaged and therefore incapable of making the patient complete. The mother is also seen as preventing the father from being the perfect and loving father the patient fantasizes that he could be (and underneath *really* is). This view also includes an impression that men are very malleable in the hands of women, which paradoxically exists alongside of the image of men as powerful and perfect.

She manifests the pattern of vicarious identificatory attachment to objects who are experienced as powerful. She feels that, through intimate contact with them, she may share in the strength and special competence she imagines they possess. This feeling about men suggests an infantile fantasy of obtaining the phallic power of the father through sexual contact with him.

Relationship Patterns Distorted by Intrapsychic Conflict. Images of the parents are distorted by the patient's unconscious Oedipal competitive feelings toward the mother. The image of the mother as old, ill, and incompetent as a wife expresses a wish to outdo and displace her. The father is seen as having deteriorated as a person owing to his wife's failings. The unconscious wish to displace the mother shows itself very clearly in the patient's current relationships with men. She often finds herself involved in triangular relationships, choosing men who are married, recently divorced, or involved with other women. The unconscious wishes that emerged in treatment made very clear that her curiosity about these women revolved around her wish to outdo them, to be better partners than they had been. In short, she acted out her fantasy that she would make the father happier than the mother could. This fantasy served partly to ward off her infantile feeling of being smaller and too young to be satisfying to the father. It emerged in treatment that her habitual and mindless use of lotions expressed an unconscious identification with the mother, whom the patient remembered as having had many somatic problems and as regularly taking medicine when the patient was young. Indeed, the patient especially remembered the father's interest in and supportiveness of the mother when she was ill.

Myth of Passivity. Her experience of her lotion habit and her experience of her difficulties in general reflect the hysterical "myth of passivity." She experienced the habit as visited on her, and her fantasy of how the symptom would disappear involved the same illusion of passivity: something would make it stop or it would go away by itself, almost by magic.

Developmental Achievements and Dominant Defenses. Even on the basis of the brief information presented, the patient's relatively advanced level of libidinal and ego development is clear. The patient's prime defenses are repression, hysterical denial, and displacement. Her limited access to childhood memories and general dearth of conscious fantasy or daydreams suggest that repression is predominant. Her need to edit and select what she attends to in men (seeking to actualize Oedipal wishes) demonstrates hysterical denial; denial that is limited to the experience of romantic objects.

The patient's developmental history suggests that the pre-genital phases have been traversed without significant fixation of drive or ego. The birth of a sibling seems to have aggravated her Oedipal struggle and resulted in an internalized conflict concerning her wish to outdo and replace the mother and guilt about this wish. The nature of the patient's symptoms, the nature of her defenses, and her extensive ego resources all suggest that she has developed to the phallic-Oedipal level without appreciable fixation.

From the material presented thus far, most of which was culled from diagnostic interviews, a hysterical neurosis can be tentatively diagnosed. What follows is, first, a report of several themes that emerged during the early phase of intensive therapy that highlight the hysterical aspect of the patient's personality style and neurotic conflicts and, second, a description of a central transference paradigm that became clear in the middle phase of the psychotherapy.

Themes in Early Psychotherapy

Illusion of Passivity. Although the patient could be very much aware of her active role in interactions that lacked strong personal significance, she proved to be far less capable of such judgments in heterosexual situations. In the latter situations, she felt that things "happened to me," leaving her feeling passive and helpless in relation to the object's actions. For example, on her first date with a man, while in his apartment, the conversation turned to an "abstract" discussion of sexual matters. Though it turned out that she had brought sex into the conversation and had, unconsciously, behaved seductively with him, she was surprised when he began making advances, and was equally surprised by his confusion and anger when she rebuffed him. Her conscious experience did not include her own contribution to the situation. She talked of not knowing what he wanted, not having thought about the implications of her going to his apartment, taking off her shoes, talking about sex on the first date, etc. Though this woman's profession concerned the commerce between people and the impact of subtle messages in public relations and advertising, this type of understanding of interpersonal situations was, via a pseudo naïveté and a restriction of ideation, unavailable. The patient was not uncomfortable with her passivity in this situation; indeed, to be like a helpless, passive child was congruent with an unconscious fantasy of being a helpless little girl in the hands of a powerful father. It served to blind her both to her libidinal wishes toward the man and to her wishes to control and manipulate him with her sexiness.

At times the patient reported that she had been "crazy" with respect to some interaction, and talked about how little she understood why she did some of the things she found herself doing. She could avoid recognizing her responsibility for one of her own acts, feeling instead that the impetus for it was visited on her from within, from her unconscious, from her "crazy" side.

The patient developed an interest in astrology, the occult, and organic cooking as each came into vogue. Though she never pursued any of these interests in depth, she called on them in a particular way when it was psychodynamically necessary to do so. Half believing it, she would explain away an unsuccessful date, an approachable man, or a heterosexual situation that was either frightening or unfulfilling by seeing herself as a plaything of the stars, the spirits, or her cooking. Here her thinking was not ritualistic and obsessive; rather, she was living out an appeal to a higher, stronger power. Her need was not to establish control over death or aggression, but to relocate the responsibility for her urges, acts, and their consequences outside herself and to live out an unconscious fantasy of being protected or excited by strong, paternal forces.

Hysterical Cognition, a Character Resistance. During the beginning of treatment, a critical character resistance was the cognitive fog that fell when conflictual matters were discussed. At such moments the time, place, or details of recent important events would suddenly be highly indefinite. This, of course, seemed to buttress the patient's sense of herself as a confused observer of events that somehow happened to her. Her conflict around seeing and looking, particularly her sexualizing the process of looking itself, had to be clarified before she could "see" much therapeutic material accurately.

The Nature of the Intrapsychic Conflict. Only in the course of long-term therapy or psychoanalysis can intrapsychic conflicts be completely understood. As the point of this case illustration is diagnosis during evaluative interviews and initial treatment of the patient, the intrapsychic conflicts only as they were discerned during the first six months of treatment will be presented.

The patient's search for an idealized Oedipal father was central. In the transference the patient replayed her tendency to see only what would uphold her image of the therapist as invincible. Her fantasies about the therapist were of the most stereotyped and romanticized kind, and she was upset and depressed when she ran into him outside of the therapy and he looked so "ordinary." Therapy and the therapist were initially cloaked in a magic the patient did not wish to have dispelled. This was the magic of the powerful Oedipal parent. The patient's repeated disappointment in men reflected her sense that they fell short of an unconscious fantasy of the Oedipal father. Many of her attempts to establish a heterosexual relationship had been directed by an unconscious wish to find a man as exciting, protecting, and powerful as her phallic-Oedipal infantile fantasy of a strong father. This longing turned out to have a strong narcissistic component as well. It emerged that the patient felt the father favored her scientifically inclined younger sister and her athletic brothers. Via an identification with the mother, the patient saw her own needs, like the mother's, as overwhelming and disgusting to the father, as ultimately alienating him. In her memories and transference reactions, the feelings of having been disappointing to the father became clear. Thus the longing for father also involved a fantasy of acceptance by him to repair this narcissistic wound. In her relationship with men she continually assumed that the men were much brighter, particularly in technical and scientific areas (which was often completely untrue) than she, yet at the same time she often behaved in a competitive and challenging way with them. This was a repetition of her experience of a relationship with the father, which she unconsciously wished would now, finally, turn out differently. She would find herself "walking on eggshells" with men, continually worried that her needs and demands would drive them away. She expected men to retreat from her just as she had experienced her distant, mildly depressed father as withdrawing from her mother. She commonly chose insecure men who were so in need of her reassurance that she felt they would not, like the father, walk off in disgust or quietly withdraw from her.

The patient's highly conflictual curiosity about other women with whom her men were involved led, in the early therapy, to an understanding of her competitive strivings vis-à-vis other women. In typical hysterical fashion, she would invite men to tell about the other women while attempting to maintain the illusion that they had volunteered the information. She would listen with a very competitive ear, scoring herself against the other women, feeling best about herself when the men implied that she was more beautiful or intelligent than the others. This information was very ambivalently sought. In addition to having to avoid recognizing her part in eliciting it, she often quickly forgot it. This forgetting was an expression of her guilt about her wish to outdo and replace the Oedipal mother and the fear of her retaliation. She would also punish herself for these competitive and murderous wishes by becoming depressed and by choosing unsuitable men.

The wish to displace the mother and guilt about this wish turned out to play a significant role in producing several other symptoms. Her habitual use of lotions and episodes of concern about her health represented a wish to substitute herself for the mother in relation to the father. The medical risk she ran in using the lotions expressed her punishment of herself for her competitive and murderous wishes toward her mother. Similarly, her preoccupations with the approval of her superiors and secondary rivalry with other supervisees involved conflict about her Oedipal, competitive feelings toward her mother. Her need for approval from mother substitutes seemed to fend off her private conviction that *she* knew more than any of them and was more attractive than any of them. The need for approval, in short, fended off and made amends for her sense of herself as better than these older women. Later on, the rivalry with other supervisees also turned out to express her competitive feelings toward her siblings.

In sum, intrapsychic conflicts were essentially Oedipal, involving both delimited symptoms (neurotic use of lotions) and less focused neurotic patterns of living (disappointment in men; neurotic preoccupation with their opinion of her; curiosity about other women). The conflicts were predominantly concerned with ambivalent strivings toward current substitutes for childhood objects, pivoting on wishes for a close, exclusive relationship with the father.

Vicarious, Identificatory Quality of Relationships. Her self-experience with those important to her was a major topic of discussion in the early portion of the therapy. She described a feeling of needing competent, "strong" people to be involved with her because then she could feel strong with them. It was not that her sense of self changed in any profound or fundamental way; rather, the relationship with the "strong" object became a focus for infantile fantasies of borrowing, sharing, or appropriating the father's strength.

Vicarious enjoyment of others' success also turned out to fend off her envy and competitiveness. She would be "happy for others" (usually women) in an unconsciously magical way, sharing their happiness or success to ward off her rage and envy at their accomplishments. In short, the unconscious idea seemed to be "If the success belongs to both of us then there is nothing you have that I need, envy, long for, or wish to take away."

Her Experience of Her "Image." It emerged that the patient had a variety of interests and tentatively explored talents that she had backed away from. Her self-exploration led to the delineation of a highly conventional image of what a young woman must be like, an image that turned out to have a powerful impact on what she felt was appropriate or proper to do. She was unaware that she had such enduring, inhibiting standards of propriety, for it was currently unstylish for someone in her position to acknowledge that they had such firm, somewhat Victorian standards. The patient, without awareness, was avoiding activities that were inconsistent with this fixed image of femininity. Jogging, playing chess, or modern expressive dancing were areas that she experienced as too undignified, exposing, or masculine to be congruent with this internal image. With her realization that she was trimming away areas of experience that could be rewarding and enjoyable in order to live up to an Oedipal fantasy of what attractive women do and are, she was relatively easily able to extend her horizons and begin some new, rewarding educational and recreational pursuits. Before therapy, she had begun to elaborate a set of pseudo interests, areas that she felt would be attractive and acceptable to others, but which she fundamentally did not enjoy. She often had the sense that she should be liking what she was doing, but did not. She felt a sense of emptiness after such activities and came to realize that it resulted from the fact that these interests were not really her own. She recognized that by engaging in such activities, she was seeking to present a certain "image," rather than seeking areas she really enjoyed. She had been more concerned with how she looked than how she felt.

Alterations of Consciousness and Attention. The patient's restricted capacity for critical, logical, and objective understanding of qualities and acts of others during affect-triggering situations has been noted. Her tendency to experience such objects impressionistically and to maintain an illusion about her relationships congruent with an Oedipal wish for firm and strong paternal protection has also been described. These trends tended to work synergetically via a characteristic alteration of consciousness and attention.

Typical of the hysterical personality, the patient shows a global shift in attention and the centrality of ideas in consciousness. At the beginning of heterosexual attachments, this shift permitted her to feel as if the object or self were living up to the unconscious Oedipal fantasies or preconscious derivative images. The shift involved a dilating of attention, a glancing attention to details, and a turning of herself over to the rush of external events. She anticipated excitement, some vague, as yet unknown pleasure. In this ego state there was commonly a peripheral awareness that she was wishing or willing the anticipated excitement, and that if she scrutinized it too carefully it would evaporate.

The ego state involved warding off sexual fantasies by suspending clear, logical thinking. The patient would be aware of a diffuse feeling of anticipation and excitement, sometimes tinged with fear, would be aware that it concerned a possible relationship with a man, but would be only vaguely and peripherally aware of her sexual fantasies or longings. She would often find herself nervous and excited in the presence of the possible romantic partner, but be struck by how completely "blank" her mind was. In short, this narrowing and dilating of attention and "fogging" of consciousness helped her avoid the realization that a fantasy could not be realized in any adult relationship.

A Central Transference Paradigm

Though most of this case study has concerned the evaluation and initial treatment stages, a transference paradigm became apparent after a year and a half of treatment which illustrates some of the hysterical features discussed in this chapter: the patient reported that she had sexual fantasies about the therapist outside the treatment sessions but simply found her mind providing no such thoughts in the sessions. She reflected little in her associations about why she, not "her mind," might be motivated to avoid such thoughts. We see at once the patient's sense of passivity in relation to the thoughts that her mind "produced."

At this point in the treatment, the patient's associations led to an understanding of several determinants of her tendency to fail to think sexual thoughts about the therapist in the sessions. The associations ran as follows: the patient remembered thinking back to the beginning of treatment, remembering her thought that patients are supposed to have sexual fantasies about their therapists, and remembered a proclamation (made in jest) to herself that she would be different and not have such experiences. She remembered thinking that sexual feelings were produced by the therapist's methods. Here we see her immediate tendency to allocate her sexual strivings toward the therapist to his "method," the therapy "situation," and what is "supposed to happen." To avoid giving in to these fantasied expectations, the patient presented herself as composed and was very concerned about how the therapist would view and evaluate her. While she viewed this as avoiding the therapist's expectation that she have sexual fantasies, it emerged later that the wish to be composed was also designed to be attractive to the therapist, to be different from his other patients, and therefore to be chosen by him for a sexual relationship. We see, then, the wish expressed in disguised form through and by the defense.

When some sexual fantasies emerged at this period in the treatment, the patient reported that she went home and deliberately worked at having sexual fantasies about the therapist "because I'm supposed to and because I want to be a good patient, a patient who pleases you" (said with an edge of annoyance). Here again the use of an illusion of passivity clearly reflects an infantile idea of femininity and disguises this hysterical patient's striving for activity and control, which, in her stereotyped view of objects, she saw as masculine. She experienced a sense of complying with the therapist, being the passive little girl who gives father what he, not she, wants. This served to avoid responsibility for the content of the fantasy, for she attributed its production to the therapist and her over-all experience was that she produced it because someone else made her do it. She did not seem annoyed that the therapist made her do it; rather, the situation seemed comfortable, in contrast to the helplessness and rage an anally fixated personality would feel in a similar situation. The patient did not, of course, recognize the active, phallic, and aggressive urges that she was expressing in the self-conscious, deliberate construction of the fantasy and the report of it. The fantasy was a controlled production, not a spontaneous one by which the patient might feel passively and suddenly excited. It was brought to the therapist with the attitude, "You want me to have fantasies, I'll have them, see!" Finally, the fact that the fantasy was not exciting expressed the patient's disappointment and annoyance with the therapist: "You are as unexciting and disappointing as all men. Your wish that I be excited by thinking about you will not come true." In this way, her own sexual wishes toward the therapist were felt to be controlled. The patient's attempts at control were themselves repressed, for to be feminine was to be uncontrolled and a bit "crazy." The stereotyped behaviors the patient saw as masculine and feminine bore the stamp of the Oedipal child's attempts to discriminate rigidly and completely between acceptable male and female behavior.

In this illustration we see the many ways in which the hysterical ego and defensive style show themselves in the transference. The hysterical personality typically shows this web of illusions and assumptions of the self as passive to fend off active, phallic and aggressive strivings. Also typically hysterical is the degree to which ego and ego defensive styles need to mirror the patient's rigid conception of sex-specific behaviors.

Therapeutic Alliance and Transference

Probably most diagnostic of the hysterical personality was the quality of the patient's transference and the working alliance that she was capable of maintaining in the face of it.

Her initial transference feelings were focused and clear inferentially, but she unconsciously sought to ward them off. The therapist was experienced in the transference as a somewhat magical, powerfully longed-for father by whom she wished to be loved. These wishes were not, as would be the case in a borderline or severely narcissistic patient, desperate wishes for actual immediate gratification. The patient never grew primitively enraged when the therapist refused to gratify needs, though of course she felt angry and disappointed as needs emerged, were clarified, and interpreted, rather than being gratified. The patient, in short, was able to recognize the "as if" quality of the transference (Tarachow, 1963), could recruit sufficient cognitive, intellectual, and impulse-delaying ego resources to take distance from her experience and progressively understand it. In spite of sometimes intense transference feelings that the therapist preferred other patients, thought poorly of her, or was angry at her, the patient never completely lost sight of the therapist's basic interest in helping her.

The transference was never diffuse, overwhelming, or desperate. For the most part it represented a reliving of the specific set of memories of her fantasies and experience of her parents in her childhood. Though transference reactions were intense, boundaries between self and therapist remained intact. Transference reactions emerged slowly, impeded by transference and characterological resistance, never erupting precipitously. This again reflects the presence of relatively extensive and enduring ego structures.

The transference, in sum, represented an attempt to act out forgotten childhood experiences, was object directed, focused, never primitive or overwhelming, and was always accompanied by some self-observational capacity along with an enduring sense of the therapist's cooperation in the self-explorative process.

This case is in no respect an unusual one. Indeed, a large proportion of outpatient-clinic and private-psychotherapy patients are probably of this kind. Such patients may present a wide range of symptoms, but their personality structures and neurotic conflicts can be observed rather easily.

For several reasons such patients are, in many respects, the most available to intensive psychotherapy or psychoanalysis: (1) they develop an object-directed, focused transference; (2) the transference is not desperate or overwhelming; (3) the capacity for self-observation is, in sound therapeutic circumstances, only transiently lost; (4) the capacity to delay and withstand anxiety and depression generated by the treatment permits a workable transference regression; (5) the intrapsychic conflicts and symptoms in such patients result from the impact of repressed fantasies and wishes, and consequently bringing such unconscious material into consciousness, which is one basic aim of psychoanalytic treatment, has a profound ameliorative effect.

The patient was presented to illustrate a typical hysterical personality suffering from a hysterical neurosis. She had most of the hallmarks of the hysterical personality and the essential properties of neurotic conflict as it typically takes form within the hysterical personality.

HYSTERICAL PERSONALITY IN MEN

The male hysterical personality is characterized by the same basic features as the female. It is marked by phallic-Oedipal conflicts, repression, narrowed and foggy ideation, diffuse affect states, and the maintenance of an ego-syntonic illusion of one's passivity. As in women, the pregenital developmental stages have been traversed relatively successfully, ego controls are generally effective, and objects are experienced as separate from the self and imaged in a relatively differentiated way.

The phallic-Oedipal conflicts usually revolve around intense unconscious phallic strivings toward the mother and a fear of a father perceived as very strong, retaliatory, and potentially castrating. Hysterical men often live out an identity as weak, childish, harmless, and passive. Overtly they seek to please, to be accepted, to be guided, and to avoid competition, though unconsciously they seek to dominate and surpass. The male hysterical personality, like the female, maintains a myth of passivity designed primarily to avoid responsiblity for sexual and aggressive strivings in order to insure continued contact with valued Oedipal objects and to avoid their wrath and abandonment. The hysterical man often tends to try to be superficially entertaining, agreeable, helpful, and "nice." He often has an overweening need to be liked, particularly by older men, who are experienced as powerful, in order to reassure himself that he will not be punished for his unconscious sexual and competitive fantasies and wishes. In such men the castration anxiety associated with the positive Oedipal position is often fended off by retreat to a negative position. This defensive position is often expressed in symptoms, object relations, character, masturbation fantasies, and sexual behavior.

CASE ILLUSTRATION

The following case illustrates the major features of the hysterical personality in a man. This presentation, like the previous one, includes only the evaluation and early portion of psychotherapy. This case should demonstrate that in important respects the hysterical personality shows itself in very similar ways in men and women.

The Patient

The patient was a tall, somewhat gangling 21-year-old graduate student in the natural sciences. He was a friendly, very inviting man, with a soft, childish appearance. He typically sat in the therapy chair with his legs spread wide apart, his arms either sprawled haphazardly over the back of the chair or hanging down between his legs. His way of sitting, reminiscent of a fidgety 10- or 12-year-old, was strikingly inconsistent with his age. He was very appealing personally and at times struck the evaluator as a cute little boy, with a mischievousness just below the surface. He spoke very easily, had a tendency to grow embarrassed quickly, and was anxious to "work hard" in the therapy. He came regularly for appointments, seemed from the outset to treat the therapist with considerable deference, but was not consciously frightened or intimidated by him. He related to the therapist much as to a wise doctor or teacher.

Presenting Compaints

The patient's initial communication of his presenting problems was strikingly vague and diffuse. By the third session they had become slightly clearer: he had been an excellent student while simultaneously working as a highly skilled technician. He performed the latter job very proficiently, far better than most men of his age in that field. His academic work for his Ph.D. was suffering, however, for he had less and less motivation to pursue it. His parents, to whom he was still quite attached, were encouraging him to give up the technical job. The latter was "fun, like a game"; he could not drop it and obviously did not want to. His real ambitions, however, lay in a career as a scientist, for which his graduate work was preparation.

He found himself having increasing trouble concentrating on his studies, was bored or anxious in class, and seemed to lose interest in virtually everything once he had become somewhat proficient at it. Typically he was enthusiastic and developed a close tutorial relationship with a new teacher, being in a "special" relationship with him; but he would quite suddenly reach a point at which he lost interest and turned his attention back to his technical job. He usually completed his academic tasks, but without the interest or proficiency he had initially shown.

Though at first he did not define them as such, he had substantial problems in heterosexual relationships. He kept his life cluttered with studies, job, and a myriad of hobbies and extracurricular activities (such as music and sports), leaving little time or energy to involve himself with women. He described himself as feeling insecure, and as feeling people, particularly women, would not accept him as himself. He approached women hesitantly and felt he had to impress them with his intelligence. He felt he needed to perform for them, feared they would find his sexual advances disgusting and rebuff them, and always waited (often in vain) for the woman to make the first move and to be the more active participant in a relationship. He said that if the woman acted first he could be sure she liked him enough to put up with his sexual interests. The patient preconsciously believed that all women really disliked sex and were disgusted by men's genitals, except for some "dirty women" who actually liked sex. This all made the patient so tentative and fearful that his interest in young women was often not apparent to them.

The patient had a great need to impress others (both men and women) that sometimes led him to exaggerate the range and extent of his accomplishments. He often needed to appear the expert in areas he knew very little about. At times he expounded on a subject about which he knew so little that he could look quite foolish. He loved to have people be pleased by his sparkling performance. This behavior struck the therapist as an attempt to imitate an infantile image of a parent giving a lecture to a child, a lecture that was way above the child's head.

Background

The patient was the fourth child of a well-to-do midwestern family. He had two sisters, two and four years older, and a brother three years older. The father was a very industrious and successful businessman, the mother an active and energetic nurse. Both parents were intellectually oriented, rather driven people, but were able to enjoy and appreciate their children for their nonintellectual qualities.

The patient had always been the brightest of the children and the mother's favorite. He was very close to her during his childhood, when she enjoyed playing with him and teaching him. He remembered feeling that she indirectly encouraged him to stay home with her rather than going out to play as much as he wanted to. He repeated this close, comfortable relationship in school, where he was very endearing to teachers, often becoming the teacher's pet. These patterns, along with being large and overweight from about eight to 16 years, left him with few friends. He rarely felt part of a peer group, was often made fun of, and increasingly retreated to his home and mother as he grew up. He always had a few close friends, however, whom he kept throughout childhood. He spoke about these friends with a warmth which reflected how much they meant to him.

He remembered his relationship with his next older sister as being much more important than that with his brother or oldest sister. He had bitter arguments with this sister about virtually anything. They mocked and degraded each other's accomplishments, these being the very ones with which each tried to gain the mother's exclusive attention. It seemed that although the mother tried to divide her attention evenly among her children, she felt a special bond with the patient and he received more attention than his siblings.

Patient's Initial View of Parents and Siblings

The patient initially described parents, siblings, and many others in glowing terms. They were all warm, sincere, understanding, etc. He had a hard time communicating what annoyed him about his parents and, in the early therapy, responded with an embarrassed, mischievous, and guilty smile to the therapist's suggestions that he had had some hostile feelings toward his parents or others. He continually stressed the warm, accepting side of his relationships with them. Though he confided a great deal in his parents, he came to realize how much he selected what he told them—choosing what would please them. He often changed his plans if his parents even mildly objected to them.

The patient viewed his parents as essentially caring, protective, and interested. He showed himself aware of the pressures on and responsibilities of his parents, of their strong and weak points, yet he tended to select from what he knew only what confirmed a pollyanna-ish view of the "happy family." His initial view was of a very harmonious, virtually unconflictual home, a picture "too good to be true." One of the initial resistances in the treatment involved the patient's need to see his parents as only kind and protective and to see his family as devoid of anger and conflict. Though he showed himself capable of seeing the realities of his family, his experience of them was significantly distorted by an unconscious fairy-talelike fantasy.

The patient saw himself as always having been closer to his mother than to his father. The father was more inclined toward athletic pursuits and though he did not put much explicit pressure on the patient to perform athletically, the patient felt off and on during his childhood that his father would have been much more pleased and involved with him if he had been more athletic. His brother and sisters, who performed less well academically, were better in sports (and had more friends) and, it seems, received more attention and positive regard from the father.

Though he spoke reluctantly and with embarrassment about his parents' sexual lives, he said he felt they enjoyed sex and were quite open about it. There was not a great deal of nudity in the house, but the parents were less than careful about locking doors, and on several occasions the patient happened in on them during intercourse. He found it puzzling that he should feel so inhibited sexually while they were so open and seemed to be so responsive to each other sexually and emotionally. He was completely unaware of being either frightened or excited upon seeing them be affectionate or sexual with each other.

His view of his parents, along with his view of other important people and affectively important events, was obscured by his cognitive and communicative style. Though he showed himself very capable of systematic and scientific thought when it came to his studies or his technical field, he was strikingly vague, global, and unspecific when he tried to think or tell about people, his feelings about them, or feelings they might have about him. Under the pressure of affects he blocked, forgot, and grew much vaguer cognitively than was usual for him.

Review of Hysterical Elements and Nature of the Hysterical Process

Even in the material thus far presented, many facets of the hysterical personality, as defined in this monograph, are to be seen in this patient. First, the requisite strengths in the personality for this diagnosis: (a) In his communications about others and affective ties to them the patient shows a capacity to empathize with others, to feel close to them, and to maintain the boundaries between himself and others. His history shows his capacity to make and keep friends and relate to them in a trusting and enduring way. There are no signs of a sense of primitive malevolence in others such as are seen in borderline or psychotic patients. (b) He has been and continues to be able to channel his energies into socially and personally productive and fulfilling pursuits. He has some work and study inhibitions, but these show a rather marked onset and seem related to some special feature of his relationships in work situations (such as having a special, parent-child relationship with teachers). The inhibitions seem connected with unconscious fantasies and not the result of any deficit in the ego's capacities to make contact with objects. (c) The autonomous, synthetic, intellectual, and other basic aspects of ego functioning are generally mature and well functioning. He shows a capacity for delay, impulse control, and resilience in ego strategies. (d) His superego is generally intact. It seems to serve as a guiding force, is not primitively severe or aggressivized, and seems to give his life an essential sense of direction. It does not have the anal-sadistic aspects found in the obsessive-compulsive superego. He does not usually evoke severe self-punishment or censure; rather, he can judge his own acts and seems capable of changing his behavior in accord with his standards. Though he often looks to others to "tutor" him and seems to work less effectively without such a guiding, parental figure, this need for a parent-child relationship seems to grow from needs to repeat an infantile relationship and is not necessary for the functioning of the ego as it would be in, say, a borderline patient, who lacks these ego capacities. (e) The therapist-evaluator sensed a ready wish in the patient to form a relationship, indeed an eagerness to relate, coupled with a responsiveness to the therapist's comments. All this reflects the patient's essentially object-related capacities.

Second, we see a delimited conflict, which involves objects and the patient's relationships with them and centers on phallic-Oedipal issues. The conflicts seem, on the basis of what has been reported above, to center on some fear of phallic superiority, of being the Oedipal victor. Whether in relationships with women or in the sphere of work, whenever he finds himself in a competitive situation he must inhibit his capacities by losing interest or he must create a "special" relationship with a protecting, parental adult which promises to remove him magically from the competitive sphere. The conflicts do not completely block activity in these spheres, but distort it in a regular and expectable way. In any situation in which he feels tempted to succeed sexually or academically, he comes to feel the situation is making him compete. This then becomes an excuse for turning his energies toward finding a "special" arrangement. His technical job provides an excellent opportunity for fulfillment within the confines of his neurosis, for the job is considered a game, is *not* valued by the parents (nor really devalued by them either), is not considered grown-up work, and holds little chance for advancement and thus little temptation to compete. His neurosis thus interferes with the best and ultimately most rewarding expenditure of his energies, but does not entirely block his outlets for love and work.

In the realm of social relationships we see an inhibition of sexual assertiveness. The patient seems to be operating on the assumption that women simply do not like sex, but that they do like relationships and that they could even like him if he impressed them sufficiently. Though he does not fantasize a great deal, his sense of relationships is based on childish images of both men and women as clean, noble, and singularly nonsexual. When the therapist (quite intentionally) used a vernacular term to refer to an emergent sexual fantasy about women to whom the patient felt attracted, he cringed and said he could not think about things like that so directly. Again the conflicts have a clearly phallic-Oedipal quality: pure and fallen women are differentiated, implying an infantile fantasy that the mother disdains the disgusting sexual father and prefers to soothe, comfort, and mother the patient. The mother will then, the unconscious fantasy goes, throw over the father and remain with the son. These conflicts distort the patient's approaches to objects, yet, as in the work situation, he is still capable of warm and reasonably close relationships. These are both important points which distinguish the hysterical personality from more severe forms of psychopathology.

The patient's neurotic resolution of these conflicts was also prototypically hysterical and can be abbreviated as: "If I remain a passive child who is taught, tutored, and led, if I steer clear of real adult activity (such as academic pursuits or sexual intercourse) which threatens to expose my competitive and murderous wishes toward Father, and if I remain a child at play (the technical job), I will be assured a place as Mother's special, bright, essentially nonaggressive child and will avoid the dangers of retaliation from Father." The patient seemed, then, to be striving to maintain his overclose relationship with his mother, yet having to inhibit his full phallic assertive potential in the bargain. He continually established relationships patterned on those with his mother, both for primary libidinal gratification and to avoid his phallic-aggressive strivings. He needed always to be in a tutee relationship with someone to assure him that he was learning *from* him and accepting him as superior; in this way he would be sure to pose no threat to the other, and thus be in no danger of retaliation from him.

Defensive Structure and Style

The patient's dominant defense mechanism was repression (to not know something he ought to know). His memories of childhood, particularly the sexual and aggressive aspects, were largely repressed. The repression was not stubborn and pervasive, and in the course of treatment he found himself able to remember more, although infantile sexual activity was clearly repressed more severely. He remembered with little difficulty, for example, the following situation: he, another little boy, and a little girl, all eight years old, would go into the woods and play house together. He and the other boy would each want to be the father and would sometimes fight about it. Though the memory aroused a great deal of embarrassment, which the patient could eventually see suggested there had been some sex play too, he could not remember it. The Oedipal aspect of this memory is obvious and noteworthy, as is its status as a screen memory in the classical sense (Freud, 1899). In this patient we see, then, selective repression of infantile autoerotic activity, and a generally repressive style in a tendency to see his childhood relationship with his parents as good, nice, warm, and excessively understanding. Related to this tendency to see parents and self in these desexualized terms, the patient presents a split in the ego common in hysteria (and not uncommon in all neurosis): he knows, indeed by personally witnessing it, that his parents do behave sexually with each other, yet he feels that they are essentially nonsexual. He keeps separate the fact of their sexual activity from an infantile attitude toward them that lives on alongside of it. The patient's mode of cognition is distorted in these specific and circumscribed situations which invoke sexual or aggressive fantasies or wishes. When the content of his thoughts is concerned with impersonal, nonaffect-laden material (such as in his technical job), he thinks in a highly systematic, careful fashion. When concerned with matters of people and feelings, he suddenly becomes vague, global, and confused. This cognitive style both buttresses and is supported by the specific defense of repression, for it too facilitates the obscuring of sexual and aggressive ideas.

The patient presents well-consolidated ego achievements of the anal stage, such as reaction formation, but makes little use of undoing, hypercathexis of words and ideas, and ritualistic-magical thinking. He does show isolation of affect, but this is a much more transient defense (that gives way easily when interpreted) than is found in an affectively dulled obsessional character or neurotic. He rarely uses the primitive defenses of projection and denial. He does use the perceptual defenses of selectively perceiving, particularly when it comes to the tutoring object (whom he must see as powerful and insuperable), but to a very different degree from the pervasive denials of the psychotic or borderline patient.

An Oedipal Compromise

The patient's behavior implied an unconscious fantasy that was brought to light in the early phase of treatment. He found himself discussing or taking positions about matters that he knew little about as if he were well versed in them. He also exaggerated reports of his accomplishments and experiences to others, telling them, for example, of the many famous musicians he had met. He felt he always needed to "impress" others and became aware that he feared he would not be fully accepted if he did not exaggerate his feats and exhibit them. He did not delude himself into believing that he knew as much as he pretended. Indeed, he often felt that he had gotten in so deep with his exaggerations that he was appearing foolish. He was preconsciously aware that he was afraid people would not take him seriously and would see him as a child unless he presented himself in this glamorous and impressive fashion. At the same time he was dimly aware that his bragging also made him appear quite childish. He was striking an internal bargain: he strove to impress, but was protected by the knowledge that the feats he claimed were mere fantasies and that therefore he was safe from retribution for them.

This need to exhibit himself had correlates in his approach to any new field of study. Soon after discovering a new field of interest, he would think of some possible discovery or invention on the very frontier of the field and immediately try to make the discovery or create the invention. He described how much of his initial enjoyment in *working* in these areas was soon replaced by a need to be really outstanding and admired. Part of the pattern of losing interest in an area of study seemed to involve this shift. The initial excitement at *doing* faded as the emphasis shifted to a need to achieve quickly and dramatically and *be* famous.

Interestingly, both the exaggerated reports of his accomplishments and the need to achieve immediately did not promote (indeed to some extent interfered with) the actual respect of colleagues and actual achievement. This seemed clearly to be one of the functions of both of these trends. In fantasy, he could live out images of himself as famous and revered, while he sought to avoid the retaliation that he unconsciously feared and expected if he were *actually* to work toward achieving his goals.

As part of his neurotic compromise, he needed to cling to infantile Oedipal fantasies of being more powerful than the father, but also needed to avoid action that might lead to real achievement that for him represented Oedipal victory. He needed to seek exaggerated goals, but only as a weak little boy, knowing all the time that he would not really be able to achieve these goals soon. This permitted him to see himself as an ambitious little boy, who looks to strong and learned tutors, who is still in the process of preparing himself, and who has not yet challenged anyone. To quiet his internal fear of a father, he could always tell himself that, in comparison to these exaggerated dreams, he had failed.

Early in treatment derivatives of Oedipal fantasies from the latency period emerged. The patient recalled a time when he wanted to be Superman and other powerful phallic figures. He also remembered family-romance fantasies from age six to eight in which he imagined that he had a very rich and stunningly successful mother and father, the latter of whom would teach him to be as successful as himself. In therapy it could be reconstructed that these fantasies became more important, as indeed did the whole world of fantasy, as the patient found himself more and more on the periphery of his peer group.

Myths of Passivity and Acting-Out in the Early Therapy

The patient's early associations to "competition" provide an opportunity to see several myths of passivity in operation, as well as the hysterical need to avoid real success discussed above.

At about the tenth session of the twice-a-week psychotherapy, the patient described how much he disliked several large classes he was in, because they were "making me be competitive." The first resistance in the treatment was the patient's conviction that something in the environment was making it a "competitive situation." After several sessions of work on this, he began to recognize that he could conceivably approach a class as a place where he could work for himself, use his own goals in the course as a standard, and that the competition he felt around him was really coming from within himself. He then associated to how there are others in the class who are "grinds," that they infuriate him because all they think about is work. "So why did he not just feel indifferent to them, why such strong feelings?" the therapist asked in a variety of ways. The patient gradually came to see that he felt immensely competitive with these students because they were the ones who might do better than he. He became more and more aware of how much he wanted to outdo them.

We see here, in this initial set of resistances, a myth of passivity: I am not competitive, the competition is forced on me by the situation (the class, the university, etc.), I am helpless to do anything about it, and I must either follow suit and be competitive or leave the situation. The function of this stance was to disown responsibility for his own competitive, specifically phallic-aggressive, strivings. To recognize these as his own raised infantile fears—primarily castration anxiety and secondarily a fear of dissolution of his tie with his mother. In addition to fearing his father, later material emerged in the treatment indicating that the patient had felt as a child that he must be passive, intellectually oriented, and not too boyish in order to maintain his overclose relationship with mother. He had felt not only that his mother would be more pleased with him as an intelligent but somewhat feminine boy, but that his more phallic-aggressive fantasies and strivings were a danger to his relationship with her. To remain close to her he had to inhibit these phallic-aggressive strivings out of fear that she would either dislike him for them or would accept his incestuous advances.

In his adult life he sought to avoid this ostensibly externally imposed competition by fleeing into "special situations" with teachers or into his job ("play"). In both cases he was affirming to himself the illusion that he was really only a helpless child. As such he might have some fantasies of fame and fortune, but these were so exaggerated as to be "harmless." Thus he fled into relationships which repeated his passive, tutored relationship with his mother in latency, and which surely harked back to a passive feminine position during the phallic-Oedipal period. In these relationships he could live out an illusion of himself as passive to avoid his competitive, phallic strivings.

To some degree the patient came to face his competitive strivings. This first emerged as he came to recognize that he could work well in a class with those older or younger than he, but not those of his own age. The latter would be at the same starting line, so to speak, and thus it would be a true test of his intelligence to compare his performance with theirs. With those younger or older he could always rationalize their successes or failures compared to himself on the basis of their ages. This led him to remember his excessively close relationships with mother and teachers, his simultaneous movement to the periphery of his peer group, and the compensating childhood fantasies (daydreams) of being so powerful or so famous that all those who were treating him poorly would be sorry, for he would turn the tables on them and *they* would suffer. He began to recognize how much these childhood vendettas and the revenge he sought in connection with them had continued to live on unconsciously and how much they seemed to infiltrate many areas of active and assertive functioning, leading to inhibition or flight from these areas. His associations also led to his anger at his next older sister for taunting him about his daydreams. His rage at and murderous fantasies about her came to light gradually, and were met first with resistance and then with anxiety.

This material was coming to light in the treatment at a regular pace. Surprisingly, the thoughts and memories did not seem intellectualized, and emerged with affect as the material deepened. The economics of the patient's psyche, however, made it necessary for him to pay a price for this, in the form of acting out. Without telling the therapist, he dropped a course and then presented a plan to drop half his semester's load. The patient had gone to summer sessions and could easily afford to drop these courses without damaging his academic career. This very reasonable explanation led therapist and patient to overlook the significance of dropping these courses, which represented a retreat from active, phallic productivity. He described a feeling that he needed to work on his problems, to expand his social skills, explore his interest in music, etc. (all of which were valid aims for him), and for this he needed to drop courses. For his therapy to be most effective, he felt, he needed to devote more time to it. He was creating a "special situation" for himself with the therapist and was dropping courses as part of a neurotic compromise: "I'll recognize my competitive, phallic, and murderous wishes, but will remain safe from these impulses and retribution for them by inhibiting action and remaining the bright, harmless student of my mother." When the therapist finally recognized and interpreted this behavior, the patient "forgot" a session and then entered five of the most difficult sessions in the early psychotherapy as he faced his fear of his competitive thoughts and feelings.

Myth of Passivity and Initiating a Sexual Relationship

Another unconscious fantasy of being passive and not responsible for personally unacceptable wishes was at work in the patient's method of choosing a living situation for himself. Needing three roommates to meet his rent, he interviewed men and women and chose one man and two women. He said he had no preconceived idea about how many men or women he would finally accept. He denied any sexual interest in living with women and talked about them as he had talked about his family, very generally and asexually as "people," not women. When he began living with them, one woman became especially interested in him. He was not sure if she was really interested and during this period an unconscious fantasy was uncovered that women really do not like men's bodies, do not really get sexually excited, and that they simply put up with sex. To be really sure if a woman likes sex, the man must be passive. Very much at this roommate's initiative, a relationship was begun, the patient emphasizing how much the woman had been the active party. By disavowing that he had set this up, finding female roommates (including one he obviously had been attracted to on first meeting), he could tell himself that it was not he who was sexual, but the women. This is another example of a myth of passivity. As this pattern was explored and interpreted and the patient began to re-own his actions, his immense guilt and shame about sexual wishes emerged. Interestingly, during this period he found himself "forgetting" to bring up in the sessions his sexual successes with this woman, one of which was losing his virginity with her.

By remaining naïve and vague about the possible consequences of having a woman living with him, he could avoid his own sexual and romantic motives. This facilitated a stance that the situation "just happened" that way, that he did not do anything actively to bring it about. Here again we see the startling incongruity between the patient's cognitive capacities in spheres such as work, in which he is capable of very precise thinking about consequences — indeed, extra-ordinarily complex probabilistic thinking — and in the realm of relationships in which his thinking proved to be much less precise. The latter can be seen as supporting the illusion of passivity, and as part and parcel of repression, which are basic to the neurotic process in the hysterical patient.

Example of Transient Anal
Regression in a Hysterical Personality

As already noted, the hysterical personality, like all neurotic personalities, shows some regression during treat-ment to anal (as well as oral) eroticism. The role of anal-level fixation and regression can be clearly seen in this patient, as can the role of these anal conflicts in his hysterical attitudes and conflicts. These anal features in hysterical patients should always be clearly differentiated from the thorough-going anal regression seen in the obsessional personality. In the hysterical personality, unconscious conflicts over anal eroticism commonly lead the patient to view his genitals and sexual functions as dirty and smelly (as opposed to clean and wholesome). In the obsessional, intense anal-sadistic aggres-sion has promoted an ego fettered by widespread reaction formations, doings and undoings, etc., leaving few areas free from ego processes designed to repudiate and control these anal-sadistic strivings. The obsessional's relationships with objects are also characterized by a treatment of them as feces, demanders of feces, or pleased authorities, not nearly as differentiated a perception of objects as in the hysterical personality.

The portion of the psychotherapy reported below illus-trates how anal material emerges in the treatment of a hysterical personality. During the early phase of psycho-therapy, the patient focused on a series of fantasies of being outstanding and "amazing" in the eyes of others. He often took jobs as a technician and then used his scientific skills, which his fellow technicians lacked, to impress them. It emerged that the unconscious idea was, "The others cannot possibly accomplish what is mere play for me." This hinted at the wish to degrade. The phallic-Oedipal wish to surpass predominated, but was merged with the anal-sadistic wish to humiliate and hurt.

These anal-sadistic aspects came most to the fore during a session early in the therapy when the patient talked of a fantasy and feeling state of being "amazing," of showing others something that would be "so big." He said this feeling state occurred first and only *secondarily* did he try to find something to attach it to. He usually came to hang these feelings on a fantasy of creating a complex research design. He was aware that the research design was merely an available content to attach to what was initially an amorphous feeling of impressing and amazing others. It turned out that the fantasy most often (though not exclusively) occurred when the patient was on the toilet. This led him to say that the moment he sits down to move his bowels, he always has to distract himself from the activity by thinking of something "lofty," often thinking of constructing one of these amazing research designs. He talked then of how base and common, disgusting and dirty it was to move his bowels. With the therapist's interpretation that his disgust seemed excessive and that it seemed that he expended substantial energy in turning his thoughts away from his toilet activity, the patient gradually came to see that there might be some pleasure in his feces that he privately felt strongly tempted to gratify. He came to remember some of his delight in anal behavior as a child, pride in producing a large piece of feces, and some anally tinged mischievousness. It was clear that the defense against these anal, perverse wishes, thinking of something lofty and amazing, also expressed a wish for an object relationship of the anal stage: to amaze his parents at the "big" accomplishment of a large bowel movement. The fantasy on the toilet of doing something "amazing" was a "clean" version of producing a large "dirty" gift of feces. The lofty nature of these strivings was the result of reaction formation and the effect of more general socialization pressures.

Phallic-narcissistic strivings are also implied in the emphasis on size. Unconsciously, then, his competitive Oedipal wishes included some anal components. At the Oedipal period, there may have been some degradation of the libido to anality and some regression on the level of the ego, resulting in unconscious fantasies of surpassing, dominating, and being admired for having a larger genital than his father, which included secondary earlier wishes to produce a larger piece of feces, to be praised for this accomplishment, and also to "shit" on others.

What then distinguishes this from the situation found in the obsessional? These anal components were part of the patient's fantasies and conflicts, but he remained substantially genital in his drive orientation. What anal strivings existed were not the intense, anal-aggressive drives seen in the obsessional. The superego was, therefore, not as aggressivized as it would be in the obsessional personality or obsessional neurotic. Nor was the ego as totally recruited into the effort to fend off aggressive impulses as in the obsessional, for the patient's reaction formations and repressions were generally quite stable. There was little breakthrough of anal-sadistic wishes which would demand an elaboration of the defensive system with, say, rituals, ceremonies, or other compulsive actions. The patient was not constantly preoccupied with such defensive efforts as undoing, obsessional doubting, and compulsive behavior as is the patient with a profound regression of libido and ego to the anal level.

The patient's phallic-narcissistic fantasies had *anal components*, but his drive development was basically phallic, his ambivalence less split and intense than in the obsessional, his aggression less anal-sadistic and more modulated, and his defenses were predominantly displacement and repression, those characteristic of the hysterical personality. Most important, his reaction formations were stable, on the whole his aggressive feelings had been put in the service of accomplishment and in the service of gratifying libidinal wishes, and large portions of his ego were free of obsessive attempts to quiet anal-sadistic aggression. The patient's Oedipus complex had been to some extent influenced by anal conflicts, but no substantial regression to the anal level had occurred during development.

Therapeutic Alliance and Transference

The patient proved in both the evaluation and the psychotherapy to be capable of a sense of trust and cooperation with the therapist. His capacity to distinguish thought from fantasy, his intact self-boundaries, the absence of primitive defenses, and the absence of unintegrated fragments of archaic experience of objects (as seen in narcissistic personality disorders and borderline patients) permitted him to be comfortable and trusting enough to at least attempt to share his thoughts freely.

This alliance, which is made possible by these various personality strengths, made it possible for the patient to experience some strong feelings toward the therapist in the psychotherapy and at the same time to recognize their unrealistic, infantile source. In the early therapy sessions, the patient experienced the therapist as an asexual, kind, but strict parent from whom sexual thoughts and feelings needed to be hidden. As mentioned above, for example, the patient found himself forgetting to mention his actual sexual success with his roommate, dwelling instead on his work, job, and parents. He described thinking outside the session of bringing up this relationship, but it simply did not come to mind. This defensive process is typically hysterical: the patient feels passive in relation to and helpless to stop the unconscious ego defenses of "not knowing" such as repression, repressive cognition, and perceptual denial.

Because of the various areas of personality strength, the patient was capable of weathering infantile feelings in the sessions without such feelings pervasively interfering outside the sessions. Of course, acting out occurred transiently, but the impact of therapy was not generally disorganizing to his life outside of psychotherapy.

Passivity is Syntonic

The patient can be distinguished from paranoid and obsessive-compulsive personalities on the basis of many features: cognitive style, defensive functioning, degree of delimitation of conflicts, transference (object-relational) patterns, among others. These features come together clinically, however, in the patient's comfort with his passivity, helplessness, and image of himself as a striving, promising child. Where obsessional or paranoid personalities would be uncomfortable, if not panicked, at recognizing their dependence, helplessness, and passivity, a hysterical patient, such as this man, is remarkably comfortable feeling this way. The acceptability of these feelings to the self permits the patient to use a myth of passivity and helplessness both as an organizing characterological theme and, in exaggerated form, as a defense.

CLINICAL AND THERAPEUTIC IMPLICATIONS
OF A DIAGNOSIS OF HYSTERIA

Why, then, be so very careful to evaluate these many areas of functioning? Of what value is a diagnosis of hysteria? What does it imply for therapy? These questions are basic and should be routinely asked of any diagnosis or diagnostic process.

First, the hysteric (hysterical personality with neurotic conflict) may tend to underestimate his actual capabilities, may seem more helpless than he is, and may attempt to draw "support" from clinicians, counselors, or anyone in a potentially helping role. It is common for evaluators to be seduced into giving "hand-holding" support to the hysteric, which obviously often promotes neurotic modes of functioning. If the patient is truly a hysteric, therapy must, from the outset, be oriented toward helping him understand his need to feel helpless and to enlist unnecessary aid. Work must be done, also early in the treatment, on the object-related purpose of these illusions about the self, particularly as they arise in the transference.

Second, the diagnosis of hysteria implies a set of psychological capacities necessary for nondirective, self-exploratory psychotherapy. The capacity for delay of gratification, for recognition that fantasies and needs concerning the therapist cannot be gratified, and for continued commitment to treatment in the face of severe anxiety and depression elicited by treatment are all included in the diagnosis of hysterical personality or hysteria.

Third, the diagnosis of hysterical personality indicates the existence of areas not afflicted by neurotic conflicts or characterological limitation.

The diagnosis of hysteria has more specific implications for the nature of the neurotic difficulties and their unconscious roots. The neurotic symptoms are delimited, tend to involve tabooed libidinal and aggressive urges toward infantile objects, and are unconsciously triangular, phallic-Oedipal in nature. The conflicts involve longings toward rather differentiated object representations. The diagnosis of hysteria rules out a variety of neurotic and borderline intrapsychic conflicts and symptoms. A profound sense of worthlessness, a chronic, gnawing hunger that must be immediately and regularly gratified by an omnipotent, pregenital mother, or a need to maintain a symbiotic relationship with a target of the reprojected maternal image, are all in the realm of more serious disturbances, and are not considered part of the definition of the hysterical personality. There are, of course, cases in which both hysterical and more disturbed elements are found. As reference points, however, hysterical personality and hysteria should by definition exclude these more severe expressions of psychopathology.

The hysterical personality's capacity for relatively mature object relationships leads the clinician to expect an organized set of true transference feelings during intensive psychotherapy or psychoanalysis. In contrast to the borderline or psychotic patient who may experience the therapist in fluid, intense, deeply mistrustful, ever-changing ways, the hysterical personality will evidence an enduring set of feelings towards the therapist that have been organized during development around a specific infantile object or set of objects. Rather than experiencing with the therapist diffuse, primitive, or undifferentiated ego states associated with the oral or early anal mother, or experiencing the therapist as a "self-object" (Kohut, 1971), the hysteric experiences the therapist as a true object. Though the transference image of the therapist may at first express itself in subtle, partial, and incomplete ways, the perception of him, at its source, is usually a transformation of a repressed experience of a relatively complex, specific, and organized fantasy of an infantile object.

Most important, the diagnosis of hysteria, if accurately made, indicates significant elaboration and consolidation of psychic structure and extensive, generally effective use of repression. The use of repression and the repressive cognitive style make the dynamic of therapeutic change within the hysteric the basic dynamic of psychoanalytic change: making conscious and accessible to the mature, adult ego what has been unconscious and expressed via derivatives, including symptoms. The hysteric has relegated what was conflictual to the unconscious, and therefore treatment that aims at bringing such unconscious material back into commerce with the conscious ego will bring about a change in the neurotic pattern. The hysteric, by definition, has an ego sufficiently intact to understand, face, work through, and ultimately integrate unconscious urges and fantasies once they are available to consciousness. By virtue of many character resources, the hysterical personality is, therefore, the personality type most amenable to psychoanalysis or intensive psychotherapy.

Finally, a diagnosis of hysteria indicates a special liability to use relationships neurotically. During treatment, the hysteric's use of relationships must be carefully assessed. His conflicts are commonly expressed in relationships, and as the hysteric uses displacement as a major defense, the therapist must be alert to the splitting of the transference or displacement of transference feelings onto current life objects. From the point of view of evaluation, the patient who seems generally to be hysterical, and who exhibits diffuse depression, should be asked carefully about the nature of his adult relationships, particularly heterosexual ones. Commonly, the true symptom turns out to be a maladaptive pattern of neurotic object choices or repeated disappointment in objects that fail to live up to infantile fantasies. It is not uncommon for the diffuse depression to turn out to be secondary to a molar neurotic pattern of life choices which the patient is not aware of.

INTERPRETATION AND COUNTERTRANSFERENCE LIABILITIES WITH HYSTERICAL NEUROTICS

It is of course impossible to deal in any specific way with the interpretive and countertransference problems raised by particular hysterical patients. Only some very general potential difficulties that this personality type presents can be described.

The hysterical personality tends to devalue words and logical deductive thinking, even though he may be intelligent and capable of such verbal thinking. To the extent that he does this, verbal interpretation loses its therapeutic effectiveness. The hysterical personality hears words as caresses, gifts, or punishments. He often uses them to try to *explain away*, rather than to truly explain, his behavior. He often experiences the interpretation as belonging to the therapist while he remains the passive listener. The de-emphasis of words is part of the hysterical personality's cognitive style. Inattention to words becomes a common defense for the hysterical personality. He often simply does not hear the therapist. The wish is to watch the therapist talk, to listen to the tone or quality of his voice, but to consider the words as an unimportant and dull part of the therapy. With some patients this attitude towards words and thoughts can be usefully interpreted as a character resistance. With others this attitude may not yield to interpretation, and treatment results may therefore be limited. With this latter type of hysterical patient, interpretations over a long period of time are not heard, previous insights not remembered, and all insights but the most superficial ones made the responsibility of the scientific, masculine therapist who "understands such complex things."

There are a few general countertransference liabilities in the treatment of hysterical personality. These patients are often blamed for being "manipulative." This type of patient is often described as a "tease," leading the therapist to react with anger (or some defense against it) or anxiety (at his own sexual response). This reaction occurs so frequently in therapists in part owing to the hysterical neurotic's tendency to express unconscious fantasies regularly in his behavior in relationships. Because the hysterical personality's ego (both its conscious and unconscious sectors) has so many relationship capacities, the patient can unconsciously very effectively engineer a certain repetitive pattern in his relationships. Because the patient can be so coercive and repeatedly "successful" in this endeavor, the behavior is often experienced by others as deliberate and under conscious control. When the patient is called "manipulative," he is considered to be willfully acting to organize or disorganize the world around himself, and when called a "tease," he is often viewed as *consciously knowing* he is being seductive and *consciously enjoying* his power to elicit and rebuff the other's response. This sometimes leads the therapist or others in the environment to respond in a retaliatory way, which for some hysterical personalities is itself part of the unconsciously motivated pattern — that is, the anger and censure are unconsciously experienced as dangerous but exciting phallic approaches by the object and punishment for excitement generated. The therapist may find himself using interpretations in a phallic-aggressive, exciting way — such as prematurely interpreting sexual wishes, failing to interpret resistance before dealing with transference and genetic material, and looking to "shock" the patient with his interpretations or questions.

The more subtle countertransference problem involves the therapist's basking in the patient's "positive" transference. The hysterical patient commonly experiences the therapist as an idealized, kind person. Other objects of whom the patient speaks cannot hold a candle to the therapist. Obviously this stance often serves to ward off the aggression and disappointment the patient feels toward the therapist and, more fundamentally, toward the parents of childhood. If the therapist has conflicts around his own narcissism or conflicts around his capacity to tolerate aggression from the patient, he may steer away from interpreting the infantile nature of the patient's idealized perception of him. The patient, particularly a female patient with a male therapist, will be inclined to compare the therapist with other men in her life, and will unconsciously try to provoke his competitive strivings toward these men. When the patient, as is commonly the case, is also subtly challenging the therapist, he may come to feel he has not "proved" himself to the patient and may respond by being exhibitionistic in his interpretations or by allowing the patient's devaluing of other men (often as an implicit comparison of these men with the therapist) to go uninterpreted.

ANXIETY HYSTERIA

Whether anxiety hysteria should be considered a necessary part of the definition of hysteria is an important question. On the basis of clinical observation and dynamic theory it seems wise to follow Freud's view that phobias are syndromes that may appear in many types of psychopathologies and should not be considered a separate and independent psychopathological type. Phobias exist in all types of neurotic, borderline, and psychotic patients. It is also probably not uncommon for phobias to develop transiently during the psychotherapy or psychoanalysis of many types of patients. A patient who evidences an unconsciously determined tendency to avoid a seemingly innocuous thing, situation, or person should be viewed as having a "phobic" symptom and should not be labeled an "anxiety hysteric." Following Freud, the term phobia should apply to a dynamic of symptom formation, not to a general description of character.

This is more than a nosological convention; it is basic to the definition of the hysterical personality proposed here. The personality description proposed here refers to a character style, not a specific symptom picture, for the hysterical personality by its nature presents different symptoms from patient to patient and era to era. Phobias are symptoms which occur quite often in hysterical personalities, but should not be considered in any way definitional of, or unique to, this personality type.

Accepting the above, are phobias more common in hysterical personalities? As noted earlier, Freud (1926) said that phobias epitomized the external anticathexes coupled with repression basic to all hysterics. This is a question that can ultimately be settled by research, research that takes an in-depth look at personality style from the points of view of development, ego defenses, cognitive style, etc. Such a study would attempt to discover the probability of various symptoms occurring within such a character structure. Such research is long overdue.

Short of a research response, can we say there is anything about the hysterical personality that would make it particularly prone to develop phobic symptoms? The tendency of the hysterical personality to invoke a myth of passivity, to use defenses of not knowing and not seeing (repression and repressive cognition), and to express conflicts motorically would seem to make it well suited for the development of phobic symptoms. The essential defenses involved in phobia are repression, projection, and displacement. While projection per se is not a dominant hysterical defense, projective tendencies are involved in the illusion of passivity in relation to external power which is basic to the definition of the hysterical personality. Displacement and repression are, of course, dominant hysterical defenses, as discussed above (p. 219). The hysterical personality can be viewed as fertile ground for the phobic symptom, but by no means do all hysterical personalities develop such symptoms.

As with all symptoms, the nature of the constituent ego processes must be carefully assessed to establish if phobia is of the truly neurotic sort found in a hysterical personality or if it reflects more serious ego pathology. The neurotic phobic person has a strong aversion to some innocuous stimuli with a simultaneous awareness of the irrationality of his fear and continual retreat from the feared stimuli. A more seriously disturbed person with a phobia may have no awareness at any level of the irrational nature of his fear. In such persons the phobia shades into a delusion. The quality of the fear itself also often reflects the more serious disturbance. Rather than the diffuse fear of injury or danger seen in hysterical phobias, the more seriously disturbed person may quite consciously and morbidly fear the imagined malevolence or murderousness of other people. A "phobia" with these characteristics would not be expected in a hysterical personality. A hysterical phobia, like any hysterical symptom, must express phallic-Oedipal conflicts, an enduring, unconscious fantasy, and reflect an ego structure consistent with the hysterical personality. Such a phobia should be distinguished from the pervasive and more primitive phobias seen in borderline and psychotic patients. The phobic fears in such patients do not contain an enduring unconscious fantasy involving phallic-Oedipal strivings and some form of castration anxiety; rather, the fear involves the overwhelming of the ego, fear of loss of objects or dissolution of the self, and primary, basic fears of the external world. Such a phobia can be compared to the panic at loud noises seen in infants.

Phobia should be viewed as one of a large variety of symptoms that occurs in the hysterical neurotic. In many patients phobias are a presenting complaint; however, the nature of the conflicts and the personality structure that underlie the symptoms must be assessed to determine if the phobia is the production of a neurotic, borderline, or psychotic personality. As with any symptom, for phobia to be considered reflective of a hysterical personality it must be based on a predominantly Oedipal-phase conflict and the ego must have the essential hysterical features which have been described.

6

CONCLUDING REMARKS

Attempts over the years to understand the nature of a series of entities called hysteria, conversion hysteria, anxiety hysteria, and hysterical personality have yielded an abundance of partial truths. Even in the earliest theories involving a wandering uterus, there was some initial understanding of this psychopathology. At this juncture one could choose simply to discard these theories because they fall short of any thorough explanation and because their flaws are often so very obvious. The problems with earlier generalizations about psychopathology and personality have led many to give up all hope of ever arriving at a useful definition of many types of psychopathologies. They prefer to assess each patient strictly according to his own individual conflicts, ego functions, object relations, etc. This sort of approach, if it is the only approach, is in my opinion incomplete. It does not comprehend the fact that there are certain sets of psychological traits that regularly occur together and that these "syndromes" or "constellations" have what might be called an internal logic, pattern, or theme. These internal patterns may yield important clues about the interaction of specific drive positions, ego functions, and object relations during development and may hold the potential for raising some important researchable questions. If these "constellations" are well defined and if their contents comprise important sectors of the personality, they can be very useful to the clinician. In providing a conceptual framework, they help to orient the diagnostician and to raise more sharply for him the points where his particular patient seems to be consistent with the pattern and where he seems to deviate significantly from it.

Why, then, has so little attention been directed, particularly within psychoanalysis, to careful attempts to define such patterns and syndromes? Clearly, a major reason is that the notion of a character type or syndrome seems to many psychoanalysts necessarily wedded to a general psychiatric nosology based on simplistic, superficial, and largely descriptive aspects of the patient. The labels yielded by such nosologies are of little help to the psychoanalyst or psychoanalytically oriented clinician. Even if such labels do not obscure the analyst's understanding of the patient, they surely do not increase it.

This monograph was begun with the hope that the many advances in psychoanalysis in the last 30 years could be brought to bear on the problems of diagnosis, particularly the diagnosis of hysterical personality. With its better understanding of the ego, its attempts to systematize and better define its concepts, its emphasis on direct observation of children, and its attempts to evaluate the various sectors of the patient's personality more systematically and comprehensively, psychoanalysis is now in a far better position than previously to understand personality constellations and psychopathologies. More sophisticated concepts of ego structure, object relations, and superego functioning are examples of the fruits of these advances which have been applied in this monograph.

It has been my working assumption in this monograph that, as these new perspectives in psychoanalysis are brought into commerce with the earlier partial truths about hysteria (and other psychopathologies), new and much more useful reference points for psychoanalytic diagnosis will be possible. As these concepts become enriched by our better understanding of personality, the concepts may be brought back into clinical, teaching, and research discourse in a clearer and more generally understood fashion. When we are all sure we are speaking the same language, our discourse in all three of these areas will be enhanced. This monograph has been an attempt to add one word to this lexicon.

REFERENCES

Abraham, K. (1921), Contributions to the Theory of the Anal Character. *Selected Papers*. London: Hogarth Press, 1927, pp. 370-392.

———— (1924), Character Formation on the Genital Level of Libido-Development. *Selected Papers*. London: Hogarth Press, 1927, pp. 407-417.

———— (1925), The Influence of Oral Erotism on Character Formation. *Selected Papers*. London: Hogarth Press, 1927, pp. 393-406.

Abse, D. W. (1959), Hysteria. *American Handbook of Psychiatry*, 1:272-292. New York: Basic Books.

———— (1966), *Hysteria and Related Mental Disorders—An Approach to Psychological Medicine*. Bristol, Eng.: Wright.

Ackerknecht, E. H. (1943), Psychopathology, Primitive Religion, and Primitive Culture. *Bull. Med. Hist.*, 14:30-67.

Ackerman, N. (1958), *The Psychodynamics of Family Life*. New York: Basic Books.

Allen, D. W., & Houston, M. (1959), The Management of Hysteroid Acting-Out Patients in a Training Clinic. *Psychiatry*, 22:41-49.

American Psychiatric Association (1952), *Diagnostic and Statistical Manual for Mental Disorder* [1st Ed.].Washington, D.C.: American Psychiatric Association Mental Hospital Service.

Angyal, A. (1965), *Neurosis and Treatment*. New York: Wiley.

Ariès, P. (1962), *Centuries of Childhood*. New York: Knopf.

Bateson, G., Jackson, D., Haley, J., & Weakland, J. (1956), Toward a Theory of Schizophrenia. *Behav. Sci.*, 1:251-264.

Blinder, M. (1966), The Hysterical Personality. *Psychiatry*, 29:227-235.

Boyer, L. B. (1962), Remarks on the Personality of Shamans. *The Psychoanalytic Study of Society*, 2:233-254. New York: International Universities Press.

Brenneis, C. B. (1967), Differences in Male and Female Ego Styles in Manifest Dream Content. Unpublished doctoral dissertation, University of Michigan. (Microfilm.)

Brenner, C. (1977), The Castration Complex in Women. Paper presented to the Michigan Psychoanalytic Society, March.

Breuer, J., & Freud, S. (1893), On the Psychical Mechanism of Hysterical Phenomena: Preliminary Communication. *Standard Edition*, 2:3-17. London: Hogarth Press, 1955.

———— ———— (1893-1895), Studies on Hysteria. *Standard Edition*, 2. London: Hogarth Press, 1955.

Bridges, W. E. (1965), Family Patterns and Social Values in America, 1825-1875. *Amer. Quart.*, 17:3-11.

Brill, N. Q. (1954), Discussion of: *Office Treatment of Ambulatory Schizophrenics*, by Don Jackson. *Calif. Med.*, 81:263-267.

Brodey, W. M. (1965), On the Dynamics of Narcissism: Externalization and Early Ego Development. *The Psychoanalytic Study of the Child,* 20: 163-193. New York: International Universities Press.

Cameron, N. (1963), *Personality Development and Psychopathology.* Boston: Houghton Mifflin.

Caro Baroja, J. (1964), *The World of Witches,* trans. N. Glendenning. London: Weidenfeld & Nicolson.

Carter, R. (1853), *On the Pathology and Treatment of Hysteria.* London: Churchill.

Cash, W. J. (1941), *The Mind of the South.* New York: Knopf.

Charcot, J.-M., & Marie, P. (1892), Hysteria. *Dictionary of Psychological Medicine,* ed. E. Tuke. Philadelphia: Blakiston.

Chasseguet-Smirgel, J. (1970), Feminine Guilt and the Oedipus Complex. In: *Female Sexuality,* ed. J. Chasseguet-Smirgel. Ann Arbor: University of Michigan Press, pp. 94-134.

Chodoff, P. (1954), A Re-examination of Some Aspects of Conversion Hysteria. *Psychiatry,* 17:75-81.

————— & Lyons, H. (1958), Hysteria, the Hysterical Personality, and "Hysterical" Conversion. *Amer. J. Psychiat.,* 14:734-740.

Demos, J. (1970), Underlying Themes in Witchcraft of Seventeenth Century New England. *Amer. Hist. Rev.,* 75:1311-1326.

Deutsch, F., ed. (1959), *On the Mysterious Leap from the Mind to the Body.* New York: International Universities Press.

Deutsch, H. (1930), Hysterical Fate Neurosis. *Neuroses and Character Types.* New York: International Universities Press, 1965, pp. 14-28.

————— (1942), Some Forms of Emotional Disturbance and Their Relationship to Schizophrenia. *Neuroses and Character Types.* New York: International Universities Press, 1965, pp. 262-281.

Easser, S., & Lesser, B. (1965), Hysterical Personality: A Re-evaluation. *Psychoanal. Quart.,* 34:390-405.

Erikson, E. (1950), *Childhood and Society.* New York: Norton.

Escalona, S. (1968), *The Roots of Individuality.* Chicago: Aldine.

Eysenck, H. J. (1957), *The Dynamics of Anxiety and Hysteria.* London: Routledge & Kegan Paul.

Fairbairn, W. R. D. (1954), Observations on the Nature of Hysterical States. *Brit. J. Med. Psychol.,* 27:105-125.

Farber, L. H. (1961), Will and Willfulness in Hysteria. *The Ways of the Will.* New York: Basic Books, 1966, pp. 99-117.

Federn, P. (1940), The Determination of Hysteria vs. Obsessional Neurosis. *Psychoanal. Rev.,* 27:265-276.

Fenichel, O. (1945), *The Psychoanalytic Theory of Neurosis.* New York: Norton.

Ferenczi, S. (1913), Stages in the Development of the Sense of Reality. *Sex and Psychoanalysis.* New York: Brunner, 1950, pp. 213-239.

Fernández-Marina, R. (1961), The Puerto Rican Syndrome: Its Dynamics and Cultural Determinants. *Psychiatry,* 24:79-82.

Fiedler, L. (1960), *Love and Death in the American Novel.* New York: Stein & Day.

Fitzgerald, O. (1948), Love Deprivation and the Hysterical Personality. *J. Ment. Sci.,* 94:701-717.

Freeman, E. W. (1891), The Revolt of Mother. In: *The Great Modern American*

Stories, ed. W. D. Howells. New York: Boni & Liveright, 1920, pp. 207-224.

Freud, A. (1936), *The Ego and the Mechanisms of Defense,* rev. ed. *The Writings of Anna Freud,* 2. New York: International Universities Press, 1966.

———, Nagera, H., & Freud, W. E. (1965), Metapsychological Assessment of the Adult Personality. *The Psychoanalytic Study of the Child,* 20:9-41. New York: International Universities Press.

Freud, S. (1894), The Neuro-Psychoses of Defence. *Standard Edition,* 3:45-61. London: Hogarth Press, 1962.

——— (1896a), The Aetiology of Hysteria. *Standard Edition,* 3:191-221. London: Hogarth Press, 1962.

——— (1896b), Further Remarks on the Neuro-Psychoses of Defence. *Standard Edition,* 3:162-185. London: Hogarth Press, 1962.

——— (1899), Screen Memories. *Standard Edition,* 3:303-322. London: Hogarth Press, 1962.

——— (1900), The Interpretation of Dreams. *Standard Edition,* 4 & 5. London: Hogarth Press, 1953.

——— (1905a), Fragment of an Analysis of a Case of Hysteria. *Standard Edition,* 7:7-122. London: Hogarth Press, 1953.

——— (1905b), My Views on the Part Played by Sexuality in the Aetiology of the Neuroses. *Standard Edition,* 7:271-279. London: Hogarth Press, 1953.

——— (1905c), Three Essays on the Theory of Sexuality. *Standard Edition,* 7:130-243. London: Hogarth Press, 1953.

——— (1908), Hysterical Phantasies and Their Relation to Bisexuality. *Standard Edition,* 9:159-166. London: Hogarth Press, 1959.

——— (1909a), Some General Remarks on Hysterical Attacks. *Standard Edition,* 9:229-234. London: Hogarth Press, 1959.

——— (1909b), Analysis of a Phobia in a Five-Year-Old Boy. *Standard Edition,* 10:5-149. London: Hogarth Press, 1955.

——— (1914), On the History of the Psycho-Analytic Movement. *Standard Edition,* 14:7-66. London: Hogarth Press, 1957.

——— (1916-1917), Introductory Lectures on Psycho-Analysis. *Standard Edition,* 15 & 16. London: Hogarth Press, 1963.

——— (1918), From the History of an Infantile Neurosis. *Standard Edition,* 17:7-122. London: Hogarth Press, 1955.

——— (1920), Beyond the Pleasure Principle. *Standard Edition,* 18:7-64. London: Hogarth Press, 1955.

——— (1923), The Ego and the Id. *Standard Edition,* 19:12-66. London: Hogarth Press, 1961.

——— (1924), The Loss of Reality in Neurosis and Psychosis. *Standard Edition,* 19:183-187. London: Hogarth Press, 1961.

——— (1925), An Autobiographical Study. *Standard Edition,* 20:7-74. London: Hogarth Press, 1959.

——— (1926), Inhibitions, Symptoms and Anxiety. *Standard Edition,* 20:87-172. London: Hogarth Press, 1959.

——— (1930), Civilization and Its Discontents. *Standard Edition,* 21:64-145. London: Hogarth Press, 1961.

——— (1931), Female Sexuality. *Standard Edition,* 21:225-243. London: Hogarth Press, 1961.

Friedlander, K. (1949), Neurosis and Home Background: A Preliminary Report. *The Psychoanalytic Study of the Child*, 3/4:423-438. New York: International Universities Press.

Fuchs, S. (1964), Magic Healing Techniques among the Behahis in Central India. In: *Magic, Faith and Healing*, ed. A. Kiev. London: Free Press of Glencoe, pp. 121-138.

Gelfand, M. (1964), Psychiatric Disorders as Recognized by the Shona. In: *Magic, Faith and Healing*, ed. A. Kiev. London: Free Press of Glencoe, pp. 156-173.

Glover, E. (1932), A Psycho-Analytic Approach to the Classification of Mental Disorders. *On the Early Development of Mind*. New York: International Universities Press, 1956, pp. 161-186.

Goshen, C. E. (1952), The Original Case Material of Psychoanalysis. *Amer. J. Psychiat.*, 108:829-834.

Greenson, R. R. (1958), On Screen Defenses, Screen Hunger and Screen Identity. *J. Amer. Psychoanal. Assn.*, 6:242-262.

Greenspan, S. I., & Cullander, C. C. H. (1973), A Systematic Metapsychological Assessment of the Personality—Its Application to the Problem of Analyzability. *J. Amer. Psychoanal. Assn.*, 21:303-327.

Grinker, R. R., & Robbins, F. P. (1954), *Psychosomatic Case Book*. New York: Blakiston.

Guntrip, H. (1971), *Psychoanalytic Theory, Therapy, and the Self*. New York: Basic Books.

Gutmann, D. (1965), Women and the Conception of Ego Strength. *Merrill-Palmer Quart.*, 11:229-240.

Guze, S. B. (1964), Conversion Symptoms in Criminals. *Amer. J. Psychiat.*, 121:580-583.

_____ (1967), The Diagnosis of Hysteria: What Are We Trying to Do? *Amer. J. Psychiat.*, 124:491-498.

Handelsman, I. (1965), The Effects of Early Object Relationships on Sexual Development. *The Psychoanalytic Study of the Child*, 20:367-383. New York: International Universities Press.

Hansen, C. (1969), *Witchcraft at Salem*. New York: New American Library.

Harland, M. (1910), *Marion Harland's Autobiography*. New York: Harper.

Harlow, H., & Harlow, M. K. (1965), The Affectional Systems. In: *Behavior of Nonhuman Primates*, ed. A. M. Schrier, H. F. Harlow, & F. Stollnitz, 2:287-334. New York: Academic.

_____ & Suomi, S. (1970), The Nature of Love—Simplified. *Amer. Psychol.* 25:161-168.

Harms, E. (1945), Childhood Schizophrenia and Childhood Hysteria. *Psychiat. Quart.*, 19:242-257.

Hartmann, H. (1939), *Ego Psychology and the Problem of Adaptation*. New York: International Universities Press, 1958.

_____ (1950), Comments on the Psychoanalytic Theory of the Ego. *Essays on Ego Psychology*. New York: International Universities Press, pp. 113-141.

_____ & Loewenstein, R. M. (1962). Notes on the Superego. *The Psychoanalytic Study of the Child*, 17:42-81. New York: International Universities Press.

Heidbreder, E. (1933), *Seven Psychologies*. New York: Appleton.

Hendrick, I. (1936), Ego Development and Certain Character Problems. *Psychoanal. Quart.*, 5:320-346.

Henry, J. (1951), Family Structure and the Transmission of Neurotic Behavior. *Amer. J. Orthopsychiat.*, 21:800-818.

——— & Warson, S. (1951), Family Structure and Psychic Development. *Amer. J. Orthopsychiat.*, 21:59-73.

Higginson, T. W. (1891), *Common Sense about Women*. London: Swan Sonnenschein.

Higham, J. (1965), Reorientation of American Culture. In: *Origins of Modern Consciousness*, ed. H. J. Weiss. Detroit: Wayne State University Press, pp. 25-48.

——— (1969), *From Boundlessness to Consolidation: The Transformation of American Culture, 1848-1860*. Ann Arbor, Mich.: Clements.

Hinsie, L., & Campbell, R. (1970), *Psychiatric Dictionary*. New York: Oxford.

Howells, W. D. (1906), Editha. In: *Different Girls*, ed. W. D. Howells. New York: Harper.

Janet, P. (1892-1894), *The Mental State of Hystericals: A Study of Mental Stigmata and Mental Accidents*. New York: Putnam, 1901.

Johnston, M. (1963), Features of Orality in an Hysterical Character. *Psychoanal. Rev.*, 50:663-681.

Jung, C. G. (1936), Dementia Praecox and Hysteria. *The Psychology of Dementia Praecox*. New York: Nervous and Mental Disease Publishing Co., pp. 70-98.

Kagan, J., & Lewis, M. (1965), Studies of Attention in the Human Infant. *Merrill-Palmer Quart.*, 11:95-127.

Kernberg, O. (1967), Borderline Personality Organization. *J. Amer. Psychoanal. Assn.*, 15:641-685.

——— (1970), Factors in the Psychoanalytic Treatment of Narcissistic Personalities. *J. Amer. Psychoanal. Assn.*, 18:51-85.

Klein, G. S. (1958), Cognitive Control and Motivation. In: *Assessment of HUman Motives*, ed. G. Lindzey. New York: Holt, Rinehart & Winston, pp. 87-118.

Klopfer, B., & Boyer, L. (1961), Notes on the Personality of North American Shamans: Rorschach Interpretations. *J. Proj. Tech.*, 25:170-178.

Knight, R. P. (1953), Borderline States. *Bull. Menninger Clin.*, 17:1-12.

Kohut, H. (1971), *The Analysis of the Self*. New York: International Universities Press.

Kretschmer, E. (1923), *Hysteria*. New York: Nervous and Mental Disease Publishing Co., 1926.

Kris, E. (1932-1952), *Psychoanalytic Explorations in Art*. New York: International Universities Press.

Lampl-de Groot, J. (1927), The Evolution of the Oedipus Complex in Women. *The Development of the Mind*. New York: International Universities Press, 1965, pp. 3-18.

Langness, L. L. (1967), Hysterical Psychosis: The Cross-Cultural Evidence. *Amer. J. Psychiat.*, 124:143-152.

Laughlin, H. P. (1956), *The Neuroses in Clinical Practice*. Philadelphia: Saunders.

Lazare, A., & Klerman, G. L. (1968), Hysteria and Depression: The Frequency and Significance of Hysterical Personality Features in Hospitalized Depressed Women. *Amer. J. Psychiat.*, 125:48-56.

Lichtenberg, J. D., & Slap, J. W. (1973), Notes on the Concept of Splitting and the Defense Mechanism of the Splitting of Representations. *J. Amer. Psychoanal. Assn.*, 21:772-787.

Ludwig, A. O. (1959), The Role of Identification in the Conversion Process. In: *On the Mysterious Leap from the Mind to the Body*, ed. F. Deutsch. New York: International Universities Press, pp. 98-110.

Macfadden, B. (1901), *The Power and Beauty of Superb Womanhood*. New York.

Mahler, M. S. (1958), Autism and Symbiosis. *Int. J. Psycho-Anal.*, 39:77-83.

Marmor, J. (1953), Orality in the Hysterical Personality. *J. Amer. Psychoanal. Assn.*, 1:656-671.

May, H. F. (1959), *The End of American Innocence*. New York: Knopf.

Mayman, M. (1968), Early Memories and Character Structure. *J. Proj. Tech.*, 32:303-316.

McKegney, F. P. (1967), The Incidence and Characteristics of Patients with Conversion Reactions: I. A General Hospital Consultation Service Sample. *Amer. J. Psychiat.*, 124:128-131.

Menninger, K., Mayman, M., & Pruyser, P. (1963), *The Vital Balance*. New York: Viking.

Michaels, J. J. (1959), Character Structure and Character Disorders. In: *American Handbook of Psychiatry*, 1:353-377. New York: Basic Books.

Miller, D. (1958), *The Changing American Parent*. London: Wiley.

Miller, P. (1965), *The Life of the Mind in America*. New York: Harcourt, Brace & World.

Murphy, J. (1964), Psychotherapeutic Aspects of Shamanism on St. Lawrence Island, Alaska. In: *Magic, Faith and Healing*, ed. A. Kiev. London: Free Press of Glencoe, pp. 53-83.

Murphy, M. (1965), National Character. In: *Context and Meaning in Cultural Anthropology*, ed. M. E. Spiro. New York: Free Press.

Nagera, H. (1966), *Early Childhood Disturbances, the Infantile Neurosis, and the Adulthood Disturbances*. New York: International Universities Press.

_____ (1975), *On Female Sexuality and the Oedipus Complex*. New York: Aronson.

Noble, D. (1951), Hysterical Manifestations in Schizophrenic Illness. *Psychiatry*, 14:153-160.

Nunberg, H. (1936), Homosexuality, Magic and Aggression. *Practice and Theory of Psychoanalysis*, 1:150-164. New York: International Universities Press, 1961.

Opler, M. E. (1935), The Concept of Power among the Chiricahua and Mescalero Apache. *Amer. Anthropologist*, 37:65-70.

Opler, M. K., ed. (1959), *Culture and Mental Health: Cross Cultural Studies*. New York: Macmillan.

Papashvily, H. W. (1956), *All the Happy Endings*. New York: Harper.

Pasamanick, B., Dimitz, J., & Lefton, M. (1959), Psychiatric Orientation and Its Relation to Diagnosis and Treatment in a Mental Hospital. *Amer. J. Psychiat.*, 116:127-132.

Pollock, G. H. (1968), The Possible Significance of Childhood Object Loss in the Josef Breuer-Bertha Pappenheim (Anna O.)-Sigmund Freud Relationship: I. Josef Breuer. *J. Amer. Psychoanal. Assn.*, 16:711-739.

_____ (1972), Bertha Pappenheim's Pathological Mourning: Possible Effects of Childhood Sibling Loss. *J. Amer. Psychoanal. Assn.*, 20:476-493.

Prosen, H. (1967), Sexuality in Females with Hysteria. *Amer. J. Psychiat.*, 124:687-692.

Purtell, J. J., Robins, E., & Cohen, M. E. (1951), Observation on Clinical Aspects of Hysteria: A Quantitative Study of 50 Patients and 156 Control Subjects. *J. Amer. Med. Assn.*, 146:902-909.

Rangell, L. (1959), The Nature of Conversion. *J. Amer. Psychoanal. Assn.*, 7:632-662.

Rapaport, D., Gill, M. M., & Schafer, R. (1968), *Diagnostic Psychological Testing*, rev. ed., ed. R. R. Holt. New York: International Universities Press.

Reich, W. (1933), *Character Analysis*. New York: Farrar, Straus & Giroux, 1972.

Reichard, S. (1956), A Re-examination of "Studies in Hysteria." *Psychoanal. Quart.*, 25:155-177.

Renaud, H., & Estess, F. M. (1961), Life History Interviews with 100 Normal American Males. *Amer. J. Orthopsychiat.*, 31:786-802.

Rossi, A. (1966), The Roots of Ambivalence in American Women. Paper presented to the Adult Education Association, Chicago, November. University of Chicago: National Opinion Research Center.

Rourke, C. (1931), *American Humor*. New York: Harcourt, Brace.

Salzman, L. (1968), *The Obsesssive Personality*. New York: Science House.

Schafer, R. (1948), *The Clinical Application of Psychological Tests*. New York: International Universities Press.

———— (1954), *Psychoanalytic Interpretation in Rorschach Testing*. New York: Grune & Stratton.

———— (1968), *Aspects of Internalization*. New York: International Universities Press.

Scott, A. F. (1970), *The Southern Lady*. Chicago: University of Chicago Press.

Seidenberg, R., & Papthomopoulos, E. (1962), Daughters Who Tend Their Fathers—A Literary Survey. *The Psychoanalytic Study of Society*, 2: 135-160. New York: International Universities Press.

Shapiro, D. (1965), *Neurotic Styles*. New York: Basic Books.

Shevrin, H., & Shectman, F. (1973), The Diagnostic Process in Psychiatric Evaluations. *Bull. Menninger Clin.*, 37:451-494.

Siegman, A. (1954), Emotionality—the Hysterical Character Defense. *Psychoanal. Quart.*, 23:339-353.

Sinclair, A. (1965), *The Better Half*. New York: Harper & Row.

Singer, M. T., & Wynne, L. C. (1963), Differentiating Characteristics of Parents of Childhood Schizophrenics, Childhood Neurotics, and Young Adult Schizophrenics. *Amer. J. Psychiat.*, 120:234-243.

Sirjamaki, J. (1953), *The American Family in the Twentieth Century*. Cambridge, Mass.: Harvard University Press.

Sterba, R. (1975), Vienna in the '20's and '30's. Paper presented to the Michigan Psychoanalytic Society, October.

Sullivan, H. S. (1956), *Clinical Studies in Psychiatry*. New York: Norton.

Szasz, T. S. (1961), *The Myth of Mental Illness*. New York: Dell.

Tarachow, S. (1963), *An Introduction to Psychotherapy*. New York: International Universities Press.

Veith, I. (1965), *Hysteria*. Chicago: University of Chicago Press.

Winokur, G., & Leonard, C. (1963), Sexual Life in Patients with Hysteria. *Dis. Nerv. Syst.*, 24:337-343.

Wisdom, J. O. (1961), A Methodological Approach to the Problem of Hysteria. *Int. J. Psycho-Anal.*, 42:224-237.

Wittels, F. (1931), Der Hysterische Charakter. *Psychoanal. Bewegung*, 3:138-165.

Wolowitz, H. M. (1971), Hysterical Character and Feminine Identity. In: *Readings on the Psychology of Women*, ed. J. Bardwick. New York: Harper & Row, pp. 307-314.

Yap, P. (1951), Mental Diseases Peculiar to Certain Cultures. *J. Ment. Sci.*, 97:313-327.

Zetzel, E. (1968), The So-Called Good Hysteric. *Int. J. Psycho-Anal.*, 49:256-260.

Ziegler, D. (1967), Neurological Disease and Hysteria—The Differential Diagnosis. *Int. J. Neuropsychiat.*, 3:388-396.

_____ & Paul, N. (1954), On the Natural History of Hysteria in Women. *Dis. Nerv. Syst.*, 15:301-306.

INDEX

Abraham, K., 51-53
Abse, D. W., 15, 73, 91-96, 110, 126, 139, 159, 161, 162, 174, 187
Ackerknecht, E. H., 172
Ackerman, N., 132
Affective experience, 218
Allen, D. W., 55, 139
Alloplasticity; see Interpersonal relations
Angyal, A., 45, 108, 109, 116-119, 135, 136, 159, 161, 189
Anticathexis, 35-37, 42
Anxiety hysteria, 40-42, 59-61, 325-327; see also Conversion hysteria; Hysteria
Apache Indians, 5, 160, 162, 166-172, 185-186
Ariès, P., 200

Bateson, G., 132, 134
Bernheim, H., 10
Blinder, M., 71, 72
Boyer, L. B., 166-170, 206
Brenneis, C. B., 149, 151
Brenner, C., 282-283
Breuer, J., 9, 11-17, 25, 46, 51, 62, 90, 98, 133, 175, 182
Bridges, W. E., 180
Brill, N. Q., 90
Brodey, W. M., 220
Brücke, E., 10, 11

Cameron, N., 59, 104
Campbell, R., 95
Caro Baroja, J., 166
Carter, R., 48
Case studies
  ego process in hysteria, 84-86, 87-89
  hysterical neurosis (female), 284-301
  hysterical neurosis (male), 301-320

modern hysteria, 192-193
  role of death in hysteria, 140-143
Cash, W. J., 180, 181
Castration anxiety, 39-40, 237-238
Character, psychology of, 29-30, 51-55; see also Hysterical personality
Charcot, J.-M., 10, 16, 48, 51, 53-54, 61, 163, 174
Chasseguet-Smirgel, J., 159
Child rearing, 201-203
Chodoff, P., 50, 61-64, 84, 101, 146, 151, 152, 161, 174, 175, 187
Cognitive style, 216, 230-232
Cohen, M. E., 68
Conflict, 17, 92, 125-127, 214-215
  Oedipal, 245-257, 268-280
  phallic-Oedipal, 234-236
  see also Repression; Resistance
Conversion hysteria, 15-17, 22, 59-64, 174-176; see also Anxiety hysteria; Hysteria
Cullander, C. C. H., 3
Culture; see Hysteria, cross-cultural perspectives on

Death, 138-144, 153
Defense(s), 27, 34-36, 92-93, 219, 224-225; see also Regression; Repression; Resistance
Demos, J., 166
Depression, 281-283
Deutsch, F., 139
Deutsch, H., 62, 98, 111, 117, 124, 128, 140-141, 193
Diagnosis
  of hysteria, 320-323
  problems of, 1-5, 212
  see also Hysteria
Diagnostic testing, 74-83, 232-234
Dimitz, J., 1

Dreams, 25-26
Drives, 213-214

Easser, S., 64-67, 94, 101, 104, 109,
115, 177, 126, 132, 134, 140, 146-
147, 149, 194
Ego
role in hysteria, 35-37, 50, 83-96,
101-103, 114-116, 215-216, 228-
230, 234-236
role in hysterical personality, 123-
124
(self-) boundaries, 105-109
structure, 217-218
style, 35-37, 149-151, 216-217
Emotionality, 104-105
Erikson, E. H., 60, 102, 148, 149, 151,
154, 201
Escalona, S., 146
Estess, F. M., 138
Externalization, 225-228
Eysenck, H. J., 70, 73, 74, 91, 203

Fairbairn, W. R. D., 54, 59, 119-
122
Family relations, 132-139, 152-153,
200-201; see also Oedipus com-
plex
Fantasy, 24-28, 32-33, 109-114, 224-
225
Farber, L. H., 45, 91, 99, 104, 110,
118, 119, 137, 140. 158, 161
Fear(s), 223-224
Federn, P., 35, 96-99, 105, 106, 144-
145, 150, 153, 162, 204
Fenichel, O., 59-62, 68, 73, 96, 105,
109, 110, 112, 120, 132-135, 139,
159, 187
Ferenczi, S., 91
Fernández-Marina, R., 142
Fiedler, L., 178, 184, 190, 194
Fitzgerald, O., 117-118, 137, 139, 146,
159
Fixation, 213-214, 248-252
Freeman, E. W., 176
Freud, A., 3, 16, 42, 43, 74, 75, 80, 15²
155, 261
Freud, S., 3, 5, 9-48, 51, 53, 54, 6(
62, 73, 74, 90, 92, 97, 98, 10!
111, 112, 120, 121, 131-133, 13!

139, 144, 154-156, 174, 175, 182,
186, 195, 203, 238, 239, 242,
255, 271, 282, 283, 309, 325,
326
Freudian theory of hysteria, 9-45
of anxiety hysteria, 40-42
of conversion hysteria, 15-17
"Dora" phase, 24-28
early, 9-12, 17-19, 22-23
Introductory Lectures phase, 28-33
seduction theory of, 19-21
summary of, 43-45
Friedlander, K., 138
Fuchs, S., 173

Gelfand, M., 173
Gill, M. M., 73-75, 109, 232
Glover, E., 90
Goshen, C. E., 90
Greenson, R. R., 98, 112, 124
Greenspan, S. I., 3
Grinker, R. R., 63
Guntrip, H., 121
Gutmann, D., 142, 149-151, 154
Guze, S. B., 68-70

Handelsman, I., 121, 122
Hansen, C., 163-164, 167
Harland, M., 178
Harlow, H., 132
Harlow, M. K., 132
Harms, E., 132, 137
Hartmann, H., 43, 50, 60, 74, 75,
80, 90-91, 102, 145, 237, 261
Heidbreder, E., 195
Hendrick, I., 101
Henry, J., 138
Higginson, T. W., 184-185, 191
Higham, J., 166, 177, 187, 189, 191,
192
Hinsie, L., 95
Hippocrates, 47
Houston, M., 55, 139
Howells, W. D., 176, 184, 185
Hypnosis and hypnoid state, 10-11, 13-
15, 93
Hysteria
case studies, 84-89, 140-143, 192-
193, 284-320

constitutional factors in, 144-146, 153-154

cross-cultural perspectives on, 130, 141-142, 156-211

definitions of, 2, 6-8, 46-128, 213; descriptive, 49, 51-53; dynamic, 49-50, 53-68; ego-process, 50, 83-116; empirical, 50, 68-74; holistic, 116-119; object relations, 119-122

diagnosis of, 320-323

etiology of, 129-155

fantasy in, 24-28, 32-33, 109-114, 224-225

Freud's theory of, 9-45

historical perspectives on, 47-48, 156-211

vs. infantile personality, 99-101

influence of family on, 132-139, 152-153, 200-201

interpersonal relations and, 127-128, 201-203, 220-223

in men, 146-151

modern, 174-176, 194, 196-198

vs. obsessional neurosis, 22-24, 37-38, 95-99, 145, 204-205, 230-232

passivity in, 103, 125, 158-160, 225-228

pre-Freudian history of, 47-48

role of ego in, 50, 83-96, 101-103, 114-116, 215-216, 228-230, 234-236

vs. schizophrenia, 94-95

symptoms of, 11-12, 15-19, 24-26, 35, 40, 51, 184-187, 228-230

see also Anxiety hysteria; Conversion hysteria; Hysterical personality; Hysteroid personality

Hysterical personality, 31-32, 42-43, 51-55, 111-114, 280-281

case studies of, 284-301, 301-320

definition of, 213

ego and, 123-124

incidence in men and women, 146

Oedipus complex in, 236-239, 245-254, 268-280

Hysteroid personality, 64-68; see also Easser, S.; Lesser, B.

Identification, 107-109, 138-144

Innocence, 223-225

Interpersonal relations, 26, 127-128, 201-203, 220-223

Janet, P., 48, 140, 174, 182

Johnston, M., 54, 59

Jung, C. G., 91

Kagan, J., 146, 148, 149

Kernberg, O., 54, 59, 67, 91, 94, 97, 99-101, 116, 117, 124, 160, 261

Klein, G. S., 102

Klerman, G. L., 70-72, 187

Klopfer, B., 166, 168-170

Knight, R. P., 90, 143

Kohut, H., 101, 261, 322

Kretschmer, E., 140

Kris, E., 168

Lampl-de Groot, J., 239

Langness, L. L., 163

Laughlin, H. P., 95

Lazare, A., 70-72, 187

Lefton, M., 1

Leonard, C., 71

Lesser, B., 64-67, 94, 101, 104, 109, 115, 117, 126, 132, 134, 140, 146-147, 149, 194

Lewinian theory, 195

Lewis, M., 146, 148, 149

Lichtenberg, J. D., 97

Liébeault, A. A., 10

Loewenstein, R., 237

Loss; see Death

Ludwig, A. O., 139

Lyons, H., 61, 63, 64, 84, 101, 146, 151, 152, 161, 187

Macfadden, B., 191

Mahler, M. S., 121, 261

Marie, P., 51, 53-54

Marmor, J., 54, 59, 68, 84, 89, 91, 101, 120, 125, 151

May, H. F., 180, 191

Mayman, M., 1. 233

McKegney, F. P., 174

Memories, pathogenic, 12-14; see also Oedipus complex; Repression

Men

hysteria in, 146-151

hysterical personality in, 301-302

Oedipal conflict in, 255-257
see also Sex differences
Menninger, K., 1
Michaels, J. J., 146
Miller, D., 200, 202
Miller, P., 179
Moebius, P. J., 10
Monroe, M., 194
Murphy, J., 171, 172
Murphy, M., 177-178, 200-201

Nagera, H., 3, 131, 155, 239-246
Narcissism, 283
Neurosis, 31-32, 280-281; see also
    Freudian theory of hysteria; Hys-
    terical personality; Obsessional
    neurosis
Noble, D., 90, 91
Nunberg, H., 169

Object relations, 119-122
Obsessional neurosis, 22-24, 37-38, 95-
    99, 145, 204-205, 230-232
Oedipus complex, 11-14, 39-40
    general features of, 257-261
    hysterical personality and, 236-
        239, 268-280
    in men, 255-257
    vs. oral, anal, phallic stages, 261-
        268
    phase of development in women,
        239-254
Opler, M. E., 167
Opler, M. K., 163

Papashvily, H. W., 177-179, 183, 184
Papathomopoulos, E., 139, 185
Pasamanick, B., 1
Passivity
    as ego strategy, 103, 125
    myth of, 158-160, 225-228
Paul, N., 68, 69
Personality; see Hysterical personality;
    Phallic-narcissistic personality
Phallic-narcissistic personality, 55-57
Phobia(s); see Anxiety hysteria; Fear(s)
Pollock, G. H., 17
Popular psychology, 195-196
Prosen, H., 55, 140
Pruyser, P., 1

Psychoanalytic theory; see Freudian
    theory of hysteria
Purtell, J. J., 68

Rangell, L., 59, 61-63, 124, 174, 188,
    192
Rapaport, D., 73-75, 80, 82, 109,
    232
Regression, 31, 37-39
Reich, W., 30, 35, 53-55, 57-59, 64-
    65, 68, 84, 102, 120, 132, 145,
    160, 187, 192
Reichard, S., 74, 90, 133
Renaud, H., 138
Repression, 17-19, 34-35, 60, 102, 229
Resistance, 17-19, 29-31; see also
    Defense(s); Repression
Robbins, F. P., 63
Robins, E., 68
Rorschach, H., 77
Rorschach test, 75, 77-80
Rossi, A., 183
Rourke, C., 181
Rycroft, C., 47

Salzman, L., 59, 124, 205, 210
Schafer, R., 73-75, 78, 108-110, 198,
    232
Scott, A. F., 180-181, 183, 184
Seduction theory (of hysteria), 19-21;
    see also Freudian theory; Oedipus
    complex
Segel, N., 283
Seidenberg, R., 139, 185
Self, 116-119, 198-200
Sex differences
    in ego style, 149-151
    in incidence of hysteria, 146-147
Sexuality, 19-21, 26-27, 30; see also
    Oedipus complex; Sex differences;
    Women
Shamanism, 166-174; see also Witch-
    craft
Shapiro, D., 15, 73, 82, 91, 101-103,
    109, 110, 116, 144, 145, 147, 148,
    150, 153, 158, 162, 193, 196
Shectman, F., 1
Shevrin, H., 1
Siegman, A., 65, 104, 105, 136, 144,
    203

Sinclair, A., 152, 179, 184, 185, 191
Singer, M. T., 138
Sirjamaki, J., 200
Slap, J. W., 97
Somatization, 184-187; see also Symptoms
Sophocles, 237
Spitz, R. A., 261
Spock, B., 195
Sterba, R., 53
Structural theory, 33-35, 228-230
see also Freudian theory of hysteria
Sullivan, H. S., 45, 118, 137, 160-162, 235
Suomi, S., 132
Superego, 221, 229
Sydenham, 48
Szasz, T. S., 159, 162

Tarachow, S., 122, 300
Testing; see Diagnostic testing
Thought, 228-230
Trauma; see Death; Oedipus complex

Veith, I., 46, 48, 71, 73, 146, 163, 167, 188, 199
Victorian era, 176-194

Warson, S., 138
Watson, J. B., 202
Wechsler Intelligence Scale, 75-77
Winokur, G., 71
Wisdom, J. O., 47, 146
Wishes, 223-224
Witchcraft, 163-166; see also Shamanism
Wittels, F., 57-59, 65, 68, 84, 103, 125, 146, 187, 192
Wolowitz, H. M., 117-119, 151, 154, 160-161, 203
Women, hysterical, 151-152
depression in, 281-283
Oedipal-phase development in, 239-254
phallic attachment to mother in, 254-255
somatization in, 184-187
Victorian, 176-187
Wynne, L. C., 138

Yap, P., 163

Zetzel, E., 66, 114, 115, 127, 146, 147, 219
Ziegler, D., 68, 69, 189

ABOUT THE AUTHOR

ALAN KROHN received his Ph.D. in Clinical Psychology from the University of Michigan in 1972. Since then he has been on the faculty of the Department of Psychiatry at the University of Michigan, on the Senior Staff of the University of Michigan Psychological Clinic, and in private practice in Ann Arbor. He is currently a candidate at the Michigan Psychoanalytic Institute. His writings include contributions on dreams and object relations, borderline psychopathology, and adolescence.

PSYCHOLOGICAL ISSUES

No. 1 — ERIK H. ERIKSON: *Identity and the Life Cycle; Selected Papers.* Historical Introduction by David Rapaport

No. 2 — I. H. PAUL: *Studies in Remembering; The Reproduction of Connected and Extended Verbal Material*

No. 3 — FRITZ HEIDER: *On Perception, Event Structure, and the Psychological Environment.* Preface by George S. Klein.

No. 4 — RILEY W. GARDNER, PHILIP S. HOLZMAN, GEORGE S. KLEIN, HARRIET LINTON, and DONALD P. SPENCE: *Cognitive Control; A Study of Individual Consistencies in Cognitive Behavior*

No. 5 — PETER H. WOLFF: *The Developmental Psychologies of Jean Piaget and Psychoanalysis*

No. 6 — DAVID RAPAPORT: *The Structure of Psychoanalytic Theory; A Systematizing Attempt*

No. 7 — OTTO POTZL, RUDOLF ALLERS, and JAKOB TELER: *Preconscious Stimulation in Dreams, Associations, and Images; Classical Studies.* Introduction by Charles Fisher

No. 8 — RILEY W. GARDNER, DOUGLAS N. JACKSON, and SAMUEL J. MESSICK: *Personality Organization in Cognitive Controls and Intellectual Abilities*

No. 9 — FRED SCHWARTZ and RICHARD O. ROUSE: *The Activation and Recovery of Associations*

No. 10 — MERTON M. GILL: *Topography and Systems in Psychoanalytic Theory*

No. 11 — ROBERT W. WHITE: *Ego and Reality in Psychoanalytic Theory: A Proposal regarding the Independent Ego Energies*

No. 12 — IVO KOHLER: *The Formation and Transformation of the Perceptual World.* Introduction by James J. Gibson

No. 13 — DAVID SHAKOW and DAVID RAPAPORT: *The Influence of Freud on American Psychology*

No. 14 — HEINZ HARTMANN, ERNST KRIS, and RUDOLPH M. LOEWENSTEIN: *Papers on Psychoanalytic Psychology*

No. 15 — WOLFGANG LEDERER: *Dragons, Delinquents, and Destiny; An Essay on Positive Superego Functions.* Introduction by Roy Schafer

No. 16 — PETER AMACHER: *Freud's Neurological Education and Its Influence on Psychoanalytic Theory*

No. 17 — PETER H. WOLFF: *The Causes, Controls, and Organization of Behavior in the Neonate*

No. 18/19 — ROBERT R. HOLT, Ed.: *Motives and Thought; Psychoanalytic Essays in Honor of David Rapaport*

No. 20 — JOHN CHYNOWETH BURNHAM: *Psychoanalysis and American Medicine, 1894-1918; Medicine, Science, and Culture*

No. 21 — HELEN D. SARGENT, LEONARD HORWITZ, ROBERT S. WALLERSTEIN, and ANN APPELBAUM: *Prediction in Psychotherapy Research: A Method for the Transformation of Clinical Judgments into Testable Hypotheses*

No. 22 — MARJORIE GRENE, Ed.: *Toward a Unity of Knowledge*

No. 23 — FRED SCHWARTZ and PETER H. SCHILLER: *A Psychoanalytic Model of Attention and Learning*

No. 24 — BERNARD LANDIS: *Ego Boundaries*

No. 25/26 — EMANUEL PETERFREUND in collaboration with JACOB T. SCHWARTZ: *Information, Systems, and Psychoanalysis; An evolutionary Biological Approach to Psychoanalytic Theory*

No. 27 — LOUIS BREGER, IAN HUNTER, and RON W. LANE: *The Effect of Stress on Dreams*

No. 28 — EDITH LEVITOV GARDUK and ERNEST A. HAGGARD: *Immediate Effects on Patients of Psychoanalytic Interpretations*

No. 29 — ERICH GOLDMEIER: *Similarity in Visually Perceived Forms.* Foreword by Irvin Rock

No. 30 — MARTIN MAYMAN, Ed.: *Psychoanalytic Research: Three Approaches to the Experimental Study of Subliminal Processes*

No. 31 — NANETTE HEIMAN and JOAN GRANT, Eds.: *Else Frenkel-Brunswik: Selected Papers*

No. 32 — FRED SCHWARTZ, Ed.: *Scientific Thought and Social Reality: Essays by Michael Polanyi*

No. 33 — STANLEY I. GREENSPAN: *A Consideration of Some Learning Variables in the Context of Psychoanalytic Theory*

No. 34/35 — JOHN E. GEDO and GEORGE H. POLLOCK, EDS.: *Freud: The Fusion of Science and Humanism; The Intellectual History of Psychoanalysis*

No. 36 — MERTON M. GILL and PHILIP S. HOLZMAN, EDS.: *Psychology versus Metapsychology; Psychoanalytic Essays in Memory of George S. Klein*

No. 37 — ROBERT N. EMDE, THEODORE J. GAENSBAUER, and ROBERT J. HARMON: *Emotional Expression in Infancy: A Biobehavioral Study*

No. 38 — DAVID SHAKOW: *Schizophrenia: Selected Papers*

No. 39 — PAUL E. STEPANSKY: *A History of Aggression in Freud*

No. 40 — JOSEPH DE RIVERA: *A Structural Theory of the Emotions.* Introductory Essay by Hartvig Dahl

No. 41 — HANNAH S. DECKER: *Freud in Germany: Revolution and Reaction in Science, 1893-1907*

No. 42/43 — ALLAN D. ROSENBLATT and JAMES T. THICKSTUN: *Modern Psychoanalytic Concepts in a General Psychology* — Parts 1 & 2

No. 44 — HERBERT J. SCHLESINGER. *Symbol and Neurosis: Selected Papers of Lawrence S. Kubie.* Introduction by Eugene B. Brody.